TREASURES

❧ OF ❧

FAITH

LIVING BOLDLY IN VIEW OF
GOD'S PROMISES

TREASURES
OF
FAITH

CHUCK and SHARON
BETTERS

prepared for

Women In the Church

Presbyterian Church in America
CHRISTIAN EDUCATION AND PUBLICATIONS
1852 Century Place, Suite 101 • Atlanta, Georgia 30345
CE&P

Unless otherwise indicated, all Scripture quotations are from the HOLY BIBLE, NEW INTERNATIONAL VERSION®. NIV®. Copyright © 1973, 1978, 1984 by International Bible Society. Used by permission of Zondervan Publishing House. All rights reserved.

Quotation of *Heirs of the Covenant* by Susan Hunt, © 1998, p. 125, is used by permission of Crossway Books, a division of Good News Publishers, Wheaton, Illinois.

Page design by Tobias Design
Typesetting by Michelle Feaster

Printed in the United States of America

Library of Congress Cataloging-in-Publication Data

Betters, Chuck, 1948–
    Treasures of faith : living boldly in view of God's promises / Chuck and Sharon Betters.
        p.   cm.
    Includes bibliographical references.
    ISBN 0-87552-096-0 (pbk.)
    1. Bible. N.T. Hebrews XI—Study and teaching. 2. Faith—Biblical teaching. I. Betters, Sharon W., 1948– . II. Title.
BS2775.5.B47 1999
227'.8706—dc21   99–32966

To our children and grandchildren,
our precious spiritual legacy and joy of our lives.

Sons are a heritage from the Lord,
children a reward from him.
Like arrows in the hands of a warrior
are sons born in one's youth.
(Psalm 127:3–4)

CONTENTS

ACKNOWLEDGMENTS

As we embarked on the task of writing a book on the great themes of faith in Hebrews 11 and 12, little did we know how intense the warfare would become. This project has been personally consuming and at times very painful. That is why we must not fail to mention some key fellow warriors who stood alongside us and interlocked their shields of faith with ours.

Thank you, our brothers and sisters at the Glasgow Reformed Presbyterian Church. You have sustained us in your prayers and by your encouragement. Few pastors have ever shepherded a more loving and faithful flock. Special thanks to Linda Smookler and Britton Goodling, fellow faith strugglers and willing and capable volunteer editors for the Leader's Guide. Thank you, all who contributed testimonies of God's faithfulness in your own faith struggles.

A mere "thank you" would be insufficient to express how we feel about our book editor, Tom Rogers. Your sacrifices and those of your family enabled us to complete this work. May your personal journey of faith find some of its reward in the lives of those who gain strength by reading this book, the writing of which bears the influence of both your hand and your heart.

Thank you, Lynn Brookside, for your flexibility and creative insight in editing the Leader's Guide. You have been a constant motivator and encourager, and a consummate professional. God is truly honored by your work and spirit.

Many thanks to Thom, Barbara, Bryce, and all of the staff at P&R Publishing Company, for your gentleness, professionalism, and biblical integrity. It took much prayer to assemble this team, and your unwillingness to give up until that team was in place has made this a book we are certain will honor God.

Thank you, Susan Hunt and the many spiritual mothers who serve as a great cloud of witnesses around the country, for your faith in our ability to write on such an awesome theme as the covenant of grace.

And what more shall we say? We do not have space to tell about all those friends and family who urged us by their prayers and notes to persevere—to keep our eyes fixed on Jesus. *To Him be all the glory!*

INTRODUCTION

"Is God really sovereign? Can I trust Him now . . . even in this?"

The steady, virulent progress of the malignant brain tumor gave real urgency to these questions for David. The disease had progressed relentlessly; a cure seemed unlikely. David knew he didn't have much time. He wanted his last few days on earth to count, to reflect a heart in tune with God's purposes. David wanted to know—he *needed* to know—if this painful death was really from God's hand. Would God care for his young wife and three children after he was gone? Would He really walk with them through the valley of the shadow of death? David needed to trust God, but how could he? *How could he?*

We understand David's questions. When our son Mark and his friend Kelly were killed in a car accident on July 6, 1993, our own struggle to survive nearly consumed us. Slowly and surely, however, God reminded us that just surviving is not enough. We needed a purpose, a reason to keep moving forward, or we were never going to make it. But, like David, we were weary, uncertain of whether we could really trust the God who was calling us to persevere.

Our search for answers led us to the book of Hebrews. This book of the Bible was most likely originally a series of short sermons written for people just like us—people tempted to give up their faith in the face of great hardship. These Hebrews, Jewish Christians for the most part who lived during the first century, were persecuted and afraid and discouraged. Some had already abandoned the faith and had returned to their former lifestyles; others were sorely tempted to do so.

Could God, through their faith, redeem their pain and give it meaning? Could that pain actually help them to encourage others in their faith or to help draw unbelievers to the heart of God (2 Corinthians 2:15–17)?

Indeed it could—but how? *By faith.* Where does that kind of faith come from? *From God.* He is the One who controls every detail of our lives; He is the One who loved us more than His own life. Such a faith can gently whisper "God does all things well" even when the heart cries out "Where are you, God? *Where are you?*"

How do we cultivate this kind of faith? The answer to that question, dear friend, is what this book is all about. It is a topic addressed by Hebrews 11 in vivid and poignant detail.

We need a faith that is real, that is alive, a faith that holds up in the nitty-gritty problems and sorrows of everyday life. Such a faith is not some abstract concept but a shining and useful tool in our hands. The Hebrew believers needed desperately to remember that God had made a "covenant," a binding promise. God had promised to strengthen His people, to love them, to be with them, to redeem them. Like us, sometimes they forgot that God *keeps* His promises.

> God is not a man, that he should lie, nor a son of man, that he should change his mind. Does he speak and then not act? Does he promise and not fulfill? (Numbers 23:19)

The author of Hebrews, in chapter 11, reminds us that since God kept His promises of the past, we can also trust Him to keep His promises for the present and for the future. In Hebrews 11 we are given a priceless vision of what God has already accomplished through the covenant and through the faithful men and women who trusted Him. We are also given an encouraging glimpse of what lies ahead for us because of that same covenant, a vision that gives our lives and work here on earth new meaning. Spurred on by this vision we can persevere, by faith, no matter what our circumstances may be.

How did the people portrayed here in this amazing chapter of Hebrews demonstrate such a life-transforming faith in God? And what do they have to teach us?

Many of the portraits in this "spiritual family album" are a little tarnished, with histories that are often quite colorful and, in some cases, even sordid. In looking at them, we sometimes felt, uncomfortably, that we were looking into a mirror. The weakness, the sin, the selfishness we saw in them we also saw only too well in ourselves. Yet in spite of their failings, God remained strong in upholding these flawed men and women, and this greatly encouraged us. Upon closer inspection, we also began to see the signs of God's faithfulness to His people, as marked by the seminal events in their lives, where God's great grace and strength somehow shone brightly through their weakness (Romans 8:28–29). You will see with us how God moved in and through these "ordinary" lives, and you will discover that our God can transform *any* life into a life of faith—even yours.

On each page of this family album, you will also see the inexorable power and grace of God as He fulfills the promises of His eternal covenant of redemption. You will catch a glimpse of God's unfolding purposes for His church. God interacts with struggling believers to build into them the faith He wants them to have. In this way we are enabled to build His kingdom, to encourage others, and to pass on a legacy of faith to coming generations.

These heroes of faith rose to prominence at pivotal moments in the sovereign purposes of God, but not without great personal struggle and doubt. We examine here their failures in order to reveal more fully the grace that moved them to victory, and some of our interpretations may stretch or surprise some readers. We urge you to dig deeper into the Scriptures to examine the pearls of grace in these remarkable lives—

these people who are our own weak, flawed, and sinful brothers and sisters but who ultimately became victorious heroes of
faith.

Each chapter begins with a personal testimony from an
ordinary person whom we consider to be a contemporary
hero of faith. Some of the names and specific details have
been altered just enough to protect confidentiality, but the
stories are wholly true. Each chapter also presents a "Faith
Principle" that emphasizes a particular aspect or benefit of
faith. This is followed by an in-depth analysis of the Old Testament person(s) who best illustrates that principle. Throughout each chapter are suggestions on how to practically live out
these principles, and each chapter also concludes with a "Digging Deeper" section, six days of daily devotions for further
study.

This book is appropriate for individual or group study (a
Leader's Guide is available). As you read, keep your Bible
open to the texts listed at the beginning of each chapter. The
writer of Hebrews assumed a knowledge of Old Testament history among his readers, and you will understand and appreciate each faith story better if you read the Old Testament passages listed at the beginning of each chapter.

Our dear friend David had questioned whether God
could be trusted through his pain. God's answer, as promised
in the sure word of Scripture, was emphatically yes. *God can be
trusted*—a truth experienced as David journeyed toward his
heavenly home, and a reality now fully confirmed in the glorious presence of his ascended Lord. You too will see, through
this study of Hebrews 11, that God is faithful and that He can
do amazing things with a yielded heart and life. What does it
mean to trust God? Will *you* trust Him? Your life will reflect
your answer to these questions. We trust that the message of
Hebrews 11 presented here will encourage you to share your
faith with others and to run with perseverance the course He
has marked out for you.

Faith does not become "living faith" until it is no longer a dry concept but a tool in your hands, one glistening with your own sweat, your own tears and, yes, even your own blood. The author of Hebrews reminds us again and again that by faith God can accomplish His great purposes through men and women who suffer, who stumble, who fail, through men and women like us, through men and women like you. *By faith* such lives become precious gems set in the crown of His great and glorious covenant. Abraham learned this, and Joseph, and Moses, and Rahab, and Samson. Come share in their encouraging journey—and ours.

Chuck and Sharon Betters

Chapter 1

LIVING FAITH

Now faith is being sure of what we hope for and certain of what

we do not see. This is what the ancients were commended for.

By faith we understand that the universe was formed at

God's command, so that what is seen was not made out

of what was visible. (*Hebrews 11:1–3*)

THE LONG ROAD HOME—SHARON BIAS

In a home filled with the terror of an alcoholic and abusive father, a place where there was little food and even less laughter, my mother would sometimes speak to me about Jesus. Alone in my bedroom, with tears streaming down my cheeks, I gave my heart to Christ. In those difficult years, I would often promise Jesus that, when I grew up, I would work hard and make enough money to help children who were too poor to buy clothes and food, I would abolish all alcohol, and I would make it so that daddies were never allowed to hit mommies.

Sometimes, when it seemed I was the particular target of Dad's rage, I thought that maybe Jesus was as angry with me as my father was. Why else was life so hard? How could a loving God allow fathers to hurt their children? Terror and resentment eventually replaced my childlike love for Jesus. As an adult, I looked for security in marriage and children and, after my daughter's birth, I finally felt like I was in control of my life. The birth of my gravely ill son, Dean, however, changed all that. Dean was born with lymphangioma. This disease disfigured his face and led to numerous complications, including constant infections, fevers, an obstructed airway, and fourteen surgeries. My husband, unable to accept our "imperfect" child, deserted us. After three years of hearing doctors tell me they could not diagnose my child's problem, I knew that time was running out. In desperation, I contacted a children's hospital and was referred to Dr. C. Everett Koop. After just one hour with him, I understood my child's rare birth defect. Dr. Koop also made it clear to me that the treatment process would be long, expensive, and difficult. At the time, all I could think was: "How much harder can this get?"

Even as I tried to deal with Dean's poor health and uncertain future, I struggled to support my small family; I often wondered how we would eat from week to week, how I would pay for Dean's mounting medical bills. After years of pain and misery, I could bear the strain no longer. I wanted to end my life. The long years of unresolved anger, fear, and depression had finally pulled me into deep despair and thoughts of suicide.

Then, from somewhere deep inside me, I remembered my mother telling me about Jesus. I began to pray, "Lord, if you're really there, if you really do love me, please help me. I'm so tired. I just can't do this anymore." Suddenly, I felt the weight of all my troubles lift as the love of Christ surrounded me. For the first time in my life, I experienced real hope.

Though none of my circumstances had changed, I knew that God had met with me in a supernatural way. Soon after that, Dr. Koop asked me several pointed questions about my faith, and he went on to share with me how I could know Jesus was with me during these difficult days. Thus, it was through my son's illness that the Holy Spirit brought me back to Jesus and through my son's caring physician that I would begin to learn how to live for Christ.

On another day, Dr. Koop showed me a room full of sick infants. I was horrified to learn that children with similar diseases were being put to death by abortion. I soon realized that God had sent Dr. Koop to prepare me for a special mercy ministry. Shortly after that discussion with Dr. Koop, I eagerly accepted the challenge to help start a Crisis Pregnancy Center. At the time, I did not know I would one day serve as its Executive Director. I often think about my childhood dreams of helping unloved and hurting children and their mothers when I see the women and children whose needs are being met through this ministry.

If the Lord had not given me the life I had as a child, would I still have the compassion I feel for others today? If the Lord had not given me a critically ill son, would I even be walking with Christ today? Would I still cry at the sight of a handicapped or sick child? And if He had not led me to meet Dr. Koop, who taught me about Jesus and His love for children, would I now be ministering to hurting people experiencing crisis pregnancies? Would I have had the privilege of seeing even my own father receive Jesus into his heart just before his death?

Years of heartache taught me much about myself and about my Savior that I would never have learned otherwise. How thankful I am that He did not give up on me even during the time I gave up on Him.

Sharon Bias

WHERE IS GOD NOW?

Do you sometimes wish your life were like a videotape so that you could fast-forward over difficult circumstances or rewind back to times of joy and contentment? If so, you will be able to relate to the following people:

John and Tracey would never experience the joy of seeing their daughter, Josie, smile or grow up. For reasons known only to God, Josie was stillborn two weeks before her due date. The doctors later explained, "We have found no reason for this death. Your daughter was perfectly healthy." The bereaved mother could only ask herself bitterly, "Well, if that's true, then why isn't Josie here with us? Lord, this all seems so mean and senseless to me. My husband and I are trying to love and follow you, but I'm not sure I know who you are anymore. Why did you give us this child only to take her away before we even got to know her? I don't want to feel this way . . . *but how am I ever going to trust you again?*"

Joe and Priscilla had reached every goal in their marriage . . . except one. When would God give them a child? After years of infertility treatments and repeated miscarriages, they were tempted to believe that God was displeased with them. Did they need more faith? Was there hidden sin in their lives? When, if ever, would God give them a child?

Though an active, committed Christian since her teens, Margie, a young woman whom we love as though she were our own daughter, had just begun to understand that her heavenly Father loved her unconditionally and would never treat her the way her physically and emotionally abusive earthly father had. She, in turn, rejoiced in being God's beloved daughter; Margie loved God, and she longed to pass that love on to her children. Yet, for reasons that are still a mystery, almost four-year-old Eric woke up from an extended coma with irreversible brain damage. Eric is now totally handicapped; he sits in a wheelchair, and any indication that he is aware of his circumstances is rare. When Margie learned we were writing this book, she came to us. "I want to be faithful to God, but I don't understand His ways and I don't feel His love in this situation. Walking in obedience is so hard when I know there will be no happy endings for my family on this earth. Tell me how to keep walking by faith when life is excruciating. Please, no clichés or 'surefire recipes.' "

Each one of these struggling believers is a present-day hero of faith. Blindsided by traumatic circumstances, they strive to honor God despite their pain. It would be easy to make this book one more "How to Have Joy in the Journey" manual for Christians. Instead, in light of the God-given determination of our friends to know God intimately and to walk by faith even when life is hard, we knew we had to share honestly from our own difficult journey.

A MARK FROM GOD

God specializes in conforming us into the image of His Son (Romans 8:29). In order to do this, He invades our lives in ways that change us forever. We will look back on some of these encounters as fond memories, such as the time we came to know Jesus, the day we married the man or woman God brought into our lives, or the moment we experienced the glorious miracle of childbirth. Like Moses, whose face shone brilliantly after just such an encounter (2 Corinthians 3:7), we also know that, from that moment on, our lives will never be the same.

At other times these invasions are more sobering and painful. Thus, we are not surprised by the anguished cries of the many people who have come to us for comfort and counsel. We know all too well the anxiety caused by too many bills and not enough money, the crushing disappointment of severe church conflict, and the terror that goes with the words,

"You have advanced breast cancer." Each of these life-changing events in our own lives, both the bitter and the sweet, has left an indelible pattern, a kind of "scorch mark," upon our souls. Through it all, however, God gently and firmly led us into a deeper intimacy with Him. Even so, none of these experiences could have prepared us for the death, on July 6, 1993, of our sixteen-year-old son, Mark, and his friend Kelly in a car accident.

At times like these, the crushing pain we suffer leads us to cry out, "God is Sovereign—but can we trust Him?" In the crucible of suffering, what we believe about God takes on critical importance. What is our reaction when God doesn't resolve our problem, when He doesn't keep His promises the way we thought He would or reconcile our marriages even when we've completed every assignment in the marriage manual? Such disappointments will quickly reveal whether our faith is based on an intimate, trusting relationship with God or merely on the blessings He so generously gives us.

Suffering drives believers to God, but what is it that we want from Him? Do we settle for pat, simplistic, "theologically correct" answers, or do we hunger for a living knowledge of our heavenly Father? Do we demand tidy formulas that explain everything to our satisfaction, or do we submit ourselves to the One whose thoughts and ways are far above ours? Do we simply want to feel better, or do we ask God to equip us to persevere with joy and to encourage and strengthen others in their struggles? Is it possible to experience joy when each new day brings another reminder that we live in a broken and suffering world?

In our own personal search for answers, we soon learned that many of the Christian world's recipes for living and clichés for dealing with pain are nothing more than man-centered formulas rather than true biblical counsel. Instead of encouraging us to live *sola Scriptura* (by Scripture alone), they promote "sola bootstrappa" striving. Such striving may give some momentary relief, but eventually it comes up empty unless it is driven by a vision of God's character and ultimate purposes. What we believe about God is what provides the basis for our worldview, the window through which we view every event in our lives and which determines our responses. Understanding God's ultimate purpose helps us see the trials in our lives, and the scorch marks they leave behind, as one of His ways to separate us from our love affair with this world and focus our attention on His eternal perspective. It is not enough to know God's ultimate purpose, however. We must also know *Him.*

KNOWING GOD

Prior to our own painful experiences, we thought we did know God. For years we taught that God is the healer of broken hearts and brings beauty from ashes. We faithfully taught that if we did what was right and godly no matter how we felt, good feelings would follow. In the hours and months after our son's death, we doubted all of it. Our minds echoed with the self-incriminating scream, "Liar!" We were deaf to God's voice, and our eyes were blind to His gracious, unconditional love. Mark's death seemed to smash our life-vision, and we no longer cared about God's ultimate purposes. We just wanted our son back.

Ever so slowly and gently God began to restore our spiritual hearing and eyesight through His Word and through the testimony of those who came before us. In addition, we are observing this same tender and long-suffering God gently but firmly move our friends from misery to experiencing His mercy and then toward ministering to others. Please know that restoration does not mean we have a bounce in our step when we visit the cemetery. God's grace is not an anesthetic.

Some days God's restoration simply means we are able to crawl to the bathroom to face the start of a new day. We are learning that is enough.

CAN GOD BE TRUSTED?

Especially significant in our personal journey has been God's gentle but firm exhortation, written to discouraged Christians and recorded for us in the letter to the Hebrews. Because of their conversion from Judaism to Christianity these new believers were ostracized and rejected by their families. Suddenly people who were accustomed to strong family roots had no familiar family structures and faced social, political, and economic persecution. They started their Christian journey with great joy, but serving God in their culture had become terribly difficult. The purpose of the letter to the Hebrews is to exhort these young believers to stay the course, to persevere, and to minister to others as they traveled the paths marked out for them by God.

In response to the Hebrews' feeling that God does not hear their prayers for relief, the writer reminds them that God speaks to their needs in a most personal way:

> In the past God spoke to our forefathers through the prophets at many times and in various ways, but in these last days he has spoken to us by his Son, whom he appointed heir of all things, and through whom he made the universe. (Hebrews 1:1–2)

Without mentioning their specific sufferings, the writer proclaims that the One they embrace as Messiah is the exact representation of God's glory and sustains all things by His powerful word (v. 3). Implied is the question, "If our Messiah sustains all things, can He not sustain you?" Through his regular use of the Old Testament as his textbook and his steadfast reliance on the sufficiency of Christ, the author of Hebrews reminds these new believers of the truth that stands in stark contrast to their feelings.

Their eyes are fixed on the darkness of the present. In response, their teacher urges them to confidently cultivate intimacy with God. They must understand the sufficiency of what Christ accomplished in their behalf and the truth of God's promises so that He may "unbolt" them from the cares of this present world by focusing their eyes on their future with Him in eternity. Because of the finished work of Christ, he implores them to experience faith-based living rather than self-sufficient striving. After constructing a firm theological foundation for walking by faith in this broken world, the writer defines faith.

WHAT FAITH IS NOT

It's easy to respond to the anguished cry of a soul by saying, "Just have faith." But what is faith? If we define faith incorrectly, we will be wrong about many other spiritual truths that rest on it, particularly obedience and suffering. It helps to establish what faith is by first understanding what it is not.

Biblical faith is *not:*

- Dormant energy waiting to be activated by some mysterious incantation.
- A way of twisting God's arm to get what we want from Him.
- Intellectual assent to man-made creeds or "articles of faith."
- Complicated and incomprehensible theories about God.
- A guarantee of a comfortable, stress-free life.

The underlying fallacy in all of these concepts is the focus on ourselves, on what we can get, and on how we can control our destinies. The writer of Hebrews points out that, in contrast to these false notions about faith, those who trust God often must walk a difficult road and sometimes seem to receive only evil in this life. Some men and women of faith

> . . . were tortured and refused to be released, so that they might gain a better resurrection. Some faced jeers and flogging, while still others were chained and put in prison. They were stoned; they were sawed in two; they were put to death by the sword. They went about in sheepskins and goatskins, destitute, persecuted and mistreated—the world was not worthy of them. They wandered in deserts and mountains, and in caves and holes in the ground. (Hebrews 11:35b–38)

Living in a broken world guarantees that everyone will experience difficulty on some level. Some suffering may be due to faithlessness and disobedience, but much of it comes as a result of having faith rather than a lack of it. This should not surprise us. When we suffer for the faith, we are following the journey of Jesus, the perfect model of faith. Jesus "endured the cross, scorning its shame," for our sakes. We have no reason to expect anything different. Other suffering comes upon us not because of our faith but for no apparent reason at all. Just having faith does not insulate us from sickness, pain, sorrow, and death.

Even those who appear spiritually strong may succumb to faulty thinking—the mistaken belief that by trying harder, believing more, or finding the right spiritual formula, we'll be able to make the pain go away. Chuck learned how his apparent ability to remove pain from his family's life had helped shape his relationship with God.

At a very early age I concluded that as long as I was in charge of circumstances, I could control my happiness. Whether a ministerial crisis, an emotional depression, or the doctor's diagnosis that my wife had advanced breast cancer, my response would be, "I can fix this!" But when I held the lifeless body of our son, Mark, in my arms, I knew fully I was not in control of my circumstances . . . and I was scared.

A skewed definition of faith subtly implies that "me plus God" equals a majority, when the proper equation is "God plus no one is the majority." The resolution of any difficult circumstance is an undeserved gift from Him. We must be wary of any definition of faith that implies that we have control over God's responses to our circumstances.

WHAT BIBLICAL FAITH IS

Hebrews 11:1 gives us a simple yet profound definition of faith: "Now faith is being sure of what we hope for and certain of what we do not see." What were the people mentioned in Hebrews 11 hoping for and what were they certain of? What was visible to them that was invisible to others?

The inhabitants of God's Hall of Faith listed in Hebrews 11 were certain of what they could not see: *God.* They were sure of what they hoped for: *God could and would keep His promises.* As a result, they ultimately obeyed God, and God in turn commended them for their faithfulness.

BIBLICAL FAITH IS BELIEVING THAT GOD EXISTS

What these people believed about God is made even clearer in verse 6:

Without faith it is impossible to please God, because anyone who comes to him must believe that he exists and that he rewards those who earnestly seek him.

The writer to the Hebrews points to creation as evidence that the Creator exists: "By faith we understand that the universe was formed at God's command, so that what is seen was not made out of what was visible" (v. 3). In other words, creation testifies to all humankind that God exists, and the visible creation depends on the invisible Creator. The knowledge that God is sovereign and in control of everything is one of the pivotal building blocks of faith.

BIBLICAL FAITH IS BELIEVING THAT GOD REWARDS THOSE WHO SEEK HIM

Believing God exists and is in control of all things is not enough. Believing God is in control sometimes deepens our pain unless we also believe that God keeps His promises (i.e., that "he rewards those who earnestly seek him" [v. 6]). Faith gives us eyes to see what is invisible to others. Where others see only suffering, faith enables us to see God's hand drawing us to Himself. Our friend Josephine expressed her commitment to this kind of faith in a note to several trusted friends.

My husband has fallen into a grievous sin; an addiction to pornography. Such an addiction can wreak destruction on a family. He has made a confession to me and our pastor and Session. He is repentant and is on the road to recovery. I am in the process of dealing with forgiveness and the restoration of our marriage. . . . I don't want all of this to be in vain. I know God promises to make beauty from ashes. He must have something for us to do for others through this crisis.

... My hope for myself is that one day I will be "clothed with strength and dignity"; I will "laugh at the days to come." I will speak "with wisdom," and have "faithful instruction" on my tongue (Proverbs 31:25–26).

The Westminster Shorter Catechism teaches us that "God is a Spirit, infinite, eternal, and unchangeable, in his being, wisdom, power, holiness, justice, goodness, and truth." Such a God is someone Josephine can trust to keep His promises.

THE PROMISE OF SALVATION

In addition to God's many promises that are in the process of being fulfilled, His promise to provide salvation for His children has already been fulfilled through Christ. Because God has kept this, the greatest of all promises, we are able to enjoy all that God has supplied for us. God's promise of salvation is the cornerstone of the "covenant of grace" (Hebrews 10:1–18). The writer of Hebrews declares,

> Therefore, brothers, since we have confidence to enter the Most Holy Place by the blood of Jesus, by a new and living way opened for us through the curtain, that is, his body, and since we have a great priest over the house of God, let us draw near to God with a sincere heart in full assurance of faith, having our hearts sprinkled to cleanse us from a guilty conscience and having our bodies washed with pure water. (Hebrews 10:19–22)

We can hear the writer exclaiming, "Therefore, in light of this amazing truth about God's grace, enjoy what God has provided for you!" Thus, we can:

- confidently pursue intimacy with our Heavenly Father (vv. 19–22),
- unswervingly believe the promises of God (v. 23),
- cultivate fellowship with other believers that encourages perseverance (vv. 24–25),
- choose to do what is right (vv. 26–31),
- remember God's past faithfulness and the joy of ministry (vv. 32–34),
- persevere by keeping our eyes fixed on eternal values (vv. 35–39), and
- be assured that God will not always seem absent (v. 37).

Rather than responses born merely of obligation, these are responses based on God's proclamation of who He is. It is a call to know God so well that we believe He is present and at work even when we cannot see Him.

Joan explains how God is enabling her to respond to His love in just this way:

"Broken" is a good way to describe my world. Alzheimer's stole my husband's mind. I finally gave in to what was inevitable and, with a shattered heart, I placed him in a nursing home. Within the same time frame I was terminated from a 14-year teaching position and also learned my daughter's husband left her with two young girls to raise. God used all of this as a means to build within me His love and kingdom. Endless hours of studying the Scriptures changed and enabled me to focus on God's many promises. I learned to praise God. In the context of 2 Corinthians 1:3–4, He gave me the privilege to "comfort those in any trouble [with Alzheimer's] with the comfort we ourselves have received from God." God has also given me a special Christian friend, the wife of my husband's roommate. Since we share similar circumstances and trust God for each day, we daily encourage each other as we "bear one another's burdens." How good God is!

God is teaching Joan to see His grace in a situation where others would see only darkness.

WHEN YOU CANNOT SEE HIS HAND

The writer of Hebrews quotes the prophet Habakkuk to remind us that faith is believing God even when we can neither see nor understand Him (Hebrews 10:38). Habakkuk records his confusion and dismay over God's apparent abandonment of Israel and exultation of Israel's enemy, Babylon. He cries out,

> How long, O LORD, must I call for help, but you do not listen? Or cry out to you, "Violence!" but you do not save? Why do you make me look at injustice? Why do you tolerate wrong? Destruction and violence are before me; there is strife, and conflict abounds. Therefore the law is paralyzed and justice never prevails. The wicked hem in the righteous, so that justice is perverted. (Habakkuk 1:2–4)

God's shocking reply confused Habakkuk even further. God intended to use Israel's bitter enemies, the Babylonians, to bring judgment on His people. This caused the prophet to continue questioning God's wisdom and love (Habakkuk 1:12–2:1), but God's answer came swiftly. Babylon would eventually also be punished; in the meantime, the Israelites were to live by faith as they waited for God's deliverance (Habakkuk 2:4). Although fearful of what awaited the Israelites, Habakkuk chose emotional, intimate worship in his response, declaring, "I heard and my heart pounded, my lips quivered at the sound; decay crept into my bones, and my legs trembled. Yet I will wait patiently for the day of calamity to come on the nation invading us . . . I will rejoice in the LORD, I will be joyful in God my Savior" (Habakkuk 3:16–18).

Habakkuk exercised true faith by trusting God even when he could not see what God was doing. He trusted God to keep His promises regarding Babylon, Israel, and—something the prophet himself would never personally see—the full redemption of God's people. Habakkuk's beliefs about God's character dramatically changed his reaction to his circumstances and gave him eyes that saw beyond the physical realm. His decision to wait by faith deepened his intimacy with God.

> The Sovereign LORD is my strength; he makes my feet like the feet of a deer, he enables me to go on the heights. (Habakkuk 3:19)

Although the Hebrew Christians were not suffering because of their personal sin, the author of Hebrews borrows a direct quote from Habakkuk, where God says,

> So do not throw away your confidence; it will be richly rewarded. You need to persevere so that when you have done the will of God, you will receive what he has promised. For in just a very little while, "He who is coming will come and will not delay. But my righteous one will live by faith. And if he shrinks back, I will not be pleased with him." *But we are not of those who shrink back and are destroyed, but of those who believe and are saved.* (Hebrews 10:35–39 [emphasis added])

A FAITH RESPONSE

In response to this, these young Hebrew believers might have said, "We know what you are saying is true, but you just don't understand how hard this is. We need to hear from someone who has walked in similar circumstances."

We understand this protest, and we have been so grateful for those bereaved parents who are farther ahead of us in this journey. Many have called back to us with the proclamation, "We know your struggle, but God is faithful. You can trust Him!" Similarly, the teacher of these young believers gave them examples of ordinary people who responded to extreme stress with extraordinary faith—people whose saving faith resulted in the eventual development of experiential faith. Faced with extraordinary testing, these people drew on a personal relationship with God that taught them He would do everything He promised. Their stories are valuable because the Old Testament hides nothing about their journeys. Throughout our study of Hebrews 11 we will watch as God progressively reveals His promises to:

- redeem His people,
- build a covenant family,
- give them His presence,
- make them a blessing to others,
- preserve their inheritance, and
- share with them His glory for all eternity.

What is more, we will see God accomplish this through ordinary people who sometimes faltered in their pilgrimages. God gave these Old Testament believers eyes to see the reality of His promises: a better and lasting possession (Hebrews 10:34), a city with foundations (Hebrews 11:10), a country of their own (Hebrews 11:14), a better country—a heavenly one (Hebrews 11:16), a "better resurrection" (Hebrews 11:35), and numerous spiritual descendants even when there was no physical heir (Hebrews 11:12, 18, 21). God's promises gave them the courage to end their love affair with this world because they knew the best was yet to come. Knowing this freed them to respond by faith to difficult circumstances.

Because they knew God intimately,

> all these people were still living by faith when they died. They did not receive the things promised; they only saw them and welcomed them from a distance. And they admitted that they were aliens and strangers on earth. People who say such things show that they are looking for a country of their own. If they had been thinking of the country they had left, they would have had opportunity to return. Instead, they were longing for a better country—a heavenly one. Therefore, God is not ashamed to be called their God, for he has prepared a city for them. (Hebrews 11:13–16)

And . . .

> These were all commended for their faith, yet none of them received what had been promised. God had planned something better for us so that only together with us would they be made perfect. (vv. 39–40)

But the stories of these men and women are not about how strong they were. Rather, their lives and experiences showcase the long-suffering, unconditional love of God. Biblical faith focuses on God's character and filters all of our circumstances through the prism of His sovereignty. We demonstrate biblical faith when we intentionally choose to surrender to God's sovereign control by allowing His plan for our lives—however different from our own plans His plan may be—in order to deepen our intimacy with Him. When we live by faith we trust that even the most difficult circumstances, though so often completely beyond our control, are still rich with possibilities and opportunities. We can have hope instead of despair because our lives and circumstances are always under God's control.

LIVING BY FAITH

Judges 2:10–12 states that a whole generation of Israelites grew up who did not know God or what He had done for Israel. "Then the Israelites did evil in the eyes of the LORD and served the Baals" (v. 11). The same statement defines our world today. Too many people do not believe God because they do not know Him, and their lives reflect that ignorance. Living by faith requires knowing God intimately. It is critical for believers to pass on the history of God's relationship to His people. Hebrews 11 is an overview of our spiritual heritage, giving an account of the way God raised up, nurtured, and preserved His kingdom through the lives of ordinary people. Intimacy with God and believing His promises gave these people eyes to see another country, another city. They knew they did not belong to this world, and so they lived as foreigners here. They were on a journey toward their eternal inheritance, and now they have reached their destination. They call back to us, through this passage, with the encouraging message: "Our God is *faithful.*"

Their examples of faith are a part of our heritage. We have found that, in our own difficult struggle with grief and loss, God's faithfulness to these men and women in Hebrews 11 helps us keep our eyes fixed on Jesus even when our present circumstances make our hearts tremble with fear and the enemy taunts us with the death of our son. We are often tempted to give in to our broken hearts and give up, feeling that the race marked out for us is just too hard. Then God reminds us of the legacy we want to leave our children, our grandchildren, and all those within our circle of influence.

What do our lives tell them about intimacy with God? And so, along with Habakkuk, we choose to believe God, and experiencing His faithfulness in our own journey drives us to call out to others:

> Though the fig tree does not bud and there are no grapes on the vines, though the olive crop fails and the fields produce no food, though there are no sheep in the pen and no cattle in the stalls, yet I will rejoice in the LORD, I will be joyful in God my Savior. The Sovereign LORD is my strength; he makes my feet like the feet of a deer, he enables me to go on the heights. (Habakkuk 3:17–19)

DIGGING DEEPER

Day One

- What is a "worldview"? How does your worldview affect your behavior? How has your personal worldview affected your reaction to irritations today?

Day Two

- Read Hebrews 11:1–6 and write out a definition of faith based on this passage. How does your definition of faith shape your worldview?

Day Three

- Read Hebrews 11:32–40. Why is it wrong to imply that suffering is a result of little or weak faith?
- What has God promised His children (Hebrews 13:5–6). Do you believe this promise? Why or why not? How does trusting this promise influence your responses to the various circumstances in your life?

Day Four

- How do the authors define "scorch mark"?
- Explain how scorch marks are opportunities to trust God.
- Identify one scorch mark in your life. How did your view of God influence your response to that event?

Day Five

- Review Joan's comments on pages 20–21. How did Joan's practical actions reflect her worldview? Why did her actions help her surrender to God's eternal purposes? How does her example help you focus on God's character and promises in your present circumstances?

Day Six

- Review the exhortation of Hebrews 10:19–39. What practical step in this passage will require faith for you to take in your present circumstances? Be specific.

Chapter 2

WORSHIP FROM THE HEART—ABEL

<table>
<tr><td>FAITH PRINCIPLE #2
BIBLICAL FAITH PRODUCES RIGHT WORSHIP.</td></tr>
</table>

By faith Abel offered God a better sacrifice than Cain did.

By faith he was commended as a righteous man, when God spoke well

of his offerings. And by faith he still speaks, even though he is dead.

(Hebrews 11:4 [see also Genesis 4:1–16])

BOLDLY FACING DEATH—DAVID SAADEH

Several years after Mark's death, God seared into our souls a vivid image of the privilege of corporate worship within our covenant community (i.e., our circle of believing Christian friends) as described in Hebrews 10:25:

> Let us not give up meeting together, as some are in the habit of doing, but let us encourage one another—and all the more as you see the Day approaching.

God gave our church the gift of thirty-seven–year–old David Saadeh, a man who had an indescribable thirst for intimacy with Christ and a longing to encourage others. We grieved with his family when they learned he had terminal brain cancer. Although David mourned the fact that he would soon say goodbye to his wife and young children, his visitors always left his presence feeling more connected to heaven.

Near death, blind, unable to stand, and barely able to move his arms, David insisted on sitting in his wheelchair near the front of the church for worship. One Sunday we began to sing the following words:

> Shout to the Lord, all the earth, let us sing
>   power and majesty, praise to the King;
> Mountains bow down and the seas will roar
>   at the sound of Your name.
> I sing for joy at the work of Your hands,
>   forever I'll love You, forever I'll stand;
> Nothing compares to the promise I have in You.[1]

Our friend's impending death made us keenly aware of the great cloud of witnesses surrounding us (Hebrews 12:1). We were weeping freely as we contemplated the day we would join all of heaven in praise to our God when, out of the corner of our eyes, we saw movement. David was struggling to rise from his wheelchair so that he could stand and lift his arms toward heaven. He told his wife, "I can't sing this song sitting down. I must stand up." Others began to weep as they realized his once healthy body would not obey. Seeing his struggle and knowing his determined heart, a man on either side of him— one an elder, the other David's doctor—helped David to stand, raising his arms for him so that he could freely worship

---

[1] "Shout to the Lord," © 1993 Darlene Zschech/Hillsongs, Australia. Used by permission from Integrity Music, Inc.

his God. In tears, the rest of the congregation rose to its feet. We sang with one voice and heart while the music swelled in loud continuous praise to God for His promises.

Like Aaron and Hur who held up Moses' arms (Exodus 17:8–13), these two men strengthened David in his feebleness and helped him display his absolute devotion to God. Members of the Body were able to encourage one another with God's truth as together they anticipated David's "Day approaching" (Hebrews 10:25) and witnessed a picture of our hope that special Sabbath.

That day, the church, the Body of Christ, reflected heartfelt worship overflowing with encouragement. David, our friend and brother, died just a few weeks later. His memorial service was an exclamation point for his earlier affirmation that the sovereign Giver of Life can be trusted, even in the face of certain death.

Chuck and Sharon Betters

WORSHIP FROM THE HEART

Faith is being sure of what we hope for and certain of what we do not see. Like the different colors of an emerging rainbow, the various aspects of this definition of faith radiate from each of the living examples of faithful men and women found in Hebrews 11, people who, one by one, experienced a hope that became a reality.

Having told us what faith is, the writer of Hebrews intentionally chooses flesh-and-blood illustrations of faith that would encourage his struggling readers. How strange it is, then, that this writer chose to encourage these believers to persevere in following God by highlighting the life of a man who was actually murdered as a result of his faithfulness.

Persecution had already caused some in the Hebrew congregation to distance themselves from the covenant community. Those who remained continued to be treated unjustly (Hebrews 10:32–34). Yet the writer of Hebrews urged these distressed believers to continue meeting together, the very thing that would likely cause them trouble. They were to worship both privately and corporately (vv. 19–25).

Then again, what *better* place to begin a description of faith than with a man noted for his worship?

> By faith Abel offered God a better sacrifice than Cain did. By faith he was commended as a righteous man, when God spoke well of his offerings. And by faith he still speaks, even though he is dead. (Hebrews 11:4)

Cain and Abel, like all of humanity to follow, were the products of sinful parents. Adam and Eve had once been in close fellowship with God. When they doubted their Creator and went on to disobey God, they brought the curse of death upon themselves and their children. As a result, Adam and Eve and their children after them lived in a broken world, un-

der the curse of God (Genesis 3:17–19). Yet God's eternal redemptive plan was already in place, wrapped in grace, and
buoyed with the promise that God would one day provide salvation through a descendant of Eve (vv. 14–15).

Eve's words at the time of Cain's birth reflected her reliance upon God for his birth: "With the help of the LORD I
have brought forth a man" (Genesis 4:1). Eve's second son,
Abel, was born not long afterward.

Though the Scriptures give few details about life in
Adam's family, we do know that although they worked hard in
the fields, they regularly set aside time to worship God.

> In the course of time Cain brought some of the fruits
> of the soil as an offering to the LORD. But Abel
> brought fat portions from some of the firstborn of his
> flock. The LORD looked with favor on Abel and his of-
> fering, but on Cain and his offering he did not look
> with favor. So Cain was very angry, and his face was
> downcast. (Genesis 4:3–5)

We know this religious observation was a common event
because the Septuagint, or Greek translation of the Old Testament, renders the phrase "In the course of time" (Genesis
4:3) to mean "at the end of the Sabbath," indicating a regularly scheduled time for family worship.

Why was God pleased with Abel's offering but not with
Cain's? It is generally believed that Cain's sacrifice was unac-
ceptable because an appropriate sacrifice required the shed-
ding of blood (see Hebrews 9:22). Yet, since Cain did not have
the benefit of the directives regarding animal sacrifice that
God gave His people in Numbers, Deuteronomy, and elsewhere, it is unfair to assert that Cain's offering was unaccept-
able because he did not adhere to practices that were only
spelled out clearly many centuries later. We believe that God
was concerned with much more here—the motivation behind

Cain and Abel's choices. Outwardly, both men offered sacrifices produced from their respective occupations—gardener and shepherd. However, the issue here is internal, involving the hearts of the two men. We know this is the case from Hebrews 11:4: *"By faith,* Abel offered God a better sacrifice than Cain did" (emphasis added). What made the sacrifice "better," what made it, indeed, acceptable to God at all, was the faith of the one who gave it. Abel's faith had produced right worship.

God, of course, sees past all artifice. He knows and cares deeply what is in the innermost recesses of our hearts, beyond the view of all others. While we tend to consider only outward appearances, the Lord looks, always, into the heart (1 Samuel 16:7). When God looked into Abel's heart, He saw trust, He saw faith. When He looked into Cain's heart, He saw anger. God confronted Cain,

> Why are you angry? Why is your face downcast? If you do what is right, will you not be accepted? But if you do not do what is right, sin is crouching at your door; it desires to have you, but you must master it. (Genesis 4:6–7)

Cain's anger here is an indication of a defiant soul, one hot with displeasure against God. We don't know the reason for this anger, but it certainly offers a warning to all of us. Great evil, God warned, was "crouching" at the door of Cain's heart. The word for crouching here is *robets*—the name of a demon according to some of the ancient rabbis. Sin is thus depicted as though it were a demon lying in wait for Cain. The moment Cain chooses to do what is wrong, the power of sin and evil stands ready to pounce on him and drag him off into even greater sin. God exhorted Cain to do what was right, warning him that his rebellious anger would lead him into deeper sin. When Cain refused to obey God, this, of course, is precisely what happened.

Cain did not repent of his anger, he did not listen to God. Instead, Cain pretended friendship with Abel. "Cain said to his brother Abel, 'Let's go out into the field' " (v. 8a). There, Cain brutally murdered his brother: "and while they were in the field, Cain attacked his brother Abel and killed him" (v. 8b).

Cain's actions confirmed God's initial judgment of his sacrifice. Cain had demonstrated an ego-driven worship that accurately reflected his own enmity against God. Throughout this passage in Genesis, Cain talks to God, argues with God, and even sacrifices to God. Cain clearly believes that God exists, but Cain's actions indicate he isn't willing to actually trust God. Cain dramatically reveals his unbelief in God's authority when, in effect, he defiantly shakes his fist in God's face and declares, "I hear you and I know you and *I will not repent.*" Cain's subsequent actions only confirmed God's initial judgment of his sacrifice.

ABEL STILL SPEAKS

Though the focus of Genesis 4 is the downward spiral of sin as evidenced by Cain's actions, the writer of Hebrews focuses not on Cain, but on Abel.

Like all of us, Abel lived in a family afflicted with selfishness, jealousy, and anger—in a word: *sin.* Backbreaking labor, pain in childbearing, and marital discord were the consequences of Adam and Eve's sin. The enmity and jealousy that result from sin spilled over into the relationship between their two sons. Cain's refusal to obey God and do "what is right" reveals the blot on Cain's soul that eventually poisoned his relationship with Abel. The Bible underscores the heinous nature of Cain's murderous hatred by constantly noting that Abel was Cain's *brother* (Genesis 4:8–12). Thus, in the midst of a family setting such as this, Abel's faith, as expressed here through his worship, must have provided an oasis of comfort and peace for him.

Hebrews 11:4 tells us that this man, this *dead* man, this first murder victim, still speaks to us, the people of faith. What is he saying?

WORSHIP IS A PRIORITY

Abel worshiped with his family despite his older brother's hatred. The threat of persecution was enough reason for some people in the Hebrew congregation to give up worshiping with their covenant community. Yet people often give up on worshiping together with far less justification, such as when life gets hard or relationships prove disappointing. God, however, tells us that the church is the very place we *should* go when life is hard. David Saadeh, the young man whose story begins this chapter, refused to give up meeting with other believers for worship, though common sense might have indicated he had every reason to stay home. He was unable to walk or even move his body; he could not see. But David believed spiritual strength and God's comfort could be found within the covenant community. Similarly, Abel's love for God did not allow him to use Cain's hatred, of which he was undoubtedly aware, as an excuse to give up on worship.

WORSHIP IS A LIFESTYLE

Worship is not, however, limited to what we do on Sunday mornings. Though Scripture only gives us one look at Abel's worship, we can be sure that he did not merely relegate his worship to set times. God commended Abel as a "righteous man" (Hebrews 11:4). The Greek word for "righteous" is *dikaios,* and it means "equitable in character or in act." By implication, it means "innocent or holy." Worship is not separate from everyday life. All aspects of our lives as believers are sacred. We worship God by the way we drive our cars, the way we speak to one another, the way we work at our jobs and interact with our employees or employers, the way we raise our children, the way we treat our spouses, and the way we show God's love in our communities. Worship is a reflection of our commitment to God through all the twists and turns of our day-to-day lives.

WORSHIP REFLECTS OUR RELATIONSHIP WITH GOD

Who or what we worship determines how we live. The Ten Commandments spell out very clearly God's priorities for us. After reminding the Israelites of His past acts of love and mercy, God sets forth the first commandment: "You shall have no other gods before me" (Exodus 20:3). This is the very bedrock of right worship.

God confronted the Israelites with a choice that offered no middle ground. Even when life is difficult, "you shall have no other gods before me." When the writer of Hebrews showcases a man at worship as his first illustration of living by faith, he makes it clear that a man or woman of faith chooses to worship God when life is good and when it is not, when children are born healthy and when they are not, when careers are successful and when they are not, when families dwell together in peace and when conflict reigns. Such worship is possible only when it is based on a solid, exclusive, priority relationship with God above all others.

By commending Abel as a righteous man, God exposed the erroneous notion that righteous living guarantees us a long and prosperous life. Like Abel, our worship must focus on the character and eternal promises of God rather than on mere temporal blessings. Broken relationships and difficult circumstances are opportunities for us to experience deeper intimacy with our sovereign Creator.

When we *know* God in a personal, one-to-One relationship, we can trust Him. When we trust God, we worship Him.

Even when blessings slip through our fingers, or never come our way at all, we can worship God if we know Him intimately. Such worship may be different from the kind we observe in a church building on Sunday mornings. Personal worship can and should also occur in solitude, sometimes with tears of joy and gratitude and sometimes with quiet cries of anguish. Such relationship-driven worship can be found throughout the Psalms. In Psalm 73:1–4, for example, the writer describes his confusion and disappointment over the prosperity of unbelievers, prosperity that was in stark contrast to his own difficult circumstances. Instead of staying in the pit of despair, however, the writer goes on to contemplate God's character and past faithfulness. The writer's concluding remarks indicate renewed confidence in his relationship with God: "But as for me, it is good to be near God. I have made the Sovereign LORD my refuge; I will tell of all your deeds" (v. 28). Our confidence deepens as our relationship with Him matures. Worship, both together with others and when we're alone with our Lord, builds that confidence, that faith.

WORSHIP BRINGS US INTO THE PRESENCE OF GOD

By citing the example of Abel's life and death, the writer of Hebrews urges these hurting, questioning believers to come boldly into the Lord's presence and to get to know Him better (Hebrews 10:19–22), come what may. He wants them, in spite of their difficult and dangerous circumstances, to bring their questions, sorrows, and fears to God. The writer knows that time spent in God's presence will in turn strengthen them so that they can indeed persevere, holding "unswervingly to the hope we profess, for he who promised is faithful" (v. 23).

God is not afraid of our questions. The psalmists often began their songs with cries of doubt and anger but, after experiencing God's presence through their worship, concluded these passages by expressing a joyful surrender to God's ways and His perfect will. Their circumstances had not changed, but simply being in God's presence had renewed their hope.

In chapter 1 we reflected on God's patience with Habakkuk and his many questions. God did not reject him for asking such questions, and eventually Habakkuk surrendered to God's answers. When we insist on understanding our circumstances or on clearing up our confusion before we come to God, we say, in essence, "I will worship and trust You only if I understand and approve of what You are doing." Instead, the cry of our souls must be, "We believe, help our unbelief!"

Sometimes we enter God's presence like angry children—accusing, bitter, fearful, shaking our fists in God's face. "Why, why have you treated me like this?" But the Lord holds us, like a father holding a screaming, panicked child; He holds us tightly until at last we relax and our cries turn to quiet sobs, and He whispers to us gently, "I know this hurts. Trust me, trust me in this."

After teaching on this subject, Sharon wept as a young mother told her this story:

My husband and I just adopted a little Chinese girl. Her initial response to us was so positive. That is why we were shocked by her terrified cries when we arrived at our hotel. She could not speak English. We could not speak Chinese. We had no idea why she was so afraid. Finally, my husband concluded, "She thinks we are going to take her back to the orphanage." We held her tightly and, with tears that matched hers, we kept whispering in a language she could not understand, "We love you. You are not an orphan anymore. You are our daughter. A new family is waiting to love you. We have prepared a home for you. You are not an orphan anymore. You are our little girl. Trust us."

In time our new daughter relaxed in our arms. I often imagine God holding us tightly in His arms and whispering the same words when we are frightened by our circumstances. But, like our little girl, we don't always understand His language or have eyes to see the place He has prepared for us.

As this little girl learns more about her new mother and father and lives in the secure and loving home they have prepared for her, she will come to trust them and live like a daughter rather than an orphan. Similarly, in those times when our circumstances seem to contradict our understanding of God's character, choosing to worship takes us into God's presence and teaches us more about who He is and what He has prepared for us. Just knowing that God holds us tightly in His grip, even when we struggle to get away, creates a deepening appreciation of His love.

WORSHIP IS OFTEN A SACRIFICE OF PRAISE

But what if your circumstances are so awful that all you have to offer God is a broken heart? For months after Mark's death, all we had to offer God were tears and questions. Doing all the "right" spiritual things didn't produce the spiritual blessings we sought.

Prior to Mark's death we looked forward to being with our covenant community, our church, joining with other believers in praising God. But how could we praise God when all we really wanted was our son back? We wanted God to relieve our agony; God wanted us to desire Him. Very slowly, we began to understand that true worship requires true sacrifice. As Hebrews 13:15 explains, "Through Jesus, therefore, let us continually offer to God a sacrifice of praise—the fruit of lips that confess his name."

A sacrifice costs the giver something valuable, something dear to the heart. So what sort of sacrifice does God want from us? Rather than delighting in "meaningless" sacrifice, God seeks a "broken spirit" (Psalm 51:16–17).

We were broken by Mark's death and we wanted to know how to surrender to God's plan. We did not simply want to go through the motions; we wanted our worship to be authentic. Although we longed for the return of our son, we began to see that God wanted us to desire Him and trust Him with our tears and pain—a sacrifice for Him to use in whatever way He pleased. Almost two years after Mark's death, Sharon wrote in her journal,

I should be planning a graduation party for Mark as I did for the other kids. . . . Oh, God, so much of life is made up of conflict resolution but there is no resolution for this ache. We worked so hard to get to this year—anticipating the joy of seeing Mark, our youngest, graduate. I'm not finished mothering Mark. How do I learn to live without resolution that satisfies my mother's heart?

You remind me: The Israelites grumbled because they had no water (Numbers 21:16–18). As Mark's absence governs my thoughts, their desire for water ruled theirs. Just as I am constantly complaining against You for taking my son, the Israelites murmured against You for not giving them water. Then You promised to give them water, and they in turn praised You for the water you would give them, thanking You in advance for the promise they knew You would keep.

Is this Your reply to me? To praise You with words that proclaim I believe You will keep Your promises to comfort before I feel that comfort? To repent of my unbelief and replace my murmuring with praise? Do You know how hard this will be for me? What can I praise You for when I feel so weak? To praise You makes me feel as though I am leaving Mark behind. I can't do this unless You enable me. Help me, Lord, to do your bidding.

Seeking to renew a grateful heart, Sharon began to write down every happy memory from her life, no matter how brief or seemingly insignificant, beginning with her childhood and acknowledging along the way that each of these wonderful memories was a gift from God. By the time she reached the events of her adolescence, the physical ache was gone from her heart. A sacrifice of praise, even though mixed with tears, had brought her relief from months of seemingly endless pain.

There were many days, however, as we were looking through the Bible and praying, that choosing to praise God did nothing to lessen our grief. We began to understand that God's grace, although sufficient, will not always eradicate—or even soften—our pain. Yet in those moments when we think we have little for which to praise Him, the Scriptures proclaim a different perspective:

> I will praise you, O LORD, with all my heart;
>   I will tell of all your wonders.
> I will be glad and rejoice in you;
>   I will sing praise to your name, O Most High.
>   (Psalm 9:1–2)

It is often difficult to remember that worship is not about meeting our own needs. Our praise and worship are to focus

on God and His works. True worship that focuses on God becomes a channel of His grace.

> Fear the LORD your God and serve him. Hold fast to
> him and take your oaths in his name. *He is your praise;*
> *he is your God,* who performed for you those great and
> awesome wonders you saw with your own eyes.
> (Deuteronomy 10:20–21 [emphasis added])

The only way we can take our eyes off our problems and
focus on God is through faith—a wholehearted trust in God
and in His promise to comfort us.

LIVING BY FAITH

Abel, though dead, still speaks to our hearts. We knew, after the death of our son, that there was nothing we could do
to bring him back. But we needed to know the One who was
sovereign over even this "scorch mark" on our souls. Mark's
death had ravaged our hearts and swept away all the things we
had drawn comfort from—all, that is, except one. Our grief
drove us to God's Word. Private worship took on new meaning
as we searched the Scriptures and asked for a better understanding of God's promises. We wanted our faith to be guided
only by His truth. The Bible had to be the grid through which
we viewed each of our thoughts and emotions.

> The word of God is living and active. Sharper than any
> double-edged sword, it penetrates even to dividing
> soul and spirit, joints and marrow; it judges the
> thoughts and attitudes of the heart. (Hebrews 4:12)

Each time the Scriptures contradicted our own conclusions about God's character, we were faced with a clear choice:
to believe God's Word or our own roller-coaster emotions.

Every decision to trust Him, in spite of our doubts, was an act of worship.

Immediately following Mark's death, gathering with other Christians for corporate worship was even more difficult than private worship. Yet, we knew that avoiding this would be disobedience to God's expressed will regarding worship and the church body. We soon realized, however, that He was using corporate worship as a means of healing, and thus it became the defining event of our week. We came to these services weary of bearing our personal sorrow, and there God used the strength of other believers to restore us. In worshiping with others, we were reminded of the finished work of Christ and His promise to help us run with perseverance the race marked out for us (Hebrews 12:1).

A gifted percussionist, Mark had served, along with his brothers, on our church's worship team. For weeks after Mark's death we avoided looking in the direction of his replacement. But when we finally did, we often saw tears streaming down the new drummer's cheeks. That young man's willingness to sit in Mark's place and to honor God through his music, despite his own sorrow, showed us that he, too, had chosen to trust God in this. Eventually, we began to long for the Sabbath rest that came to us on Sundays, when we gathered with other members of the Body—people who not only prayed for us but wept with us. We experienced blessings even in the darkness that had invaded our lives. God's people prayed as one for us, asking Him to heal and strengthen our broken hearts.

Although confused by the loss of Mark and his girlfriend, Kelly, our believing friends believed God's promises to comfort and heal us. His presence in our lives was painful and, yet, also sweet. Listening to other believers express their faith in worship, through hymns and Scripture songs, became a kind of "lifeline" for us, connecting us to God's heart. We often wept as we listened to those around us praising God for His trustworthiness and expressing their need for intimacy. At other times, our grief and sense of loss would return, unbidden, overwhelming, and we would falter before singing the words, "I surrender all."

Our corporate worship became an opportunity to renew publicly our desire to surrender to God's love and purposes. We eagerly anticipated the preaching of the Word, knowing that, through it, God would be giving us a glimpse into His Own heart. We thought of the "great cloud of witnesses" (Hebrews 12:1) worshiping in heaven as we worshiped here on earth. We realized anew that our worship here on earth, though wonderful and encouraging, gave just a hint of the glorious worship taking place in heaven. And although we still struggled with questions and doubts, we experienced God's presence in ways that brought peace for that moment. We began once again to embrace worship as a marvelous privilege—the privilege of coming into the very presence of God.

In biblical worship, worship of the heart, we focus on God and not on our circumstances, and we express our longing to know Him intimately. Our next two examples of faith, Enoch and Noah, will, like Abel, teach us that all aspects of our lives provide us with an opportunity for true worship.

DIGGING DEEPER

Day One
◆ Read Genesis 4:1–16. Describe Abel's broken world. What was Abel's response to his broken world? If you feel your world is broken, describe this brokenness and how you have responded to it.

Day Two
◆ Describe your private worship. How does private worship affect corporate worship?

- Read Isaiah 58. How do your everyday activities reflect a worshipful lifestyle?

Day Three
- Read Isaiah 58:13–14. What do these verses concerning the Sabbath tell us about our priorities and behavior in corporate worship?
- What practical preparations can you make to help yourself and/or your family appreciate and benefit from corporate worship?

Day Four
- Consider once again Isaiah 58. Stop and pray after you read each verse. Ask God to reveal any ways your public worship is being negated by behavior in your private life. Confess your sin to a trusted friend and ask him or her to hold you accountable as you seek God's change in your life.

Day Five
- Review your answers to yesterday's exercise. Outline one action you will change to reflect your commitment to worship God in your daily life.

Day Six
- Read Hebrews 10:19–25. According to this passage, what should you do when you are tempted to give up on life and on your relationship with God?

Chapter 3

THE WALK OF FAITH— ENOCH AND NOAH

FAITH PRINCIPLE #3
BIBLICAL FAITH PRODUCES RADICAL OBEDIENCE

By faith Enoch was taken from this life, so that he did not experience death;
he could not be found, because God had taken him away. For before he was taken,
he was commended as one who pleased God. And without faith it is impossible
to please God, because anyone who comes to him must believe that he exists
and that he rewards those who earnestly seek him.

By faith Noah, when warned about things not yet seen, in holy fear
built an ark to save his family. By his faith he condemned the world
and became heir of the righteousness that comes by faith.

(Hebrews 11:5–7 [see also Genesis 4:17–6:10])

WALKING THE TALK—LANI QUIMBO

"You say you are a Christian, but you can't even help your
own family! Some Christian you are!"

My sister's angry words felt like someone had just thrown cold water in my face. After I got off the phone, I thought carefully about the situation. My father was dying, but I saw no way I could help care for him. My sister wanted me to leave my job in Manila, where the unemployment rate was very high and jobs were scarce, and come home to my family's remote village to help care for my father. But I was afraid to give up my job in the city, afraid to make such a drastic change. I was not only newly married but also pregnant. My husband and I were very involved in our church and with other Christian activities in and around Manila. While I had often prayed that my parents and older sister would come to know the same grace God had shown to me, they had remained hostile and resistant, and we soon realized we could not even discuss our newfound faith with any of them. Perhaps in this circumstance God was giving me an opportunity to share His grace through my actions rather than my words. Thus, after much prayer, we decided to go home to help with my father's care.

It proved to be a trying experience. My father was involved with witchcraft and was depending on magical charms he was wearing, healing charms given to him by local witch doctors. He was hostile to me, and every time I tried to share the gospel with him, he would angrily exclaim, "Don't you know that I am Satan's right hand in hell?" By God's grace, I eventually persuaded my mother that these tokens were evil, and she finally convinced my father to get rid of them.

Early one morning my father repeatedly cried out, "Lani, why is my soul so painful?" I answered him gently, "Papa, the pain you feel in your soul is like the pain in your body. The pain in your body is caused by your sickness. The pain in your soul is caused by your sins." Then he asked me, "How can I get rid of my sins so that the pain in my soul will go away?"

"Only Jesus can take away your sins, Papa," I said. "Confess them to Jesus, repent, and ask Him to forgive you. Jesus will forgive you and take away your sins. You must receive Him as your Savior and Lord." My father asked me to help him do this, and we prayed together. When I left him, he had a smile on his lips.

The next morning my father died peacefully. Soon after my father's death, my mother and older sister also committed their lives to Christ. My husband and I are so glad we gave up our jobs and left our church in Manila to be with my family in their time of great need. The initial hostility of my family to our faith forced us to stop talking about our beliefs and instead to "walk the talk." We are now both attending seminary in the United States, and we are preparing to go back to the Philippines as missionaries to share with others there the good news of Jesus Christ.

Lani Quimbo

TWO MEN WHO WALKED WITH GOD

Enoch and Noah lived in cultures similar to ours, cultures characterized by death, evil, and destruction. Yet they trusted God and lived accordingly. They could do this because:

◆ they believed that God existed even in an evil world,
◆ they believed that God rewards those who seek Him,
◆ they obeyed God's commands even when His promises were hard to believe, and
◆ they obeyed God's commands even when the rest of the world did not.

Most of us are so familiar with the stories of Enoch and Noah that we fail to appreciate the difficulties these men faced. We must not romanticize them or take for granted their remarkable faith-response to God's call to "radical obedience," a call to obey God and stand boldly against an evil culture.

ENOCH WALKED WITH GOD

Eight times in Genesis 5 we read the sure consequences of sin's entrance into the world: "and . . . *he died.*" Yet here in the midst of this "list of the dead" may be found a brilliant nugget of God's grace:

Enoch walked with God; then he was no more, because God took him away. (Genesis 5:24)

Enoch did not experience the finality of death. Instead, he was supernaturally ushered by God directly into the kingdom of heaven.

Genesis 5:21–24 implies that Enoch may not always have walked with God. Although this passage may be translated otherwise, the birth of his son Methuselah appears to have changed the direction of Enoch's life. And how did this event change Enoch's lifestyle? The name Methuselah means "when he dies it will come." The "it" here refers to God's judgment. It may well have been that God warned Enoch, a warning reflected in the name Enoch gave his son, that He was about to judge the world for its sin. Jude portrayed Enoch as a preacher of righteousness and judgment who admonished the ungodly to turn from evil (Jude 10–15). Enoch's preaching fell on deaf ears, however, and the people of his day continued to practice such evil that God's heart was actually grieved and filled with pain (Genesis 6:6).

God mercifully and supernaturally removed Enoch from the world before the destruction came. Others searched in vain for the missing prophet (Hebrews 11:5 [see also Jude 14–15]).

Like Elijah, Enoch did not experience death but was escorted directly into heaven. In one sense his final victory over death points us to Christ, for while Jesus would endure the shame and indignity of death, He ultimately overcame death by His resurrection into the glorious presence of His Father. Jesus, the Author and Perfecter of our faith, thus fulfills everything Enoch's godly life symbolizes for us. For even though all of us, except those still living the Day Christ returns (1 Thessalonians 4:13–18), must undergo death, Enoch's experience of bypassing of death shows us what ultimately awaits each and every believer. Surely, the most marvelous moment in our faith journey will be that moment we step from the physical world into heaven.

As He did in the life of Enoch, God sometimes graciously pulls back the veil and gives us a glimpse of what awaits us— the exchange of our present bodies for incorruptible ones. In Susan Hunt's *Heirs of the Covenant,* Chaplain Steve Leonard describes one of these remarkable moments in a letter to family and friends after the death of his wife, Bronwyn:

Bronwyn was a valiant covenant saint to the very threshold of heaven when she gloriously passed from our presence, giving us a glimpse of her greeting there. She "crossed the river" on Sunday night, the "day of all the days the best." Throughout her whole life, she loved the Lord's Day and so entered into eternal rest on that day of rest.

It was so like *Pilgrim's Progress*—for Bronwyn, suffocating for air as fluids filled her lungs, crossed the river and "stepped on the far shore." Linnea (her daughter) told her mother how much we would miss her, but that in minutes she would be with the Lord Jesus and Papa (Dad R.), and Moses, Abraham, et al. . . . Bronwyn got a joyful and childlike look on her face—she opened her eyes wide—and, speaking without gasping for air for a number of minutes, nonstop she talked of Paul, Mark, Joshua, and Caleb (not her sons who bear those names), and Dad—and even though so overwhelmed at the large greeting said a number of times, "Everybody is here." And "Hallelujah."

When Linnea said, "Mummy, you won't be gone from us long; we are going to follow you soon," Bronwyn said clearly and firmly, "Hurry!" And so we must. Hurry to Christ. Hurry to the Word. Hurry to prayer. Hurry to believe and obey. Hurry to heaven.

God used this account of Mrs. Leonard's entrance into heaven as a way to encourage our hearts. Indeed, God's Word confirms that He will "redeem my soul from the grave; he will surely take me to himself" and that He will "guide me with [His] counsel, and afterward . . . take me into glory" (Psalm 49:15; 73:24). Reading about this woman allowed us to picture Mark and Kelly "stepping" into heaven, firmly trusting in God's promises. Although their physical lives ended in a terrible car accident, we believe the place where they died is holy ground. A friend erected two white crosses at the accident site as a symbol of our confidence that—at the exact place where Mark and Kelly left their physical bodies behind—Jesus brought them into their Father's eternal presence (John 14:1–4). In the same way, Enoch's example encourages us as it encouraged the Hebrew Christians. It reminds us that, although we may face a horrible physical death, the death of our bodies means the freedom of our souls. Like the Hebrew Christians, we can know that Jesus will walk with us through the valley of the shadow of death, just as God walked with Enoch. No child of God ever faces death alone.

The details of Enoch's life are sketchy, perhaps intentionally so. He was a preacher, husband, and father, whose daily life was characterized by an intense love for God. He was an ordinary man, made extraordinary by the presence of God in his life. Enoch pleased God because he believed God and, as Jude tells us, Enoch's warnings came true (Jude 14–16). When Enoch's son Methuselah died at 969 years of age, the rains of the flood that would destroy the whole earth at last began to fall. God's warning of coming judgment and the actual fulfillment of that judgment in the great flood spanned the lifetime of Methuselah, the oldest man who ever lived (cf. Genesis 5:25–27 with Genesis 7:6, 11).

Enoch was not the only prophet who offered a warning. Noah, a descendant of Enoch's line, also walked with God and he, too, offered a warning from God (Genesis 6:9 [see also 2 Peter 2:5]).

Noah Built an Ark

How things had changed since the creation of the world! In Genesis 1:31 we read, "God saw all that he had made, and it was very good."

But now by the time of Noah,

> The LORD saw how great man's wickedness on the earth had become, and that every inclination of the thoughts of his heart was only evil all the time. The LORD was grieved that he had made man on the earth, and his heart was filled with pain (Genesis 6:5–6).

God determined to destroy every living thing on the face of the earth or, rather, almost everything. In the midst of that blighted and sin-sick world, there remained a beacon shining from the darkness. "But Noah," Enoch's great-grandson, "found favor [or grace] in the eyes of the LORD" (Genesis 6:8).

Noah's daily walk of faith set him apart from his contemporaries. Like his great-grandfather Enoch, Noah obeyed God and enjoyed the intimacy that results from God's pleasure. How was Noah able to live in such an evil world without being corrupted by his culture?

MARCHING TO THE BEAT OF A DIFFERENT DRUMMER

God spoke to Noah about things that were totally unfamiliar to him—things not yet seen. God warned Noah of a future he could not possibly comprehend: a devastating flood was coming, and Noah was directed to build an ark, a vessel suitable not only for his family but also for many animals as well. Noah must have been overwhelmed at times by this task. What was a flood? What was an ark? Two of every kind of animal?

But God's warning came wrapped in a promise: He Himself would preserve Noah and his family through this great catastrophe (vv. 11–22).

Noah could not go to a shipyard to observe such a vessel under construction, since there was no such vessel anywhere on earth, so he followed God's instructions to the letter. The ark would be gigantic: equivalent to four and a half football fields in length, one football field wide, and four stories high. Imagine the ridicule Noah and his family must have endured! Yet Noah believed God, and he worked tirelessly to build the ark, so certain was he of the coming flood.

THE WARNING AND THE WORK

On New Year's Day, 1998, we were in our home enjoying the company of our children and grandchildren. At one point, Chuck casually remarked, "Does anyone else smell smoke?" We ignored this first warning of impending danger. Then someone else said, "I think I smell smoke, too." Suddenly everyone jumped into action, as our son Daniel ran up the steps, flung open his bedroom door and screamed, "My room is on fire! Get everybody out of the house!"

As the women gathered up the younger children, the men flew into action. We were ill-prepared for a fire—we had no exit plan and no fire extinguishers. Pandemonium reigned as Chuck began throwing burning objects to the floor, flailing at the fire with blankets and pillows, heedless of the cries of our sons and son-in-law who begged him to get out of the house. The smoke finally got so thick they could hardly breathe. These young men were able to crawl to the bedroom, searching along on their hands and knees for their father, convinced Chuck was not responding to their pleas because he had passed out from the smoke. By the time they pulled him from the room—still conscious—all that was left was smoldering debris.

As Chuck explained later, "All I could see was the fire threatening to destroy our home. I knew if I could just put out the flames we could contain the damage. I guess my adrenaline was pumping, because I never heard your screams."

The smoke had warned us that danger was near and, once Chuck was aware of the danger, nothing could stop him from acting quickly and with all his energy to respond to the crisis.

God's proclamation of a coming flood was the "smoke" that warned Noah. When that warning came, Noah did not hesitate, he did not question God. He simply obeyed with all his heart. Danger was near, but God would save Noah's family if he built the ark as instructed. All Noah had was God's promise, but that was enough. For Noah, the coming flood was just as real as if it had already occurred, so sure was he of God's promises, and Noah knew if he obeyed God that his family's safety was just as certain. Noah's response was holistic and immediate. He set aside life as he knew it and responded in quiet, trusting obedience to God's warning. Noah's obedience meant sacrificing his time, his money, his labor, and his pride. In the face of severe personal hardship, Noah nevertheless did as God instructed.

We have to wonder as we consider Noah's story: Did the taunts and smirks of their neighbors hurt Noah and embarrass his family? Were there days he wanted to quit? Did his children question his behavior? Was he lonely? Did he sometimes wonder if one man could really make a difference amid such evil? Whatever doubts he may have had, he kept building the ark because he trusted that God could not lie. But believing God did not make the task easy or less costly. His obedience did not reap immediate rewards; he worked on the ark for a great many long and difficult years—a long time to undergo both ridicule and personal sacrifices. All the while, Noah's family watched as Noah obeyed God in reverent fear. When the day finally came, they willingly followed him into the ark (Genesis 7:5–7).

In an ungodly world, Noah served God not only as a carpenter but also as a preacher of righteousness (2 Peter 2:5). He and his family were secure but, although his culture was doomed, he still could not keep God's message to himself. No one believed Noah, however, and so the people of Noah's day had no excuse, for "by his faith [Noah] condemned the world" (Hebrews 11:7).

A COUNTERCULTURAL FORCE

The Hebrew Christians lived in a culture similar to Noah's, as do we. As a result, we are all under tremendous pressure to "blend in" and conform to popular culture. But true faith cannot be hidden. It's unlikely God will instruct any of us to build a physical ark but, in his letter to another group of early believers who lived in a period of persecution, Peter described how to live boldly and confidently (1 Peter 1:13–20):

- Prepare your minds for action.
- Exercise self-control.
- Always look forward with hope to the coming of Christ.
- Be obedient in the present.
- Resist the lure of temptations.
- Enjoy intimacy with God.

Living out such a practical faith is as foreign to some of us as a worldwide flood was to Noah. We can imagine some of the early believers' protests to these instructions because we hear the same protests today.

- "You're asking too much of me."
- "I'm just so busy; I don't really have the time to focus on this right now."
- "This might lead to trouble with my friends or my spouse. I don't want to rock the boat."

- "You don't know what I've been through; my past makes that kind of obedience impossible."
- "Why can't things just be like they used to be?"
- "Come on, now. Who can be that 'holy' in this day and age?"

Noah could have used some of these same excuses, but he didn't. Instead, he believed that if God called him to do something, then God would also equip him to do it.

People struggling to experience genuine faith must learn to put their hope fully in God's promises rather than the comforts promised by this world, and their obedience will forever mark them as strangers in our culture. It is something we need to both expect and be prepared for.

RADICAL OBEDIENCE

Redemption moves us out of our comfort zones and into a kind of "radical obedience" to God, obedience that will prove to be a countercultural force. This kind of obedience comes in many different forms. God instructed Noah to build an ark; God instructs us to "go and make disciples." Neither task is an easy one; obeying God, indeed, will often prove to be very costly. In every case, our obedience will be reflected by the influence we have on others even as our own lives are changed by God.

> Then Jesus came to them and said, "All authority in heaven and on earth has been given to me. Therefore go and make disciples of all nations, baptizing them in the name of the Father and of the Son and of the Holy Spirit, and teaching them to obey everything I have commanded you. And surely I am with you always, to the very end of the age." (Matthew 28:18–20)

Francis of Assisi once told his contemporaries that the way to share Christ was to "preach the gospel all the time and, if necessary, use words." Hundreds of years later, the Quimbos (the couple whose story begins this chapter) realized that this exhortation still rings true. As a result of their "preaching without words," their family finally understood and accepted the gospel. This couple chose not to isolate themselves from the real needs of their family just because they were too busy in their safe and comfortable local church. Rather, they answered God's call to stand alone against the culture through meeting their family's physical needs.

Just as Noah's family observed his steadfast faithfulness and then followed him into the ark, the other members of the Quimbo family followed Lani and her husband into the ark of salvation. Just as Noah cut and hauled cypress wood and applied pitch for many years, the Quimbos and others like them demonstrate through their lives and actions the hope of the gospel. Their experience of God's love, mercy, and grace drives them to live out a life of faith, openly and boldly, as an example to others. The enemy will use every weapon in his arsenal to keep us from demonstrating God's mercy, and there will doubtless be many heartaches and disappointments along the way. But just as Noah's endurance prepared a safe place for his family, our endurance provides a safe place for broken people to meet the risen Christ.

THE SIGN OF GOD'S PROMISE

The story of Noah is a story of God's grace. God sent the flood because He "saw how great man's wickedness on the earth had become, and that every inclination of the thoughts of his heart was only evil all the time" (Genesis 6:5). Yet in mercy He went on to promise that "never again will I curse the ground because of man, even though every inclination of his heart is evil from childhood. And never again will I destroy all living creatures, as I have done" (Genesis 8:21). And He sealed this promise with a bright and beautiful symbol of His grace:

> And God said, "This is the sign of the covenant I am making between me and you and every living creature with you, a covenant for all generations to come: I have set my rainbow in the clouds, and it will be the sign of the covenant between me and the earth. Whenever I bring clouds over the earth and the rainbow appears in the clouds, I will remember my covenant between me and you and all living creatures of every kind. Never again will the waters become a flood to destroy all life. Whenever the rainbow appears in the clouds, I will see it and remember the everlasting covenant between God and all living creatures of every kind on the earth." (Genesis 9:12–16)

The rainbow still reminds us of God's promise. How appropriate it is that, when Jesus takes us to heaven, the rainbow of God—whatever that might actually be—will proclaim that He was faithful to all the promises He has ever made.

> At once I was in the Spirit, and there before me was a throne in heaven with someone sitting on it. And the one who sat there had the appearance of jasper and carnelian. A *rainbow, resembling an emerald, encircled the throne.* (Revelation 4:2–3 [emphasis added])

God's grace is woven throughout Noah's story. God knew many of Noah's descendants would eventually choose sin over loyalty to their Creator. Not long after God saved Noah and his family, we see that even Noah himself succumbs to drunkenness and disgrace (Genesis 9:20–21). His descendants later declared their rebellion against God when they brazenly proclaimed,

"Come, let us build ourselves a city, with a tower that reaches to the heavens, so that we may make a name for ourselves" (Genesis 11:4). Faithful to His promise to Noah, God did not destroy these arrogant people, instead confusing their languages and scattering them "over the face of the whole earth" (v. 9).

LIVING BOLDLY IN VIEW OF GOD'S PROMISES

God gave Enoch and Noah a true and lasting, saving faith. This faith was not inherent in them but a gift of God placed in their hearts, hearts that had been prepared by the Spirit of God and made ready to receive His Word (Ephesians 2:8–9; 2 Timothy 1:9; 3:15; Romans 10:17). God's promise to preserve the earth is what energized their obedience. Their lives—lived out in the context of corrupt cultures—provided encouragement to the Hebrew Christians, that they should rest assured that God would preserve and sustain them despite their difficult circumstances. And they knew, as well, that God's promise would hold true in life or in death. Like the Hebrew Christians, we too must remain confident of God's promises as we:

- develop a worldview that emphasizes the coming of Christ (Revelation 22:7, 12),
- make the most of every opportunity (Ephesians 5:16),
- focus on what is important and resist pettiness (vv. 15–16),
- live at peace with others, especially fellow believers (Hebrews 12:14),
- encourage those who lead us (Galatians 6:6),
- strive to live in holiness (Romans 12:1–2; Hebrews 12:14),
- serve others through mercy ministries (Matthew 25:34–40),
- live every day in submission to His will (Luke 22:42),

- experience the richness of His grace (1 Corinthians 10:13), and
- passionately share the good news of Jesus (Matthew 28:18–20).

You may be thinking, "But I'm just one person. The needs around me are too great! I don't have the energy or the courage it takes to live such a life." And you would be right. You most certainly cannot do this in your own strength. But God can do it in you. God promises to give you the strength and the understanding to live a life that pleases Him (Philippians 2:13).

Instead of allowing the enormous needs of our world to overcome you, concentrate on the here and now, the situations right in front of you. God may not call you to build an ark or to preach in a foreign land, but He does call you to obedience in this moment. He calls you to walk with Him as they did. And you only need to do that one minute at a time. You walk with God when you obey Him, whether in the mundane tasks or in the magnificent opportunities that God provides. You walk with God by the way you act while you travel to church, as well as by the way you worship there; by the way you treat your neighbors, by the way you use your time. Enoch and Noah show us, through the examples of their lives, that we cannot separate the holy from the secular. It is all one and the same. Our walk with God is reflected by everything we do, every word we speak.

The first eleven chapters of Genesis—the "Book of Beginnings"—cover the events of approximately two thousand years. The story of Abraham—our next example of faith in action—reveals the way God gives each of His children the gift of faith (Ephesians 2:8–9) and pursues personal intimacy with them. A closer look at how God enabled this man of faith to make difficult choices will give us hope as we continue on the journeys God has marked out for each of us.

DIGGING DEEPER

Day One

- What is a "worldview"? Read Hebrews 11:1–7 and write out the worldview of Enoch and Noah.
- Read Genesis 5:24 and Genesis 6:8. How did the behavior of these men reveal their worldview?

Day Two

- Read Amos 3:3. What is one indication that you are "walking with God"?
- How did Noah demonstrate that he "agreed with God"? How was his behavior "radical obedience"? In what area of your life has God called you to "radical obedience"? Be specific.

Day Three

- Read Genesis 6:1–22. How did Noah respond to the specific details of God's instructions? What specific scriptural instructions has God given to you that appear strange and at times impossible to obey?
- What is God's response to your questions and doubts? Read 1 Corinthians 10:13. How does knowing that if God has "called" you to a specific task, He will also "equip" you to perform it, encourage you?

Day Four

- Read Hebrews 12:1–15. Consider the next twenty-four hours of your life.
- In the context of your expected activities, what is the "race" marked out for you today? Each time you are tempted to "walk alone" instead of "walking with God," ask Him to remind you of His promise in 1 Corinthians 10:13.

Day Five

♦ God warned Noah that a flood was coming and then outlined how Noah was to prepare for the coming calamity. Read 1 Peter 1:13–20. What warning has God given to us, and how are we to respond?

Day Six

♦ Read Ephesians 5:15–21. How are we to respond to the "opportunities" of everyday life? How does the behavior described in this passage reflect "radical obedience" in our present culture? How will your obedience to this passage demonstrate "radical obedience" for you personally?

Chapter 4

SEEKING GOD'S CITY— ABRAHAM AND SARAH

```
FAITH PRINCIPLE #4
BIBLICAL FAITH SETS US FREE TO SEEK THE CITY OF GOD.
```

By faith Abraham, when called to go to a place he would later receive as his inheritance, obeyed and went, even though he did not know where he was going. By faith he made his home in the promised land like a stranger in a foreign country; he lived in tents, as did Isaac and Jacob, who were heirs with him of the same promise. For he was looking forward to the city with foundations, whose architect and builder is God.

By faith Abraham, even though he was past age—and Sarah herself was barren—was enabled to become a father because he considered him faithful who had made the promise. And so from this one man, and he as good as dead, came descendants as numerous as the stars in the sky and as countless as the sand on the seashore.

All these people were still living by faith when they died. They did not receive the things promised; they only saw them and welcomed them from a distance. And they admitted that they were aliens and strangers on earth. People who say such things show that they are looking for a country of their own. If they had been thinking of the country they had left, they would have had opportunity to return. Instead, they were longing for a better country—a heavenly one. Therefore God is not ashamed to be called their God, for he has prepared a city for them.

By faith Abraham, when God tested him, offered Isaac as a sacrifice. He who had received the promises was about to sacrifice his one and only son, even though God had said to him, "It is through Isaac that your offspring will be reckoned." Abraham reasoned that God could raise the dead, and figuratively speaking, he did receive Isaac back from death.

(Hebrews 11:8–19 [see also Genesis 11:31–22:24])

GRACE FOR THE MOMENT—
MICHELLE MCCONOMY

I was the mother of wonderful three-year-old twin boys and a beautiful little girl. But, nearly four years after our first child, Joshua, was stillborn, I was still bitterly angry at God. Because I felt He had failed to protect me from that terrible loss, I could not trust Him to protect me from similar losses. Reading the Scriptures and honestly asking Him questions left me feeling even more abandoned, so I gave up expecting to feel His love or His presence in my life. The anger I always carried around so deep within me eventually began to break out; I started to lash out at my husband and my children, and I knew I needed help.

Through events only God could have arranged, I started meeting with a godly older woman who seemed able to see right into my soul. My anger toward my family was bad enough, but this was only a symptom of the greater problem;

my anger toward God was the real poison destroying my life. My friend recognized this, and she patiently began to show me the way back into fellowship with God by sharing the details of her own pain-filled life and how God had taught her to trust Him through those hard times. Yet my heart, seared and defiant, continued to resist.

Finally, one Sunday morning, the many months of loving support and encouragement from my friend and the ministry of the church broke through to me. God transformed me from a broken despairing woman into a woman who felt His presence deeply. Suddenly I knew He loved me, and I never wanted to go back to my old way of living. Every day He surprised me with new revelations of His love and specific care for my family and me. I soon began to realize that He knew me even better than I knew myself.

God also patiently began teaching me to hold onto life loosely; I started to realize that my life might change at any moment, as it had the day I lost my son, and that I needed to be prepared. I began to see all of my circumstances in the context of eternity, and I knew I could count on the Lord to be with me through any hardships that might lie ahead. I had the feeling that God might be preparing me for something difficult, but I wasn't afraid because He was also teaching me that I could trust Him to give me the grace I would need when that moment came.

September 14, 1998, started out like an ordinary day for us, but it turned out to be a dramatic turning point in our lives. That was the day a pediatric oncologist told us one of our three-year-old twins, Jacob, might have cancer. I was terrified. "What will happen to Jacob if he does have cancer? Will he need chemotherapy? Will he need radiation? How sick will he get? Will he lose all his hair? How long will it take for him to get better?" The question behind the other questions, of course, was one I could hardly even contemplate: *"Will* Jacob get better?" The thought of an empty space at the table, of putting away his favorite things, of having only memories of him to hold onto, was more than I thought I could bear. Yet, in response to each of my questions God's gentle answer was always, "My grace is sufficient for you."

"Yes, yes," I would cry, afraid. "But what about *Jacob*?"

"Your times are in My hands, Michelle, both past and future. Know that I love both you and Jacob and that I will give you the grace you will need for *this moment.*"

As the doctor described for my husband and me the surgery needed to remove our son's cancer-ridden kidney and the subsequent tests to determine whether the cancer had spread, I thought, "How can I put my three-year-old son through the pain of surgery? What if something happens to the other kidney, then he will surely die." Again I could hear God saying, "My grace is sufficient for you for *this moment. Trust Me, Michelle. Trust Me in this.*"

Fear seized my heart again when the radiographs of Jacob's lungs indicated that the cancer in his little body might have spread. I wondered how this would affect his chances of getting better. What if they think they've cured him but his cancer returns? Each time I found my anxious thoughts running far ahead of God—into all the might-happens and what-ifs and dark and fearsome possibilities—He would bring me back to His truth. As long as I remained with God for *that moment,* He gave me the strength to handle whatever challenge I faced.

Our journey in this terrible land of cancer has only just begun. We are still waiting for test results to determine the extent of Jacob's cancer. We are strangers in an alien country. The language where we live includes the words "malignancy" and "terminal" and "life-threatening." We don't want to be here; we want to take our children and go elsewhere, anywhere. Our journey through grief, following Joshua's death, taught us much about God's character and His loving faithfulness, and now we know that the future, whatever it may bring, is in His hands. In this journey we are on, in this landscape filled with tubes, and monitors, and small children lying on hospital beds, we are trusting the Lord to teach us once again how to rely on Him for our future by giving us the grace we need for the moment—*this moment.*

Michelle McConomy

THE FIRE THAT SETS US FREE

Because of a devastating fire that had swept through the area, our first visit to Yellowstone National Park was tarnished by the image of miles of great lodge-pole pine trees reduced to giant, charred toothpicks. Elsewhere in the park, fires still raged unchecked because the ecologists had determined that this destruction would actually help to renew the forest. Unless fire periodically destroys the tall trees, the smaller saplings do not get the necessary sunshine and so die out. It also takes fire to break open the hard shells that encase these pine seeds. Without fire, the old trees would simply die off without leaving any young plants to grow up and take their place in the forest.

On our second visit to the park, which occurred about five years later, the "before and after" effect was striking. The once-charred and blackened forest now teemed with new life. Miniature lush green pines pushed up through the under-brush, pushing aside the old logs and burnt branches. The fields were filled with wildflowers, their brilliant colors drawing a vast array of birds, butterflies, and bees. Herds of bison and elk roamed the green and flower-filled meadows, now abundant with the food these animals needed. The fire had truly done its work; it had renewed the land.

The stories of Abel, Enoch, and Noah are rich examples of perseverance. Yet they can leave us feeling unsuited for God's purposes. Except for the passage describing Noah's drunkenness and disgrace (Genesis 9:18–29), the biblical record does not say anything about their weaknesses and failures. One might mistakenly conclude that these men were somehow holy and unique, men for whom living by faith came much more easily than it does for the rest of us.

As though he had anticipated this possibility, the writer of Hebrews next turns to Abraham and Sarah. The life journey of these two people, in contrast to the other individuals we have considered thus far, is told in great detail, and the faults and sins of these two individuals are in full view. Their story, too, is a record of God's grace, but here that grace is repeatedly applied—like fire—to clearly flawed, self-centered human hearts. This is the story of a man and woman who struggled, who sinned, and yet, in spite of their many failures, who persevered. In Abraham and Sarah God's divine blaze, with precision but also with pain, cleared the way for a brighter, clearer, stronger faith. In this way, God unshackled them from their love for this world and set them free to seek the city of God.

LEARNING THROUGH DISOBEDIENCE

Abraham, the Bible tells us, spent much of his life traveling. After he was called by God to leave his native land, Abraham simply moved from place to place, living in tents, always leaving—every campsite just another place to rest for a short while. Yet, even though he had no place on earth to call "home," Abraham's home was real to him nonetheless; for his true home was based upon a promise from God to him and to his descendants, a home that lay somewhere in the distant future. Thus it could be said that Abraham lived between two worlds—the world he actually lived in, always as a stranger, and the world he spent his life seeking.

> By faith Abraham, when called to go to a place he would later receive as his inheritance, obeyed and went, even though he did not know where he was going. By faith he made his home in the Promised Land like a stranger in a foreign country; he lived in tents, as did Isaac and Jacob, who were heirs with him of the same promise. For he was looking forward to the city with foundations, whose architect and builder is God. (Hebrews 11:8–10)

Abraham was a moon worshiper (Joshua 24:2) when God singled him out and gave him these specific instructions in Genesis 12:1:

- Leave your home in Ur of Mesopotamia (present-day Iraq).
- Leave your father and your other relatives behind.
- Go to the land I, the Lord, will show you.

God also gave him a magnificent, six-part promise (vv. 2–4):

- I will make you a great nation.
- I will bless you.
- I will make your name great.
- I will bless those who bless you.
- Whoever curses you I will curse.
- All peoples on earth will be blessed through you.

Was Abraham just born "holy"? Did he immediately believe God's promises and obey this strange call to pack his bags and move far away, even though he didn't even know where he was going? We might imagine that, once he met with God, Abraham spent the rest of his life coasting trouble-free through this world, "living as a stranger and loving it," and, of course, never ever faltering. We can almost see Abraham singing en route to Canaan, "This world is not my home, I'm just 'a passin' through. My treasures are laid up, somewhere beyond the blue!"

But Abraham did not instantly or completely obey God's call. There was a lapse between the time God gave Abraham his original instructions and the time he finally packed up and began his long trek. We know this because "the LORD *had said* to Abram [his name when this story begins], 'Leave your country, your people and your father's household and go to the land I will show you'" (Genesis 12:1 [emphasis added]).

Stephen, the first martyr, in his account of this story, also provides us with a clue as to the timing of God's call to Abraham.

> To this he replied: "Brothers and fathers, listen to me! The God of glory appeared to our father Abraham *while he was still in Mesopotamia, before he lived in Haran.* 'Leave your country and your people,' God said, 'and go to the land I will show you.' " (Acts 7:2–3 [emphasis added])

Abraham's obedience was not only belated, it was defective in other ways as well. Instead of traveling only with his immediate family, when he finally left Ur and headed toward Canaan, he took his extended family with him (Genesis 11:31; 12:4). He settled with them in Haran, not Canaan. It wasn't for another five years, after his father, Terah, died, that Abraham finally moved on to Canaan. In Hebrews 11:8, the words "Abraham, when called to go . . . *obeyed and went*" literally mean, *"while* he went"—in other words, that Abraham was learning obedience *en route,* while on his life's journey.

DESCENT INTO EGYPT

In Canaan, God revealed more of His plan for the Patriarch's family. Upon Abraham's arrival in the city of Shechem, God told him, "To your offspring I will give this land." Abraham demonstrated his growing love and intimacy with God by building altars to the Lord in both Shechem and Bethel (Genesis 12:7–8). He may have concluded at this point that his journey to the city of God was going to proceed smoothly. But trouble, in the form of a severe famine, came into the land, putting Abraham's growing trust and friendship with God to the test (Genesis 12:9–10). How would God feed Abraham and his family? Abraham was still just getting acquainted with

God and the great promises accompanying His call, and thus Abraham's faith was weak. As a result, rather than seeing the famine as an opportunity to trust God, Abraham immediately fled to Egypt.

God had promised Abraham, in no uncertain terms, "I will bless you, Abraham, you and your family. And, in turn, all people on the earth will be blessed through you."

And Abraham had concluded in effect, "Hmmm. I guess I'm just going to have to take care of myself in this situation."

One could argue that Abraham had made a purely common sense decision here. After all, wasn't he responsible for the needs of his household? In Egypt, his family would have food, and he would one day return to Bethel a much richer man than when he left. But there is nothing here to indicate that God ever directed Abraham to go to Egypt. While in Egypt, there were apparently no supernatural encounters with God, no altars built to honor Him. Rather than reflecting a godly concern for his family's welfare, this "side trip" seems to indicate a lapse in Abraham's faith; in any case, his decision to do the expedient thing at this point set his entire household on a path to more trouble.

Remember that Abraham had been steeped in paganism before God first came to him, and, like all of us, he had much to learn. God had not called Abraham to a life of "common sense" but to a life of faith, and Abraham failed to grasp this at first. Even so, God used Abraham's mistakes, like this one, as purifying fires to burn away the remaining unbelief from his heart and to prepare him for what lay ahead: the ultimate test of his trust in Jehovah, the God of Glory.

LIES AND MORE LIES

While in Egypt, Abraham continued his downward spiral. As is so often the case with us, Abraham compounded his problems, getting deeper and deeper into trouble. After first running to Egypt, instead of waiting upon God for help and direction, Abraham proceeded to compromise his wife's honor and, in the process, put all of their lives in jeopardy in order to achieve personal gain and possibly to save his own skin. He told Sarah,

> "Say you are my sister, so that *I* will be treated well for your sake and *my life* will be spared because of you." (Genesis 12:13 [emphasis added])

Sarah was so beautiful that Abraham feared the king of Egypt, the Pharaoh, might kill him in order to take Sarah as his own. Abraham's ruse, however, was discovered, and even the pagan king of Egypt was indignant and outraged at Abraham's dishonorable behavior. Abraham and Sarah left Egypt in disgrace.

Years later, Abraham, incredibly, tried the exact same ploy with Abimelech, king of Gerar. Once again, Abraham lied about his relationship to Sarah. Once again, he was caught in the act. Genesis 20:11–13 records Abraham's string of excuses when an outraged King Abimelech caught him red-handed in this act of subterfuge.

Abraham first has the gall to blame Abimelech for the entire mess, actually excusing his own deceit by blaming it on the faithlessness of others: "I [Abraham] said to myself, 'There is surely *no fear of God* in this place, and they will kill me because of my wife' " (emphasis added). Then Abraham tried to get himself off the hook on a technicality: "Besides, she really is my sister" since she was "the daughter of my father though not of my mother; and she became my wife." And, finally, he blamed his lie on God Himself: "And when *God had me wander from my father's household,* I said to her, 'This is how you can show your love to me: Everywhere we go, say of me, "He is my brother." ' " Abraham is suggesting here that, since God called him on this journey in the first place, it was God who had put him in the position of having to make up all these lies just to "get by." At no point, of course, does Abraham ever simply say, "I did wrong. I'm sorry."

God had promised Abraham, "I will make you into a great nation. I will make your name great. I will bless those who bless you. I will curse those who curse you."

And Abraham had concluded, "If I don't take personal control of this situation, I might die."

How could this man of God sin so blatantly? Perhaps Abraham, having received God's great promise about his destiny, nevertheless decided God needed "a little help" at the particularly rough spots they encountered along the way. However, through all of this, God did not give up on Abraham; indeed, it was God who alerted both the king of Egypt and King Abimelech (through curses of disease and barrenness, respectively) to Abraham's lie. Abraham's attempt to control his situation might well have resulted in the very thing he most feared—his own death—had not God intervened time and again to save him.

The riches Abraham accumulated in Egypt proved costly and were clearly the spoils of disbelief; they resulted in trouble and sorrow for his house and a blot upon his reputation. The wealth and lifestyle of Egypt, so tantalizing to Lot, soon became a source of conflict between Abraham and his nephew. Upon division of the land, Lot chose the property nearer the Jordan because it reminded him of Egypt (Genesis 13:10). Lot pitched his tents near Sodom and eventually decided to live within that wicked city (Genesis 13:12–13; 14:12). After Lot and Abraham separated, leaving Abraham finally alone in the very place God had wanted him all along, the Lord instructed Abraham, "Lift up your eyes from where you are and look north and south, east and west. All the land that you see I will give to you and your offspring forever" (Genesis 13:14–15). Intimacy between this former pagan and God had at last been restored, though the consequences of his trek into Egypt were not yet over.

Roller-Coaster Faith

God had already kept many of His promises to Abraham: he was now wealthy, his name was at last respected, and his family had been protected. God had also promised to make him into a great nation and give him a homeland (Genesis 12:2; 15:4–7). Abraham asked God how He planned to accomplish all of this.

Rather than rebuking Abraham for these questions, God took him for a walk under the stars and affirmed His promise that, old as Abraham was, he would nevertheless have his own physical heir: "Look up at the heavens and count the stars—if indeed you can count them. . . . So shall your offspring be" (Genesis 15:5). Abraham still had his doubts, and he did not hesitate to ask how he could believe God (v. 8). But instead of rebuking Abraham for doubting His promises, God provides Abraham with a sign and a seal that He would keep His word.

God ordered Abraham to prepare a sacrifice by cutting sacrificial animals into pieces and laying the pieces in two parallel rows on the ground. This ancient Eastern ritual was actually a formal contract. Whoever walked between the two rows of pieces was legally required to fulfill all the terms of the contract, even if it cost him his own life. In this unfolding drama, God legally sealed the terms of His contract—or covenant—with Abraham by walking down the center of the sacrifice Himself, in the form of a burning pot. Then Abraham knew that God would accomplish all that He had promised (cf. Genesis 15:8–21; Hebrews 6:13–19).

Hebrews 6:13–19 declares that, in this remarkable scene, the God of Glory, since He could swear by none higher than Himself, swore by His own head to fulfill all the terms of the covenant. In so doing, He not only addressed Abraham's need, but ours as well. This is undoubtedly the most significant turning point in Abraham's life. But this spiritual high point, sadly enough, was to be short-lived.

Abraham, even though back in close fellowship with God, nevertheless fell victim once again to acting expediently rather than depending on his Lord. His wife, Sarah, concluded that God had never actually said the child of promise would come from *her* body, only that the seed of promise would come from Abraham. Therefore, since she was already well beyond child-bearing years, Sarah offered her Egyptian slave, Hagar—another "aftereffect" of their infamous flight into Egypt—to Abraham to serve as a surrogate mother. Abraham, thinking once again that God might need a little "help" to fulfill His great promise, agreed to this plan.

Hagar conceived and immediately began to taunt Sarah for her infertility. Sarah, in turn, proceeded to blame her husband for the entire mess, conveniently forgetting that this plan had been her idea in the first place. And Abraham failed to deal with the situation honorably and justly; instead he allowed Sarah to mistreat the pregnant slave girl. Finally, Sarah treated Hagar so badly that the young woman fled for her life.

God, however, met Hagar in the desert with great grace and tenderness, and He promised to strengthen her. He also promised Hagar that her child, to be named Ishmael, would bear descendants of his own that would be too numerous to count. Ishmael would be an ever-present reminder that "God hears," for this is what the name means. Not only did God hear Hagar; she also claimed that God saw her. Thus did Sarah's Egyptian slave give God the name, "You are the God who sees me" (Genesis 16:13). At God's direction, Hagar went back to Sarah and bore her son, Ishmael. For thirteen years, Abraham and Sarah treated this "wild donkey" of a boy as the child promised to them by God.

THE MIRACLE CHILD

But God had a better plan. When Abraham was ninety-nine years old, God once more confirmed His covenant as an everlasting promise for generations to come. He commanded Abraham to use circumcision to identify his descendants as belonging to God (Genesis 17:11), and He planned to bless Sarah with a son so that she would be the mother of nations, and kings of peoples would come from her (vv. 15–16). Abraham couldn't believe it. He laughed at the very thought of two senior citizens—both "as good as dead" (Hebrews 11:12)—actually bearing a child. God, however, was serious:

> Your wife Sarah will bear you a son, and you will call him Isaac. I will establish my covenant with him as an everlasting covenant for his descendants after him. . . . My covenant I will establish with Isaac, whom Sarah will bear to you by this time next year. (Genesis 17:19, 21)

But Abraham's joy at such news was short-lived. What was he to do about Ishmael? Abraham loved him. God promised Abraham that though He would care for Ishmael, it was to be through Isaac, the son Sarah herself would bear, that the promises of the covenant would be realized.

THE PURGING OF AN OLD WOMAN'S FAITH

While Abraham's faith was strong that God would indeed provide an heir, God still had work to do in Sarah's heart. God sent three visitors to Abraham on the plains of Mamre. Two were angels (Genesis 19:1), and the third was the Lord Himself (Genesis 18).

Barren Sarah eavesdropped as the Lord told Abraham that she would deliver a son the following year. She laughed derisively at the thought (Genesis 18:12), and can we blame her? How could she take seriously anyone who claimed that her old shriveled womb would carry the child God had promised them? The Lord, aware of Sarah's laughter, confronted Abraham: "Why did Sarah laugh and say, 'Will I really have a child, now that I am old?' Is anything too hard for the LORD? I will return to you at the appointed time next year and Sarah will have a son" (vv. 13–14).

God knew Sarah's heart response. He had heard her laugh even to herself. But instead of admitting her faithlessness, in fear, she denied it. God responded, "Yes, you did laugh" (v. 15) because He knew full well what was in her heart. Yet Sarah ultimately believed God. The *New American Standard Bible* has the best rendering of this passage from Hebrews: "By faith, even Sarah herself received ability to conceive, even beyond the proper time of life, since *she considered Him faithful* who had promised" (Hebrews 11:11 [emphasis added]).

How tenderly God dealt with this elderly woman's unbelief. After exposing her private, mocking, bitter laughter, God gently rebuked her for her unbelief with this question: Is anything too hard for the Lord? God's proclamation and His past faithfulness, combined with His intimate knowledge of Sarah's inner being, persuaded her that His promise could indeed be trusted. Though she appeared to be physiologically incapable of bearing a child, she still considered Him faithful. In turn, God would grant her "real laughter"—the sweet, glorious, joy-filled laughter that came the day her long-awaited son, Isaac, whose very name means "laughter," was born to her.

GIVING UP WHAT IS MOST PRECIOUS

Time and again Abraham had failed the trials of faith brought his way by God: by running to Egypt; by lying—not once, but twice—to try to protect himself; by attempting to fulfill God's promises for an heir by coming up with, in collusion with Sarah, a half-baked idea of their own. Each of these spiritual tests left an indelible "scorch mark" that deepened his understanding of God's character. But had these experiences prepared him for the ultimate test, had they prepared him to obey God above all, to put the commands of the Lord God before everything else he held dear?

Years after that miraculous day when Isaac was born, God made an astonishing demand of Abraham: "Take your son, your only son, Isaac, whom you love, and go to the region of Moriah. Sacrifice him there as a burnt offering on one of the mountains I will tell you about" (Genesis 22:2). What? Kill this child, so precious to him, the son for whom Abraham had longed all his life?

Abraham had failed so many lesser tests of faith, and yet, this time, Abraham obeyed immediately and completely:

> By faith Abraham, when God tested him, offered Isaac as a sacrifice. He who had received the promises was about to sacrifice his one and only son, even though God had said to him, "It is through Isaac that your offspring will be reckoned." Abraham reasoned that God could raise the dead, and figuratively speaking, he did receive Isaac back from death. (Hebrews 11:17–19)

The Greek word for "reasoned" is *logisamenos* and implies a calculated or computed reasoning. Abraham reasoned, but not blindly. He reasoned that Isaac's existence was a miraculous fulfillment of God's word. God had also promised that Isaac would have descendants. Yet to obey God meant Isaac would die before he had established his own family. The "old Abraham" would have taken Isaac and run to a safe place, concluding that God was mistaken about this need for a sacrifice and that he, Abraham, would just have to "reinterpret" those instructions. The transformed Abraham, a man now of deep and mature faith, knew that God could not go back on His word.

There had never been a resurrection, but Abraham's message to the servants who accompanied them to Mount Horeb was clear. "Stay here with the donkey while I and the boy go over there. We will worship and then *we* will come back to you" (Genesis 22:5 [emphasis added]).

We can only imagine the wrenching emotion Abraham must have felt as he sadly approached the place chosen by God for this dramatic exhibition of his faith and Jehovah's faithfulness. On the mountain, Abraham built the altar, arranged the wood, and bound Isaac. When Isaac questioned his father as to the whereabouts of the sacrifice, Abraham replied that "God himself will provide the lamb" (Genesis 22:6, 8). As Abraham raised the knife to slay this young boy, his own dear son, God's angel suddenly intervened: "Do not lay a hand on the boy," the angel said. "Do not do anything to him. Now I know that you fear God, because you have not withheld from me your son, your only son" (v. 12). The wording here— "you have not withheld *from me* your only son"—suggests that this angel may well have been the preincarnate Christ.

God had promised, "All peoples on earth will be blessed through you." And Abraham had concluded, "God is sovereign—I *can* trust Him."

By God's sovereign will, the fires of Abraham's life had burned away the last vestiges of his unbelief. Because of the promises of the covenant, true faith fixed this man's eyes on what was yet to come, enabling him to give up to God the one thing that was most precious to him in all the world: his one and only son. Abraham would name that mountain "The LORD Will Provide" (v. 14). Abraham had believed that the God of life would resurrect his son, Isaac. In so doing, Abraham anticipated, though "through a glass darkly," the coming resurrection of God's own one and only Son. Indeed, it was in that same mountain complex that, many centuries later, God sent His Son Jesus to die on the cross. God did indeed provide the sacrifice.

LIVING BY FAITH

Abraham's encounter with God and his search for the promised city eventually set him free from his love affair with this world, his dependence on shortsighted, quick-fix, expedient living. Though casual readers might conclude that Abraham spent his life looking for sons and a place to settle down, the writer of Hebrews assures us, by his deliberate placement of verses 13 through 16 in Hebrews 11, that this is not the case.

Abraham eventually learned that the land promised to him was not composed of sand and dirt—a property to be claimed during his time here on earth. Instead, he sought "a better country—a heavenly one," and so, too, should we. As a result, Abraham spent his life as a stranger and pilgrim on this earth (Genesis 23:4). Like Michelle McConomy, whose story begins this chapter, Abraham learned to hold the "things" of this world loosely, even the loved ones so precious to us. For though wealthy enough to build a city of his own, he knew such a city could never compare to what God was preparing for him and his descendants. He saw his destination from afar (Hebrews 11:13) and longed for the place of God's continual presence. God used purifying fires to burn away Abraham's disbelief and self-sufficiency, revealing in the process God's own great and everlasting faithfulness after the pain and smoke had cleared. This story is not so much about Abraham as it is about God's faithfulness to equip men and women to travel the paths He has laid out for them.

In the same way that Abraham lived in two worlds—the physical world and the world of promise, the world to come—God calls the readers of this marvelous book of Hebrews to the same journey. Like Abraham, we too will stumble and stray; we may fall into deep sin or perhaps just make dubious and disreputable compromises; we will look for shortcuts and end-runs and quick fixes when the way marked out for us by God just seems too difficult. We will both make mistakes and deliberately disobey, and at times the difficulties we face will threaten to overwhelm us. But Abraham's God is our God; His promises to Abraham apply to us as they did to him (Galatians 3:29). Only by embracing the promise of the eternal city of God and His continual presence can we really hold life loosely—as Abraham learned to do—and surrender to God all that is most precious to us. We will live as strangers here on earth, always on the move, always heading toward our real "home." C. S. Lewis makes this point in *Mere Christianity* when he writes:

> If you read history you will find that the Christians who did most for the present world were just those who thought most of the next. The Apostles themselves, who set on foot the conversion of the Roman Empire, the great men who built up the Middle Ages, the English Evangelicals who abolished the Slave Trade, all left their mark on Earth, precisely because their minds were occupied with Heaven. It is since Christians have largely ceased to think of the other world that they have become so ineffective in this. Aim at Heaven and you will get earth "thrown in": aim at earth and you will get neither.

Is it reasonable to aim at heaven in this impersonal, postmodern, high-tech world we live in? For Michelle McConomy and her husband, Bill, it is *only* by "aiming at heaven" that they are able to press on in their own difficult journey. As of this writing, they have received the good news that aggressive chemotherapy has successfully eradicated the cancer in Jacob's body. But this proved to be only a brief respite. Shortly after receiving this encouraging news, Michelle miscarried a baby boy and nearly died from the associated hemorrhaging. Michelle—struggling to trust God in the face of repeated sorrows—told us,

> I'm so weary of the journey. Just when I relax and take in fresh breaths of His Spirit, another wave crashes. Yet I don't have the same anger I had when we lost Joshua. I still grieve for my lost children, and I still ask a lot of questions, but I know I'm cherished by a loving God. I no longer feel there's a wall between God and me. Each new hurt and loss confronts me with a question: Am I seeking what I think will make me happy, or am I seeking more of Christ? Each time He reminds me that this life is not all there is. God is teaching me that I can experience His intimate presence as I journey toward heaven, especially in times of grief.

The question that confronted Sarah looms for us as well: Is anything too hard for the Lord? The tension of life is this: It is by grace that we learn to live both in a broken world and in God's glorious, healing presence at the same time. Such a life is marked by a living faith, unbolted from our deadly and destructive love for this world and the "easy answers" it seems to hold out to us. Such a faith frees us to live, to love, to serve, and to share, as we journey here on earth, until we come at last to God's eternal city of rest—until, in other words, we come *home*.

DIGGING DEEPER

Day One
- Read Genesis 12:1–4. What was God's promise to Abraham?
- Read Galatians 3:29. What is God's promise to all believers? How does this promise encourage you in your daily life?

Day Two

◆ Read Hebrews 11:8–10. Abraham "obeyed as he went." The only source of information that Abraham had about God was God Himself. What resources to help you mature as a believer do you have that Abraham did not have?

Day Three

◆ Read Genesis 12:10–20. Why did Abraham go into Egypt? Why was this decision a mistake?

◆ What is your first response when you are surprised by difficult circumstances? What does Abraham's story teach you should be your first response?

Day Four

◆ Read Genesis 22. What do Abraham's actions indicate he now believed about God? Has God asked you to surrender to Him a specific part of your life? How does Abraham's story encourage you to trust God and surrender to His purposes?

Day Five

◆ Consider the C. S. Lewis quote on page 84. What are you aiming at—heaven or earth? Do you feel so caught up in this world that you don't think much about the next? How will thinking about heaven enable you to persevere in your journey?

Day Six

◆ Read 1 Peter 1:3–12. Why can a child of God view trials as temporary, necessary, and even valuable? How does aiming at heaven shape this view? How does this passage remind you to surrender to God's greater purposes?

Chapter 5

COSTLY OBEDIENCE— ISAAC

FAITH PRINCIPLE #5

BIBLICAL FAITH MEANS SURRENDERING TO GOD'S WILL.

By faith Isaac blessed Jacob and Esau in regard to their future.

(Hebrews 11:20 [see also Genesis 24; 25:19–28:9])

LORD, CHANGE ME—DENISE BODIE

When I held my newborn son for the first time, I knew I had to raise this child to honor God. My husband, Paul, did not share my desire, however, and the more I nagged and begged him to come to church with me, the more our fragile marriage deteriorated.

I eagerly accepted an invitation to attend a women's Bible study, though I was sure the study topic—*Lord, Change Me,* by Evelyn Christenson—wouldn't be especially beneficial for me. God had already saved me, so why on earth did I need to change? I had already "arrived"; I already knew what I needed to know, and I was already the person I needed to be—*wasn't I?*

Our next study of the love story in the book of Ruth, however, began to stir up more discontent in me regarding my husband and the state of our marriage. The other families in the church, every one of which seemed so "together" and harmonious, were a constant reminder of what I did not have in my own life, and I regularly cried out to God, "If only You would save my husband, my life would be perfect!" My desire for my husband to become a Christian began to matter more to me than anything else. Week after week I asked my friends to pray for my husband's salvation; week after week nothing happened. One of my friends, who was not a Christian, encouraged me to get a divorce, but my friends from the Bible study urged me to seek biblical counseling, and so I did.

The counselor's proposed course of action shocked me. Instead of showing me how to change my husband, this woman showed me my own need to change, and she helped me learn new ways to handle conflict in a way that honored God. I wanted to run home from each session to share with my husband what I was learning, but my first study in 1 Peter 3 stopped me. I interpreted this passage to mean: "Stay focused on your Father in heaven, not on your husband. Learn contentment where you are, and don't miss the blessings of each day." (My husband later told me that he hated God the most whenever I would try to "nag him to faith," so learning to be a "silent witness" was a valuable lesson indeed!)

It would be a lie to say that I skipped down the road to obedience with a joyful and obedient spirit, or that I mastered all of God's lessons on the first try. The journey was painful, long, and hard. At times, God's directions in His Word did not make sense to me and so I obeyed reluctantly—kicking and complaining and crying all the while. God placed me in a group of godly women who taught me that all Scripture—even Proverbs 31—applied to me. They encouraged me to persevere and to love my husband unconditionally.

After eleven years of prayers and tears, I was overjoyed to

see how God, in His own time, brought Paul to Himself. My husband's salvation was the answer to my prayers, but learning to live with a Christian man brought struggles of its own! I am a strong-willed woman, accustomed to traveling through life "spiritually single." Now, however, I am learning how to surrender to the leadership of my godly husband, who started the journey long after I did. It isn't always very easy to let go, to surrender to God's will for us, but I am learning, slowly, step by step, day by day, how to do this.

Paul and I don't know what future God has in store for us, but we are learning that He gives us many wonderful surprises as we learn to respond to His Word in obedience and as we surround ourselves with godly people who, in turn, encourage us to live by faith. As Paul and I continue to run the race that God has set before us, we are learning to rest in these truths: that God is in control, that He is ever faithful, and that He will work out His good and gracious plans for each of us in His own time, in His own way.

Denise Bodie

One "Ordinary" Man

At first glance, Isaac resembles a "back-pew" Christian who was raised in the church, exposed to sound doctrine and exciting, living faith in the persons of his mother, Sarah, and his father, Abraham. Like his father, Isaac was always on the road, living in tents, and doubtless his father taught him about God and His promises as the family traveled together (Hebrews 11:9; Genesis 26:2, 24). Isaac, despite the benefit of his father's example and teaching, remains something of a spiritual mediocrity. His life story can seem a little drab, sandwiched as it is between colorful Abraham and the rascally, sensational Jacob.

Isaac, however, was no "ordinary" man in God's eyes. Isaac was the necessary link God had chosen through whom to transfer His covenantal promises from one generation to the next. As with other members of God's family, Isaac's life and behavior reveal a sinful heart eventually transformed by—and surrendering to—God's grace.

A History of Faithfulness

Isaac's life was remarkable in many ways. As we learned in the last chapter, he was the "child of promise"; his birth was nothing short of a miracle, and he was raised by a father who was the very "friend" of God (Isaiah 41:8). He was the child through whom all of the promises of the covenant would be transferred to God's people.

Isaac's father was a wealthy man, and so all of his personal and material needs were met. Isaac was a loving and obedient son, not even protesting when his own father laid him out upon an altar of stone and prepared to offer him up as a sacrifice to the Lord God. Isaac, too, heard God's angel speak to his father, and he saw with his own young eyes how God provided a sacrifice, a ram, that would be killed in his place (Genesis 22:11–13).

Isaac grieved for his mother as he helped Abraham bury Sarah at Machpelah. As Abraham neared death, he decided it was time to secure a wife for his son, as was the custom for parents in those days. Abraham charged his trusted servant, probably Eliezer (Genesis 15:2), with the difficult task of traveling to Nahor, Abraham's native land, to find a wife for Isaac from among Abraham's extended family there. When Eliezer expressed doubts regarding the mission's potential success, Abraham explained that God would guide the servant (Genesis 24:7). Eliezer, through prayer and faithful obedience, eventually found Rebekah, Abraham's great-niece (v. 48). All of the main characters in this remarkable story reflected a remarkable awe of God and trust in His ways. When Rebekah's brother, Laban, and her father heard the details of Eliezer's quest for a wife for Isaac, they responded, "This is from the LORD" (v. 50). And, when asked if she was willing to leave her family, to go to a distant land, and to marry a man she had never even met, Rebekah herself showed an astounding degree of faith and trust by saying, simply and quietly, "I will go" (v. 58).

Isaac had witnessed firsthand God's faithfulness to his father, so he surely believed that God would lead Eliezer to the right woman, the woman of God's own choosing. Though we are not given much detail about the first meeting of Isaac and Rebekah, we do know that Rebekah's presence was a healing balm for a man who mourned the passing of first his mother (v. 67) and, soon thereafter, his father, Abraham. Rebekah brought into Isaac's life a love that comforted him and encouraged his grieving heart.

BORN TO CONFLICT

God had promised that through Isaac a mighty nation would arise, a nation that would one day possess the land of

Canaan, and that through his family all nations would be blessed. For twenty years, Isaac and Rebekah waited for the promised child, but Rebekah was barren. Isaac, however, had apparently learned much from Abraham—both from his father's mistakes and from his great faith. Isaac was only a little boy when, at the instigation of his mother, Abraham finally ordered Hagar and her son (Isaac's half-brother), Ishmael, from their camp. But Isaac most surely remembered the pain caused by his father's adultery and all of the ensuing turmoil. Isaac, therefore, did not try to come up with some "creative solution" to his dilemma. Instead, he turned to God in prayer (Genesis 25:21), asking for God's help. Thus, Rebekah's inability to have children, painful though it was for both Isaac and Rebekah, served a greater purpose in their lives. Like the circumstances surrounding their first meeting, the birth of their children, when it finally came, would also be the result of intense prayers. Isaac's turning to God for help in this circumstance reveals that Isaac had truly embraced his father's God as his own.

God answered Isaac's prayer. Rebekah conceived, but the unusual amount of jostling in her womb troubled her. When she took her concerns to God, this frightened mother learned that she was not carrying one child but two: twin boys destined to become the fathers of two great nations (vv. 22–23). Perhaps even more startling was God's revelation that the first-born child would eventually serve the second (v. 23).

This was unsettling news to Rebekah. In their culture, birth order was of paramount importance. Leadership of the clan was always passed on to the oldest son, and this authority was conferred formally through the patriarchal blessing. Yet God had declared that Esau, the older twin, would serve the younger twin, Jacob. This divine choice was not based on Jacob's inherent merit or value but on God's sovereign purposes (Romans 9:11–13). By overruling the traditional rights of the firstborn and declaring His choice before the boys were even born, God was making it clear that He alone, not tradition or circumstance, was in absolute control of this family.

This unusual situation served to bring Isaac to a difficult crossroad. Although the Scriptures are silent as to whether Rebekah told Isaac about God's plan for the twins, it is unlikely she kept this information from him. The twins' birth only served to illustrate the unusual nature of their relationship to one another. Esau emerged from the womb, red and hairy, followed by Jacob, who was hanging onto his brother's heel (Genesis 25:24–26).

A FAMILY IN CRISIS

The twins had markedly different personalities: Esau was a skillful hunter, a man of the woods and fields, whereas Jacob was more of a homebody. The Bible tells us that "Isaac, who had a taste for wild game, loved Esau, but Rebekah loved Jacob" (v. 28); this is the first hint that, although the marriage of Isaac and Rebekah started out with love, something had subtly changed. This was now a home troubled by the destructive sin of favoritism, and this favoritism for their children had begun to drive a wedge between them. Isaac, who loved good food, preferred Esau, who knew how to satisfy his father's cravings. Esau, however, cared little about his role and responsibility as the firstborn son.

The brothers' growing animosity toward one another was certainly evident the time Esau, famished from a day's hunting, carelessly traded away the birthright he scorned to Jacob for a mere pot of stew (vv. 29–34). Esau also showed his disregard for his parents by marrying a Canaanite woman, someone who was probably not a believer in the Lord God and who was certainly a "source of grief" to his parents (Genesis 26:34–35). Isaac was constantly battling these same Canaanites over control of his wells and property rights. They were a people who, for the most part, had rejected both Isaac's family and his God. Yet Esau proceeded to sadden his parents by marrying first one and then another of these unbelieving women.

Isaac's heart, not unlike his home, was divided. He attempted to serve two masters. On the one hand, his cultural context demanded that Esau receive the patriarchal blessing and inheritance. On the other hand, God could not have been clearer: the blessing was to go to Jacob. Esau was a son out of control, displeasing to God and an embarrassment to the moral and spiritual values of his family and their God. Blinded by his pride in Esau's toughness and hunting abilities, Isaac was unaware that he and his family were headed for a time of great sadness and a crisis that would sorely test them all.

JACOB HAVE I LOVED

The birthright, so despised by Esau, involved a threefold patriarchal blessing and accompanying responsibilities. The recipient of the birthright was entitled to two material rewards—a double portion of his father's possessions and control over all business and family matters. The firstborn was also destined to bear a third responsibility, one that makes Isaac's story so pivotal in redemptive history. The oldest son was to care for the spiritual welfare of the clan, to transmit and teach all of God's covenant promises to the next generation. Esau, by marrying Canaanite women and carelessly trading away his birthright, had clearly indicated his disdain for the God of his parents.

Believing he was near death, Isaac told Esau to prepare a special meal for him, after which he would bestow the patriarchal blessing on him. Rebekah overheard Isaac's instructions, and once Esau had left for the hunt, she put a plan of her own into action, a sneaky and deceitful plan that shows us how much her relationship with Isaac had deteriorated by this point (Genesis 27:5–10). Moreover, she drew her favored son, Jacob, into her scheme as her accomplice. Jacob at first demurred, fearing their lie would be discovered. In response to his fears, Rebekah uttered words that would later return to haunt her: "My son, let the curse fall on me. Just do what I say" (v. 13).

Jacob agreed to the plan and, pretending to be Esau, presented himself before Isaac. The near-blind and somewhat suspicious old man called his son near so that he could touch him. Jacob, prepared for this, offered Isaac his arm—covered with a goatskin to feel like hairy Esau's own thick arms. Isaac, still uncertain, peering at the young man uneasily though weak and rheumy eyes, asked him point blank, "Are you *really* my son Esau?" And Jacob replied, "I am." After eating his meal, Isaac once more called his son near. As Jacob kissed his father, Isaac caught a whiff of the clothing Jacob was wearing, clothing he had "borrowed" from his brother, Esau. Isaac was reassured by the smell of the woods and fields, a smell so reminiscent of Esau. Then, rather than pausing to seek God's direction, rather than prayerfully and carefully looking into the matter further, Isaac allowed his physical senses to guide him. Convinced that Jacob was indeed his firstborn son Esau, the aged patriarch bestowed the twofold material part of the patriarchal blessing on Jacob, but he still withheld the more crucial spiritual part of the blessing (vv. 27–29).

In our view, Isaac's incomplete transfer of the patriarchal blessing was further evidence that he knew of God's declaration that the younger son must serve the older. We believe that, instead of accepting God's plan for Jacob to receive the entire blessing, Isaac compromised at this point. He attempted to satisfy the desire of his own heart and honor tradition by giving Esau what was important to him—money. We believe Isaac planned to obey God by later giving to Jacob the spiritual portion of the blessing that linked the son of promise to the covenant God had made with Abraham.

Jacob, now the recipient of this material blessing, quickly left his father's tent before his deception was discovered. Esau then entered, bringing with him the tasty meal he had prepared for his father. Isaac, realizing with shock what Jacob had done, "trembled violently" (v. 33), but nevertheless affirmed that the blessing he had given to Jacob must stand. Isaac would later extend the critical final part of the patriarchal blessing to Jacob as well.

When Esau realized that Isaac would not rescind the blessing and that Jacob was destined, according to the terms of the blessing, to rule over him after his father's death, he burst out with a loud and bitter cry: "Bless me—me too, my father!" (v. 34).

Esau was seeking money and power, not spiritual leadership. Hebrews 12:17 describes God's reaction to his tears: "When he wanted to inherit this blessing, he was rejected. . . . though he sought the blessing with tears." These were not tears of repentance for offending God and for despising the birthright; these were tears of sorrow and regret over an enormous loss of wealth and prestige. Isaac responded to Esau's painful outburst by giving him a "blessing" that sounds more like a curse: Esau would not know the economic prosperity of his brother; he and his children would live as scavengers; and he and his descendants were destined to serve Jacob and his descendants. Isaac, by faith, also sees into the future and prophesies that Esau's descendants will eventually throw off the rule of Jacob's descendants (Genesis 27:39–40).

It is for the giving of both of these blessings, the one to Esau but especially the one to Jacob, that Isaac is honored in Hebrews 11:20: "By faith Isaac blessed Jacob and Esau in regard to their future."

What had transpired in those few moments to mark Isaac as a man of faith? The phrase, "in regard to their future," is best translated: concerning the events that were inevitable or predestined. Isaac's partiality to Esau was at cross purposes with his responsibility to obey God. Perhaps he trembled because he suddenly understood that he had pitted his desires against God's will. All at once Isaac remembered that this was not about meeting Esau's needs or his own desires. This blessing was about God's plan to redeem His children. Isaac surrendered to God's purposes with an amazing, affecting combination of both awe at God's sovereign ways and sadness for himself and for his tragic, favored, but now lost son. Isaac did not understand—indeed, could not have fully understood—what God intended for the distant future but, at that moment, Isaac reflected a deep and profound faith in God's plan of redemption, despite his own tragic personal circumstances.

Esau, in contrast, did not acknowledge God's hand in this situation. He blamed Jacob and plotted to kill his brother (Genesis 27:41), thereby showing his utter disdain for his father and the words of his father's blessing (that he would one day serve Jacob) and, ultimately, his contempt for the will of God. There is no evidence of surrender in Esau's life—none whatsoever. Rebekah, upon learning of Esau's nefarious plan, instructed Jacob to visit her brother Laban for a while until Esau had calmed down. Then she lied to Isaac, telling him that she had sent Jacob away because she was afraid he would marry a Hittite woman, as Esau had done. Isaac then gave Jacob the final and most important part of the covenant blessing (Genesis 28:1–4) and sent him away to find a wife.

SHARED SIN, SHARED CONSEQUENCES, UNCONDITIONAL LOVE

Each player in this story attempted to "control" God's plan, coercing events and circumstances to achieve his or her own shortsighted ends. Isaac and Rebekah had begun their marriage with an understanding of their part in God's plan of redemption, and they had both certainly loved each other and trusted God. So what happened?

Isaac and Rebekah lost sight of the fact that privilege comes with responsibility—and such responsibility can be costly. Instead of training their sons to revere God and preparing them for the roles God had ordained, the parents each chose to focus attention on their own favorite child. Isaac attempted to compromise God's instructions. He plotted ways to satisfy himself in Esau and convinced himself that he was still submitting to God's plans. Rebekah, for her part, had slowly grown accustomed to deceit. Years earlier, Isaac had followed his own father's bad example; he had risked Rebekah's life in order to protect his own, by using precisely the same lie Abraham had used—claiming Rebekah was "his sister" (Genesis 26:7–11)—and to the very same man, no less (Abimelech, king of Gerar). Perhaps Rebekah concluded from this episode that it was acceptable to deceive and manipulate her husband provided it was all done for a "good cause": to secure the full patriarchal blessing for her beloved Jacob. In turn, Jacob, the chosen one, repeatedly lied to his father, and he failed to trust God to give him what was promised. Esau, the pleasure seeker, dishonored God in his life, married whom he willed, scorned his birthright, and then had the temerity to cry "foul"—and almost immediately started plotting the cold-blooded murder of his own brother.

Isaac's family members suffered the consequences of their sin. Rebekah had told Jacob she would carry on her shoulders the curse for their deception, and carry it she did. She would never see her beloved son again. The favoritism of the parents would lead, eventually, to the formation of two warring nations, to incalculable hurt and suffering for generations to come. Esau left the family in anger, plotting murder, and thereby revealing, once again, his own godless heart. Finally, Isaac, for his part, would not see Jacob again until he was on his deathbed, some forty-three years later.

THE SWEET FRUIT OF SURRENDER

Despite all of this foul play and family turmoil, God chose to commend Isaac, in Hebrews 11, for finally realizing his part in God's plan of redemption and for acting accordingly. In the end, God graciously protected Isaac from choosing Esau to be his successor. Ultimately, faith empowered Isaac to set aside his own desires for himself and his family with faithful obedience. He blessed his sons according to the sovereign word of God. Isaac understood the spiritual truth conveyed many years later by the prophet Isaiah:

> "For my thoughts are not your thoughts, neither are your ways my ways," declares the LORD. "As the heavens are higher than the earth, so are my ways higher than your ways and my thoughts than your thoughts." (Isaiah 55:8–9)

Although this family suffered severe consequences for its sin, God did not reject them but continued to carry out His covenant plans through them. Isaac, in the end, trusted God, surrendering to His will and accepting the promises of the covenant. Like his father Abraham before him and his son Jacob after him, Isaac longed for a "better country." He, too, saw that country only from afar, but at last he entered into that country, just as God had promised (Matthew 22:32).

SURRENDERING IT ALL

Isaac had loved Esau and longed for him to experience the blessings due the firstborn son. Just as his own father, Abraham, was forced to relinquish Ishmael, Isaac was forced to give up Esau even when his heart cried out against it. It was painful and difficult for this doting father to obey God in this matter even when Isaac could not understand why God would choose Jacob over Esau. Yet Isaac's ultimate refusal to rescind the blessing to Jacob demonstrates his decision to trust God with his family's future, no matter what might be in that future. God was working in ways that Isaac could not see but was learning to accept by faith (Hebrews 11:1–2).

In our opening story, Denise learned that the ends do not justify the means. God wanted her to walk in obedience before her husband. Instead, she attempted to coerce her husband's salvation, and she was met, not surprisingly, with resistance and anger. She felt her behavior was justified. After all, she was the one who knew God; why should she submit to an unsaved husband? Her Christian friends reminded her, however, that, as a believer, her life was not about what she wanted, it was about God's bigger plan.

Eventually, Denise had to learn to walk in faith, with quiet repentance and a humble heart, even to the point of surrendering to God the very thing she wanted most in the world: her husband's coming to Christ. In other words, God was teaching Denise to believe His ways are right and true and best, even when her circumstances did not immediately change as a result of her obedience. When we are asked to give everything to God, it not only means giving up the sinful habits we're so attached to, it also means "giving up" the good and right things we cherish, the things we hope for: a child of our very own, the husband or wife we wish we had, the good health that has so long eluded us. We may long for these things, and we may pray for them. But we must always remember that our Lord knows what we really need most. So, are we willing to trust Him? Are we prepared to give up every-thing—*everything*—this world has to offer, in order that we might gain everything He has to give? Surely, this is what it means to "surrender."

In our own personal journey through grief after Mark's death, a good friend reminded us that we needed to view our lives as a part of the bigger picture of God's redemption. After months of listening, as we struggled to reconcile our love for God with our deep grief, this woman quietly said, "We need to really pray about how God is going to use your experiences to help build up the church." And we were angry. *"You pray about it! All we want is to feel better."* But our friend had planted the seed that eventually brought us to our own point of decision, a place where we were able to ask: How can our response to our son's death help build up God's kingdom? And, once we identify how God wants us to react, will we be able to do it?

Every Christian faces the same questions every day. Will we see the hard places in our lives as opportunities to reflect our confidence in our God, or will we attempt to manipulate God into doing things *our* way?

If we could have manipulated His actions in our lives so that life would be what we had planned, we would have. Our hearts cried out to God that parents should not have to bury their own children. Like Isaac, we wanted God to plan out our lives in ways that meet our needs, ways that satisfy our expectations. When death crashed into our home that day and left us bleeding and broken, thinking, so sadly, again and again, of all that might have been, we wrestled with God, and we often asked Him to open our eyes to His purposes so that we could trust Him once again. We wanted to take comfort in God's promises, but instead our grief raged like a storm against His wisdom.

Yet, in spite of our distrust, God extended His goodness to the two of us in ways we could never have imagined. He is teaching us even now, slowly, gently, with great and loving patience, how to surrender to His purposes. It is an ongoing, daily process. Each day we ask Him to help us accept Mark's death as a means through which God is building His kingdom. And we ask Him to help us live obediently, reflecting our trust in Him so that the church will benefit from our jour-

ney. Isaac eventually understood that he must run with patience the race marked out for him by God (Hebrews
12:1–4). Like Isaac, we are learning, even when we do not understand God's actions, to apply this same faith principle of
surrender.

God identified Isaac as His own and, in so doing, provided one more snapshot in this "faith family album" in Hebrews 11—an album filled with pictures of people who knew
God's character and came to accept His unconditional love. It
is easy to sympathize with Isaac. We see ourselves in him. Like
Isaac, we are often tempted to reject God's authority and to
come up with our own solutions. Going our own way often
seems so much easier, so much more likely to satisfy our
needs. But, as He did with Isaac, our sovereign God knows
how to correct our steps, and He shows us—through the life
of Isaac and through the circumstances of our own lives—that,
in the long run, obedience really is better.

Faith often forces hard choices on us that may not
make sense, especially when God's directions to us in His
Word require the giving up of our "rights." God, in fact,
through the book of Hebrews, was asking these suffering
first-century Christians to continue to do the very things that
brought them pain: to grow in intimacy with Christ, to believe His promises, to identify themselves as members of the
covenant community, and to keep on ministering to one another (Hebrews 10:19–25). Isaac's recognition of the supremacy and power of God's sovereign will reminded these
first-century believers that their obedience, costly as it was,
boldly proclaimed to a watching world that they, too, trusted
God. God commended Isaac—the critical human link that
would pass His promises on to Jacob—and thereby reminded the Hebrew Christians that they, too, were critical
links in the family of God. They, like us, simply needed to
persevere—relating the truth of God to the next generation
of believers, *whatever the cost might be.*

DIGGING DEEPER

Day One
◆ With pen and notebook in hand, read Genesis 24:1–28:9 and write out your impressions of Isaac's character.

Day Two
◆ Review the description of faith in Hebrews 11:1–3. Read also Genesis 24. How do each of the following people demonstrate faith? Abraham; Abraham's servant (Eliezer); Isaac; Rebekah

Day Three
◆ Read Genesis 27. What did each of the following people in this troubled family do that was wrong? Isaac; Rebekah; Jacob; Esau
◆ Do you feel a particular "kinship" with any of these people? Why?

Day Four
◆ Describe one hard place presently in your life. How are you reflecting your trust in God in response to these circumstances? How can you intentionally build the kingdom of God through these circumstances?

Day Five
◆ How did Denise, in our opening story, make an idol out of a "good thing," her desire for her husband's salvation? What good thing are you attempting to attain or hold onto? Ask God to show you if you are in danger of putting your desire(s) ahead His plans.

Day Six

- Read Romans 8:29–39. Write out and personalize this passage as a prayer. Put the prayer someplace you will remember. When you are struggling with God's purposes, pray this prayer.

Chapter 6

FROM SNEAK TO SERVANT—JACOB

FAITH PRINCIPLE #6

BIBLICAL FAITH REVEALS OUR NEED FOR GOD'S HELP.

By faith Jacob, when he was dying, blessed each

of Joseph's sons, and worshiped as he leaned on the top of his staff.

(Hebrews 11:21 [see also Genesis 28:10–48:22])

WOUNDED BY THE SHEPHERD—STU LINDNER

I knew how to get what I wanted in life: I was a former high school and college athlete and a U.S. Air Force Academy graduate; my Air Force career was exemplary, and I had become a successful business owner and top sales professional. Success was my signature. But there was a powerful undercurrent of secret sin in my life: sexual immorality. The environment of my workplace made it easy to satisfy my desires through numerous adulterous relationships. I knew that what I was doing was wrong because I had been raised with Christian values, but I still felt trapped and addicted. In the midst of this darkness, God placed a "light": my barber, Charles.

Every time he cut my hair, he read from his Bible and he prayed with me. As much as I looked forward to our prayer time and as close as I became to Charles over the years, I never shared with him the pain and overwhelming sense of guilt that adultery was causing in my life. And so I did nothing; I was caught in a snare of my own making, and I successfully kept it hidden from everyone . . . everyone, that is, but God.

So it was that God removed His hand of protection from me for just a moment, a split second, the day I collided with a truck while flying along at nearly 50 mph on my motorcycle. Suddenly the strong, healthy body of which I had always been so proud was completely shattered. The paramedics told my wife, Patty, that I was the worst motorcycle accident survivor they had ever seen. My specialists, at a loss over the severity of my injuries, even encouraged my friend Charles, who had immediately come to see me, to pray for me.

God performed miracles that night in the emergency room. As Charles led Patty in prayer, glass fragments that the doctors were unable to remove suddenly disappeared. A week after the plastic surgeon described for us the reparative surgery needed to restore my broken cheek bone, he was shaking his head in amazement at the remarkable healing of my repaired face. Later, when my doctors removed the bandages from my legs, they expected to begin making the skin grafts usually required by massive infection. Instead, they were stunned to discover just how much the lacerations had already healed.

Six weeks in traction brought me face to face with Jesus Christ and what His death on the cross really meant for me. God spoke to me, particularly through the book of Romans, to show me my sin. I asked Him to forgive me and to help me turn away from my selfishness and the sinful habits of my former lifestyle. At that moment both joy and sadness washed over me—joy for my new life, sadness for how it must have grieved the Lord to have had to smash the body of someone He had so lovingly created.

I had read somewhere that a shepherd would sometimes break the leg of a lamb intent on running away. Unless the animal was literally forced to lie still, it would never stop wandering off and would eventually be killed by predators. While the lamb was healing, the shepherd would tenderly care for and carry the injured animal and, in turn, the lamb would form a deep, lasting bond with the shepherd. Once it had fully recovered, the lamb would never wander away again. God, I believe, was acting as the faithful Shepherd, one who must sometimes break the leg of a sheep that is intent on running away. Each pain-filled moment I cried out for God's comfort. I would feel His nearness in the night as I closed my eyes to sleep. Peace with God finally brought rest to my restless soul. In shattering my body, that accident also shattered the idol that had blinded me for so long to Christ's love and the love of my wife. God not only opened my own eyes to His forgiveness; Patty, too, committed her life to Christ on the night of the accident. My love for my wife deepens every day, and our marriage is now strong and growing.

Even though God has forgiven my sin, the scars of my selfish lifestyle, like the scars in my physical body, remain with me always. Memories of that former bondage have given me a heart for prison inmates who are trapped by the same bars of sin. The physical aches and pains I still endure are a constant reminder that help me resist temptation. Our sons were very young when God turned my life around through this accident. They are now teenagers and are better equipped to resist temptation; Patty and I have honestly shared the details of my past with them, as well as our testimony of God's redeeming love. Instead of longing for what I was, what I once had, I remember daily that God used my suffering to bring me to Himself. I have learned to thank Him when discomfort restricts my physical activities, for I know that my sufferings "are not worth comparing with the glory that will be revealed" in me (Romans 8:18).

By His grace, I now hold onto life loosely and pray that I will live each day left to me in a way that glorifies "the God before whom my fathers Abraham and Isaac walked, the God who has been my Shepherd all my life to this day" (Genesis 48:15). My prayer for our sons is that "the Angel who has delivered me from all harm" will bless these boys as well (Genesis 48:16).

Stu Lindner

LEAVING A LEGACY

Observers must not give in to the temptation to tear away a cocoon encasing a caterpillar. To do so pulls the struggling caterpillar past the very step this small creature needs to push vital fluids into its wings and to transform it into a soaring, healthy butterfly. As we journey beside our next example of faith, Jacob, we will be tempted to tear away his cocoon of selfish machinations, grab him by the throat, and scream, "Jacob, how many times does God have to speak to you before you really hear Him?" But our patience with Jacob will grow as his journey illuminates our own failures. In so many ways, Jacob is someone we can identify with personally. He will teach us, through the example of his own life, how God's grace can rescue us from ourselves, from our own foolish and self-centered behavior. We will long to experience the same deep wells of God's forgiveness that Jacob discovered. In Jacob's story we are reminded that, as believers, we will inherit the same glorious legacy.

The reference to Jacob in Hebrews 11 is so brief and flies by so quickly you might easily miss it altogether. But there is a priceless message buried here:

> By faith Jacob, when he was dying, blessed each of Joseph's sons, and worshiped as he leaned on the top of his staff. (v. 21)

This verse takes us into Jacob's death room, where we witness the final moments of his life. But before we enter that holy place, we must reflect on the events and circumstances God had used to bring Jacob to this culminating point in his life's journey.

THE JOURNEY BEGINS

"Manipulate" means "to control or play upon by artful, unfair, or insidious means, especially to one's own advantage."

The subject of this chapter, Jacob, was indeed a master manipulator, passionately attempting to maintain control over every life choice he made.

Thus it was that, instead of seeking reconciliation with his brother, Jacob decided to seek the most "practical" solution to his problem and fled for his life. He left the comfort and safety "among the tents" and sought his fortune elsewhere. At one point, when he stopped to rest along the way, God confronted Jacob and reaffirmed some powerful eternal promises:

> I am the LORD, the God of your father Abraham and the God of Isaac. I will give you and your descendants the land on which you are lying. Your descendants will be like the dust of the earth, and you will spread out to the west and to the east, to the north and to the south. All peoples on earth will be blessed through you and your offspring. I am with you and will watch over you wherever you go, and I will bring you back to this land. I will not leave you until I have done what I have promised you. (Genesis 28:13–15)

Jacob made the stone he was using for a pillow into an altar, and he named that place "Bethel" ("House of God"). But Jacob still did not quite trust this voice in the night. Instead, he vowed that, *provided* God kept His promises, the God of Abraham and Isaac would then also be Jacob's God. In other words, when it came to his relationship to God, Jacob wanted the goods first. Over the next twenty years he continued to try to play "let's make a deal" and "show me the money" with God and everyone else he met until, years later, he finally returned to Bethel, an older and somewhat wiser man.

When Jacob finally arrived in Haran, he gratefully accepted the hospitality of his uncle Laban. Jacob, ever the wheeler and dealer, agreed to work seven years for Laban in return for the privilege of marrying Laban's daughter, the beautiful Rachel. Seven years "seemed like only a few days to him," the passage tells us, so great was Jacob's love for Rachel (Genesis 29:20). When the seven years of labor were completed, the young bridegroom enjoyed his wedding night with his new bride only to discover the next morning that Laban had beaten him at his own game. The veiled woman Jacob had married the night before was not the lovely Rachel but her older sister Leah.

How ironic it is that Jacob's anguished question for Laban carried the same accusation his father Isaac had once made against him, "Why have you deceived me?" (Genesis 29:25). Perhaps some appreciation of the pain his own act of deceit had caused his father came back to Jacob at that moment as he listened to Laban's mealy-mouthed explanation for this ruse. What a shock it must have been for Jacob to discover that he had just married into the family of a man every bit as cunning and devious as himself. Jacob, however, refused to accept Leah as his only wife. Rachel was beautiful; Jacob loved her and her alone, and he intended to have her, no matter what. Thus, Jacob agreed to work for Laban for yet another seven years in order to marry Rachel as well.

THE COMPETITION OF TWO WIVES

Polygamy led to intense family conflict as Jacob's obvious preference for Rachel proved to be a source of great grief for Leah and, eventually, great anger for Leah's sons. Yet in tenderness and in response to Jacob's obvious rejection of Leah, God gave her many children; indeed, she bore Jacob's first four children—Reuben, Simeon, Levi, and Judah—whereas Rachel remained barren. Jealousy of Leah's ability to have children erupted into a sinful and destructive competition between the two sisters. Rachel, in a maneuver reminiscent of Jacob's grandmother, Sarah, suggested to Jacob that he sleep with her maidservant, Bilhah, and this woman in turn bore Jacob two more sons: Dan and Naphtali. Then, at Leah's instigation, Jacob in turn slept with Leah's own maidservant, Zilpah, who bore Jacob two more sons: Gad and Asher. Rachel remained childless while Leah gave birth to another two sons, Issachar and Zebulun, as well as a daughter, Dinah. Then, at long last, God graciously gave Rachel and Jacob a son, Joseph; finally, many years later, Rachel bore a second son, Benjamin.

Jacob, sadly, ended up following his own parents' poor example of child-rearing by openly showing special love and preference for Joseph, the apple of his eye, the firstborn son of his beloved wife Rachel. That favoritism would eventually produce a severe case of sibling rivalry among the other brothers, a rivalry that would, in time, lead to terrible and destructive consequences for everyone in this troubled family.

JACOB'S HOMECOMING

Even as his wives and concubines bore him more and more children, Jacob also prospered materially. Though Laban continued trying to swindle Jacob, God protected Jacob, his chosen man, and Jacob's flocks flourished greatly. Laban and his sons concluded that Jacob had outwitted them, and their attitudes toward him began to turn sour. In the midst of that controversy, God in grace spoke to Jacob:

> Then the LORD said to Jacob, "Go back to the land of your fathers and to your relatives, and I will be with you." (Genesis 31:3)

Jacob still didn't really trust God's voice, however, apparently relying more on the opinions of his two wives than on a clear command from God. Providentially, however, both Rachel and Leah urged him to obey God in this instance—less because they believed God, as it turns out, than because they so greatly distrusted Laban, their wily father.

Though God promised to be with this family on their return home, Jacob was still extremely nervous and afraid. Going back home meant escaping from crafty and not-to-be-trusted Laban only to face the vengeful and murderous Esau. Surely, Jacob feared, one or the other of these formidable adversaries would catch up to and destroy both him and his family.

Believing God's promise to protect us is, of course, especially hard when we are faced with real danger. When our friend Janice was a teenager, her brother died. Now a young mother, she is learning what God's promise of His presence really means in her own daily life. She described for us a response markedly different from Jacob's reluctant, fearful obedience:

> We think we need to *feel* things in order for them to be true, but we don't. We have to hold onto what Scripture teaches us. Our feelings are deceptive and unreliable. There are many times that I don't *feel* His protection. That's when I come to a point where I have to admit my unbelief and just commit myself to trust God anyway, even when I'm afraid I might lose one of my children the way my mother did. God doesn't lie to us. Sometimes we have to take a step of faith even when all we see before us is a big black hole.

In spite of Jacob's faithlessness, God by grace protected him as he fled from his father-in-law's angry pursuit, and God even warned Laban in a dream that he must not harm his son-in-law. Laban and Jacob were reconciled, and Jacob was able to leave that place in peace, taking his large family back to his homeland, the land of his father Isaac—the land of his "blood enemy," his brother Esau.

CONFRONTING THE PAST

Jacob remembered well the murderous wrath of Esau, and, with great trepidation, he prepared to confront his brother. Fear of the outraged and swindled Esau, now a mighty and powerful leader in his own right, warred against Jacob's desire to trust his God. Jacob was just *so* afraid. In desperation, he reminded God of His promises: "Save me, I pray, from the hand of my brother Esau, for I am afraid he will come and attack me, and also the mothers with their children" (Genesis 32:11).

After sending gifts ahead to Esau to appease his anger, Jacob concluded the time had come for him to face head-on the consequences of his past. The night before he confronted Esau, however, Jacob, lagging behind his family as they crossed a stream called the Jabbok, was left standing alone. Suddenly, out of the darkness, a man stepped out and threw Jacob to the ground. Throughout his life, Jacob had "wrestled" his enemies, outsmarting them, duping them, dodging and parrying and scheming his way through life, always getting what he wanted, always somehow "winning" in the end. He had successfully deceived his father and his brother and so won the birthright and the patriarchal blessing. He had learned to beat Laban at his own game. And he probably even thought he'd cut a "sweet deal" with the living God back at Bethel—saying, in effect, "You take care of me, Lord. Prosper me, protect me, and *then* I'll be your man!" (Genesis 28:20–22). But this time, God initiated a wrestling match of His own, one that would teach Jacob that He—and He alone—controlled Jacob's destiny.

Jacob began to realize that this was no ordinary person he was wrestling. Wounded, Jacob still clung helplessly to his opponent. He realized, probably for the first time in his life, how helpless he really was without the supernatural help of the living God. Jacob, humbled and severely wounded, pleaded for God's blessing. In answer to that pain-filled prayer, God changed his name from "Jacob" ("he grasps the heel") to "Israel" ("he struggles with God"). In this remarkable, one-of-a-kind wrestling match, God finally humbled Jacob, this man who, for the first time in his life, was completely overmatched. Jacob was left with a permanent injury in his hip, an ever-present reminder—a "scorch mark," if you will—to show him that God was truly the Master and he, Jacob, was the servant.

After this "mountaintop" experience, one might have expected to see a completely different man, a "new Jacob." For by now God had given Jacob a double inheritance through Isaac's blessing, and God had reaffirmed this promise to Jacob both in his dream at Bethel and later at the river Jabbok, where Jacob wrestled with God. Moreover, God had also promised to protect Jacob. In response to Jacob's prayer for help against his brother, He even softened Esau's angry heart. But when Jacob saw Esau approach, Jacob lost his nerve, and his trust in God's protection went, so to speak, right out the window.

Instead of believing that God had changed Esau, as in fact God had done, the younger brother judged Esau's warm greeting by that old familiar standard: Esau must be lying, Jacob suspected, thinking, in effect, "It's just the sort of thing *I myself* would do." Jacob cravenly addressed the ungodly Esau as his "lord," bowing obsequiously before him, even though God Himself had long before promised that it would be Esau who would one day serve Jacob. Finally, Jacob lied. He promised to join up with Esau later when he really planned, in direct disobedience to God's instructions to return home, to go to the city of Shechem instead, safely out of Esau's clutches. Although at Shechem Jacob and his family were certainly back in the land of Canaan, they were not yet living where God had told them to go: the place near

Bethel where his father and the rest of his family were settled. Jacob, once again, had improvised, bringing along God "in tow." The family of Jacob would suffer deep consequences for this seven-year detour into Shechem, a detour made in defiance of God's expressed wishes for Jacob. Dinah, his only daughter, would later be raped in that place, and Jacob's sons, in taking upon themselves a horrible and bloody act of vengeance, would in turn bring near-disaster upon them all.

TIME TO CLEAN HOUSE

On the heels of this disheartening chapter in Jacob's life, God once again called upon Jacob to return to his home:

> Then God said to Jacob, "Go up to Bethel and settle there, and build an altar there to God, who appeared to you when you were fleeing from your brother Esau." (Genesis 35:1)

This time Jacob complied. In doing so, he had come full circle. Thirty years before, he had vowed that if God would protect him he, in turn, would surrender to God, becoming God's faithful and obedient servant. Jacob, battered and discouraged by the aftermath of the sojourn in Shechem, this time commanded his family to get rid of all the foreign gods and to repent of their idol worship. Jacob then led his family in worship and finally came home to Bethel.

God once more spoke to Jacob, calling him again by his new name, "Israel" (Genesis 35:9–15). This use of "Israel" reminded Jacob that he had struggled with—and had been overcome by—God. The Lord's words to Jacob were gracious, displaying His compassion and forgiveness for an undeserving, broken man.

LOSING AND FINDING A BELOVED SON

But Jacob's troubles were not yet over. His beloved Rachel died while giving birth to Benjamin, their second child. And as for the older son, Joseph? The price Jacob and Joseph would one day pay for their special relationship makes Hebrews 11:21 even more poignant. Instead of learning from his own parents' sin of favoritism, Jacob expressed his preferential love for Joseph at every opportunity, including giving him a beautiful, expensive coat of many colors. As it would turn out, the "apple does not fall far from the tree": Jacob's other sons, jealous and angry, carried on the sins of their father as they schemed and plotted their brother's downfall. These malcontents finally and brutally got rid of their hated brother Joseph, selling him off as a slave while telling their father the boy must be dead.

Even as Jacob mourned the "death" of this, his favorite son, God, in sovereign grace, was bringing about three powerful miracles—the deliverance of Joseph, the creation of a safe place in Egypt for the covenant family of God to survive and grow, and the redemption of his fallen brothers. Behind the scenes, even in the midst of the intense pain of this splintered family, God was doing something wonderful. For surely, as it says in the book of Jeremiah, God had "plans to prosper [them] and not to harm [them]," plans to bring life and hope and a better future for them all (Jeremiah 29:11).

Through circumstances we will study more fully in the next chapter, God eventually miraculously reunited Jacob with his dear son Joseph, the son he thought had died so many years earlier. Before rushing to this joyous reunion, Jacob first worshiped his God. When the Lord spoke to him this time, Jacob believed God.

"I am God, the God of your father," he said. "Do not be afraid to go down to Egypt, for I will make you into a great nation there. I will go down to Egypt with you, and I will surely bring you back again. And Joseph's own hand will close your eyes." (Genesis 46:3–4)

Seventeen years after Jacob's trip to Egypt, seventeen years after that joy-filled reunion with Joseph, Jacob would remember those words. On his deathbed, Jacob understood that he had one more important thing to do before he died: he was to convey the promises of the covenant to his family after him.

PASSING ON THE LEGACY

Jacob knew his earthly days were drawing to a close, and he remembered God's promise that he, Jacob, would one day return to Canaan, the land of his fathers. During his final years in Egypt, so very far from that homeland, Jacob asked Joseph to promise to take his father's remains back to Canaan (Genesis 47:28–31). To be buried there with Abraham and Isaac would declare to all the world that he, Jacob, and his offspring did not really belong in Egypt, a land of comfort and ease for them in that day, but also a land filled with people who hated the Israelites, people who did not accept or honor the Lord God. Like Abraham and Isaac before him, Jacob "was looking forward to the city with foundations, whose architect and builder is God" (Hebrews 11:10). He wanted to leave a legacy of hope and a message of warning to his progeny—that Egypt was not and would never be their "home."

Jacob then worshiped God, having been assured that Joseph would honor his father's last request. The description of the elderly Jacob leaning on his staff in worship is a poignant one, for here was a man truly overcome by the grace God had shown him throughout his whole life—in times of humble obedience and in times of crafty self-reliance. This remarkable picture is not a sterile, "church as usual" sort of scene. Jacob's intimacy with God at that moment was deep, intense, reflective, emotional. The "old Jacob," wily, scheming, and self-sufficient, was gone forever. Though Jacob's body was, by this time, old and frail, surely here was a man at last made new.

A Double Portion

Learning that his father was dying, Joseph brought his own two sons, Manasseh and Ephraim, to visit Jacob one last time. The aging grandfather hugged and kissed the two boys. Jacob's reminiscing reveals at this point what was on his mind as he faced death: the promises of the covenant God had made with Abraham, memories of his own pilgrimage, the sorrow of losing his beloved Rachel, and the legacy he wanted to pass on to Joseph's sons. Jacob still seemed in awe that Joseph really was alive when he exclaimed, "I never expected to see your face again, and now God has allowed me to see your children too" (Genesis 48:11).

Joseph then arranged the boys to stand in front of their grandfather so that Jacob could bless them according to their ages, giving to Manasseh the rights of the firstborn. When Jacob appeared ready to give the younger son, Ephraim, those rights, Joseph protested as though his father was about to make a big mistake. But Jacob was insistent; he knew exactly what he was doing and, by God's direction, he proceeded to give the greater blessing to the younger son.

The Blessing

Jacob's blessing expressed to the two boys reveals much about the relationships between Jacob, his God, and his grandsons:

Then he [Jacob] blessed Joseph and said, "May the God before whom my fathers Abraham and Isaac walked, the God who has been my Shepherd all my life to this day, the Angel who has delivered me from all harm—may he bless these boys. May they be called by my name and the names of my fathers Abraham and Isaac, and may they increase greatly upon the earth." (Genesis 48:15–16)

Jacob's soul had taken hold of the faith of his father and grandfather, Isaac and Abraham. He could finally acknowledge God as his own Great Shepherd, the One who had firmly but gently guided him each step of the way, even when that guiding also involved sorrow and pain. Jacob trusted his faithful Shepherd to also guide his grandsons and their children after them. By giving his own name, "Israel," to his grandsons, he made them equal to all of his other sons. And though they literally dwelt in Egypt, Jacob wanted his grandsons to always dwell, in their heart of hearts, in the promised land of Canaan. God had given Jacob a glimpse of the future, and it was as real to him as though it had already happened. In the book *Gleanings from Genesis,* pastor and theologian A. W. Pink describes this remarkable moment:

Deliberately, Jacob crossed his hands "guiding his hands wittingly" (48:14), or, as the Hebrew reads, literally, "he made his hands to understand." Note it is expressly said that "Israel" did this: it was the new man that was acting, not the old man, "Jacob." And "by faith" he blessed both the sons of Joseph. Truly, it was not by sight or reason. What was more unlikely than that these two young Egyptian princes, for this is virtually what they were, should ever forsake Egypt, the land of their birth, and migrate to Canaan! How unlikely, too, that each should become a separate tribe. And how improbable that the younger should be exalted above the elder, both in importance and number, and should become "a multitude of peoples" (48:19). How impossible for him to foresee (by any human deduction) that long centuries afterwards Ephraim should become representative of the kingdom of "Israel," as distinct from "Judah." But he had heard God, rested on His word, and believed in the sure fulfillment of His promise. What a grand display of faith! Nature's eyes might be dim, but faith's vision was sharp. In his bodily weakness the strength of faith was perfected.

Jacob was a man who, for the better portion of his life, thought mostly of himself, was continually disobedient and sneaky, and refused time and again to really trust God. These flaws, however, became the very tools that God used to teach this man what faith in Him is really all about. The Lord repeatedly showed grace—and patience—to a man who would not be humbled until each of his props was pulled away, painfully, one by one. By the end of his life Jacob had finally learned to rest in the work that God had done, the work that He had in fact been doing all along. Jacob thus "finished well." As Paul would write many centuries later:

> Being confident of this, that he who began a good work in you will carry it on to completion until the day of Christ Jesus. (Philippians 1:6)

Jacob was, by the end of his life, able to take a longer view of things. No longer was he consumed with solving some immediate problem by whatever dubious means were at hand. Now he was concerned for the legacy entrusted to him by Isaac and Abraham and, ultimately, by God. Jacob was now fully surrendered to the sovereign and magnificent ways and will of the Most High. Jacob's blessings for his sons, prophecies recorded in Genesis 49, reveal that he was beginning to see what others still could not see. With confidence and faith, he shared with all of his sons their futures, as revealed to him by God. No longer smug and self-reliant, Jacob was now looking to Another for help:

"I look for *your* deliverance, O LORD." (v. 18 [emphasis added])

When Jacob finished giving instructions to his sons, he breathed his last and then joined "his people"—in paradise (v. 33).

UNBOLTED LIVING

One of the brilliant threads woven throughout Hebrews 11 is the eternal perspective of each character. Jacob's worship and anticipation of "resting with his fathers" reminded the early Hebrew Christians that there was so much more to life than the painful trials they were presently undergoing. Even as biblical promises bring comfort to dying Christians today, God's repeated promises of the covenant comforted Jacob in his last days. God had promised him:

- ◆ that He, the Lord, would give to Jacob's descendants the Promised Land,
- ◆ that Jacob's family would greatly increase and prosper through the years,
- ◆ that all peoples on the earth would be blessed through them, and
- ◆ that He would never forsake them.

In the fullness of time, God would keep each and every one of these promises to Jacob (Genesis 28:13b–15; 35:11–13; 46:2–4).

By the end of Jacob's life, his family had certainly grown quite large and prosperous. Joseph's leadership in Egypt had proved to be a tremendous blessing, not only to the people of that nation, but for all the surrounding nations as well, which turned to Egypt for assistance during a severe famine. Finally, Jacob had learned by this point in his life that God had been with him every step of the journey and had never forsaken him. Thus, Jacob had already seen the fulfillment, in part, of God's promises to him—and yet this was only just the beginning, just the "tip of the iceberg" of what God intended to do through this special family.

Jacob's life story shows us the journey of a man who suffered the consequences, again and again, of trying to make his own way in this world, by hook or by crook. Yet this story ends on a bright and encouraging note: we see a man humbled, a man redeemed, a life joyfully surrendered in worship to the living God. The Lord had shown Jacob the utter futility of attempting to control his own destiny; not even the cleverest of Jacob's schemes could compare to the magnificent joy of accepting God's will and God's own purposes for his life. The consequences of Jacob's various deceptions only served to expose this deeply flawed and struggling sinner's great helplessness. Jacob, finally "getting it," learned to cling to the God of his fathers for everything he needed in life. Through a painful and, at times, very difficult learning process, Jacob experienced firsthand God's great and deep covenantal love. Jacob, at the end of his life, was determined to pass on to his children and grandchildren the truths he had himself finally and truly embraced, the great promises of the covenant, the great love of a sovereign and gracious God.

Like Jacob, Stu Lindner, whose story begins this chapter, learned to cling to God when every other prop of his self-made "success story" was stripped away from him. Outwardly, he had apparently been enjoying the fruit of his natural giftedness and the spoils of his secret sin. But deep within Stu's soul there was only frustration and despair over his inability to break free of sexual addiction. As a result of the motorcycle "accident," this man, now redefined by a broken body, confined to a hospital bed for six weeks, alone in the darkness of the night and the emptiness of his life, was forced by God Himself to see his own helplessness and great sin. Only when Stu surrendered to God, relinquishing that tightly held control to the Lord of all things, did God's great peace and confidence fill this broken man's heart. Gratitude for God's compassion and redeeming love now fuels Stu's renewed devotion to his family and his ministry to prison inmates. His service to others is a continuing fulfillment of God's promise that we, His people will be a blessing to many.

As we struggled to drive home the truths of this chapter, we received the following note from a young woman who has encountered numerous severe difficulties and great sorrows in her own life journey:

> Tonight I lay in bed and you came to mind. You have spoken in the past about how God was "pruning" you. For over eight years I've been in deep anguish as I have tried to live with the consequences of my husband's sin and as I've tried to understand what you meant. Tonight, the pruning really made sense to me. I actually could picture God holding shears and cutting away the dead branches of my life (at least He was trying and I kept pulling away). He is trying to teach me how to grow up, how to see that all that I am going through is actually Him trying to clean house in my heart and soul.
>
> In no way have I "arrived," but I am beginning to think that I should write out my personal testimony so that I can see where God has brought me (and,

boy, has He been patient!) and how He has been so faithful to me through all the stages in my life. I am sure I will continue to struggle as God continues to cut off all that stands between us to make me the woman He wants me to be. But maybe someday His patient faithfulness to me will serve to encourage someone else.

Jacob had known success, status, and wealth, and, though it took many long years, he finally learned that all the riches and comforts this world has to offer cannot even begin to compare with what God has prepared for those who love Him. By the end of his life, Jacob treasured intimacy with God above all else. He had learned that the life of a servant, the life of one who follows and obeys the living God, is far better than a life of selfish scheming and lonely independence. You might say that Jacob had learned as "Israel," as one who *struggled,* that it was better to be the most lowly and obedient servant and travel in fellowship with God than to be the wealthiest and most successful man on earth and yet walk alone. At the end of his now fully surrendered life, Jacob could say, with the psalmist:

> Better is one day in your courts
> > than a thousand elsewhere;
> I would rather be a doorkeeper in the house of my
> > God
> > than dwell in the tents of the wicked.
> For the LORD God is a sun and shield;
> > the LORD bestows favor and honor;
> no good thing does he withhold
> > from those whose walk is blameless.
> O LORD Almighty,
> > blessed is the man who trusts in you.
> > > (Psalm 84:10–12)

DIGGING DEEPER

Day One

♦ Read Genesis 28–50 in one sitting, if possible. If not, at least read three chapters a day to get a biblical overview of Jacob's life.

♦ Write out questions to bring up in your small-group discussion.

Day Two

♦ What event in Jacob's life is the most dramatic to you? Why?

♦ Describe Jacob's spiritual battle. What was his root problem? Describe your own spiritual journey. If you are battling with God, what is your root problem?

Day Three

♦ Why should Jacob's journey encourage you to persevere?

♦ Of all the points in Jacob's life, why did the writer of Hebrews choose to highlight Jacob at worship and Jacob blessing his grandsons as examples of living "by faith"? In what circumstances do these two incidents encourage you to walk by faith? Why?

Day Four

♦ Jacob repeatedly tried to control his own circumstances. What do God's responses to Jacob tell you about His character?

♦ How do these aspects of God's character encourage you to persevere when you fail?

Day Five

♦ How do the following Scriptures encourage you to believe that the grace God showed to Jacob is extended to you as well? Isaiah 43:1–7, 18–21; 45:15–25; 49:13–16

◆ Describe one area of your life where you have questioned God's grace. How will you respond to these doubts in light of the examples of God's grace in Jacob's life?

Day Six

◆ At the end of his life, Jacob longed for his children to embrace his God, and he exhorted them to do exactly that. What are your children or the children of the church learning from you about your priorities, about what is really important in life?

◆ If you were to die an hour from now, what would your friends and family say most characterized your life? (Hint: They will base their conclusions more on the way you have responded to life's challenges than on your behavior when life is going the way you planned.)

◆ Are you satisfied with the spiritual legacy you are building? If not, ask God to give you a heart for intimacy with Him.

Chapter 7

RESTING IN GOD'S WILL—JOSEPH

FAITH PRINCIPLE #7
BIBLICAL FAITH BRINGS US GOD'S PEACE.

By faith Joseph, when his end was near, spoke about the exodus

of the Israelites from Egypt and gave instructions about his bones.

(Hebrews 11:22 [see also Genesis 37–50])

DOWN FOR THE COUNT—DAVE TIBERI

On February 8, 1992, I sat glued to my television set as a local Christian boxer and good friend of mine, Dave Tiberi, entered the ring to fight for the IBF Middleweight Championship of the World. He was the decided underdog up against the reigning champion, James Toney. In fact, the gambling world would not even take bets on the fight since it was generally felt Tiberi had no chance of winning. Toney was described by Dan Dierdorf, the ABC ring announcer, as "a man who says he was born angry," whereas Tiberi was described as "a man of God."

I couldn't help wincing as Dave took a sharp and brutal right hook square on his forehead in the first round. Dave later told me he had never been hit so hard in his life and thought he was a goner. That, in fact, is just what Toney had promised to do to Dave before the fight: "I want to kill him." It may have been pre-fight hype, but that was one incredible, powerful punch.

I started yelling, "Go down, Dave! Don't be a hero. Go down! You are going to get killed!"

Dave, however, did not go down. Instead, he kept fighting and, as the fight progressed, he actually seemed to gain strength. He will tell you that this strength came from the Lord Jesus. Dave desired nothing in those crucial, pain-filled, exhausting moments other than to do his best. Of course, he wanted to win the title, but there was more at stake here for Dave. He wanted very much to bring glory to God in this bout. To be the middleweight champion of the world would give him name recognition and significant opportunities to honor God. Dave was certain, as he once told me, that "boxing is my angle to witness to people."

With each round, it became more and more obvious to everyone, including the ringside announcers, that Dave had not only survived that early shot to his head but—to everyone's surprise—was now actually outboxing his opponent and winning the fight. Though Sharon had no interest in watching two men "beat each other's brains out," she was drawn into the room by my shouting and excitement, and so she joined me "just for a moment" to watch the fight. By the eighth round, we were both thoroughly engrossed, both yelling and jumping and cheering for Dave. By the twelfth round, I was practically screaming at the television, "Stay away from Toney, Dave! You won! You won!"

When at last the final bell sounded, I was ecstatic. "You did it, Dave! You did it! You won!" So, too, were the announcers, the news reporters, and most sports fans around the world.

Two of the three judges who scored the fight, however, somehow saw it all quite differently, and they awarded the match to James Toney. We and many others along with us were absolutely astounded by that decision. Our friend Dave was devastated.

Sharon and I had just witnessed one of the greatest injustices in boxing history. The awarding of that decision to James Toney eventually led Senator William Roth of Delaware to ask for a Senate investigation of the sport of boxing. This unjust decision confronted Dave head-on with a tremendous test of his faith. At that moment, Dave did not have "Genesis 50:20 vision," the ability to appreciate and accept all that happens—even our greatest disappointments and personal crises—as part of God's good and perfect will for us. Blindsided by the judges' decision, Dave was not prepared for what this severe and painful disappointment would bring him. After the fight a frustrated and confused Dave could only tell interviewers that he had been "deprived." The ringside announcer, less restrained, called it "a disgusting decision."

God, however, was able to take that act of injustice and use it for good in Dave's life. Defeat forced Dave to carefully consider how he might be able to glorify God even in the midst of his disappointment. As Dave later told me, "each time God helped me to obey Him by responding honestly but without malice to my circumstances, I experienced a little bit more of His peace. I began to realize that He had intentionally arranged this entire situation for His own eternal reasons."

Thus it was that the loss of that fight actually gave Dave greater name recognition and opened up more ministry opportunities than a win could possibly have done. The godly influence of this man is now an ever-widening circle to a growing television audience and to inner-city young people. He deliberately located the Dave Tiberi Youth Center in the middle of the biggest drug district of Wilmington, Delaware, where no other youth ministries existed. Dave's godly response to his unfair treatment has earned him the right to share the hope of Christ with teens who have been similarly

betrayed by people and by systems that were supposed to uphold justice and protect them. God is transforming this
earthly loss into eternal victories. He has used this experience
not only to deepen Dave's peace in his own journey but also
to deepen and strengthen the faith of many others.

Chuck Betters

THE SCHOOL OF ADVERSITY

The idea that "nothing is important but that which is eternal" permeates the life and writings of missionary to India Amy Carmichael. Called by God to go to that country in the early 1800s, Carmichael spent the better part of her life rescuing Indian children from temple prostitution. The Dohnavur Fellowship of India, the mission she founded, still exists today. Her many writings reflect the deep suffering she and her fellow laborers endured as they cared for these homeless and mistreated children. Yet by seeing her life's work in the context of eternity, Carmichael was able to find purpose even when the suffering around her and the immensity of the task she faced seemed overwhelming.

Joseph, like this faithful young missionary, also experienced sufferings that taught him to view life in the context of eternity. Though bruised and battered in his life's journey, Joseph ended life on this earth as he had always faced it, looking forward to the fulfillment of the promises of God. When he was 110 years old, Joseph prophesied the future exodus of the Israelites from Egypt at a time when these people had no reason to leave that country (Genesis 50). Though he had lived in Egypt for all but the first seventeen years of his life and though he would eventually die in that country, Joseph insisted that his family must one day return his remains to the land of promise, the land of Canaan. In his dying moments, Joseph continued to think of himself as a son of the covenant, a member of the blessed family of Abraham, and not as an Egyptian. Moreover, he urged his family to remember that when hard times came, God would come to their aid. How could Joseph demonstrate such deep faith in a God who had allowed him to be sold into slavery and unjustly imprisoned, forgotten by everyone? How could he urge his family to take comfort in God's presence despite all the hardship he had personally endured?

Joseph's story reveals a brilliant young man who, through deep suffering, was used of God to accomplish great things. C. H. Spurgeon, a great preacher of the mid-1800s, himself no stranger to sorrow or suffering, declared,

> My witness is, that those who are honored by their Lord in public have usually to endure a secret chastening, or to carry a peculiar cross, lest by any means they exalt themselves, and fall into the snare of the devil. . . .
>
> By all the castings down of His servants God is glorified, for they are led to magnify Him when again He sets them on their feet, and even while prostrate in the dust their faith yields Him praise. They speak all the more sweetly of His faithfulness, and are the more firmly established in His love. . . . Glory be to God for the furnace, the hammer, and the fire. Heaven shall be all the fuller of bliss because we have been filled with anguish here below, and earth shall be better tilled because of our training in the school of adversity. (as quoted by Richard E. Day, *The Shadow of the Broad Brim*)

The "school of adversity" did indeed train Joseph for great work. For Joseph would one day not only help supply a famine-stricken world with food but, more importantly, he would be used by God to provide a safe place for his family, the Israelite people, the "covenant community" of that day, to grow and prosper. Harsh slavery and the grim existence of prison life would transform Joseph's idyllic and easy faith, the faith of a favored and coddled son, into an authentic, pulsating, intimate faith in the God of Abraham, Isaac, and Jacob.

THE ROOT OF THE PROBLEM

In order to appreciate fully the life and experiences of Joseph, it is necessary to "back up" a little to consider the days of his childhood and youth.

As a good father disciplines his child, so God had disciplined Joseph's manipulative, deceptive father until the wily Jacob had finally come full circle. Jacob had at last settled where God wanted him—in Canaan. Upon leaving Shechem, Jacob destroyed the many idols his family had come to rely on. Now Jacob's long "wrestling match" with God had finally ended, and he was learning to follow the God of Abraham and Isaac. But Jacob's years of wandering and manipulation had proved costly. He was now the father of children by four different women. The older children born and raised during his rebellious period had observed him all too closely, and now they began to emulate their father's old patterns of lying and deception.

However, God's discipline of Jacob had also produced a harvest of righteousness and peace (Hebrews 12:11), first in Joseph and then, eventually, in his other sons, that would only bear fruit many years later. In a sense, in Joseph and his brother Benjamin, Jacob was given a "second chance" at parenting. Joseph's godly responses as he passed through the fires of his own suffering speak well for Jacob, indicating that he had taught at least his favored son rightly and well.

Seventeen-year-old Joseph and one-year-old Benjamin, the children of Jacob's beloved and favorite wife, Rachel, were clearly his favorites. Even though Rachel had died during the birth of Benjamin, these two boys brought great joy and some measure of comfort to their father. Unfortunately, Jacob also made this painfully clear to his other sons and even gave the young Joseph an ornamental cloak that the others saw as a mark of "royalty"; Joseph was clearly the "crown prince" of the family dynasty. His older half-brothers actually hated him so much that they "could not speak a kind word to him" (Genesis 37:4–8).

Joseph himself added fuel to those fires of jealousy when he described a couple of dreams he had had to his family. These dreams pictured, through obvious symbolism, his brothers one day bowing down before him. Joseph's second dream suggested that not only his brothers but also his parents would one day bow down before him. His brothers' jealousy only worsened in response to this, and even Jacob rebuked Joseph, though the old man also kept the matter in mind (Genesis 37:11).

GETTING RID OF THE DREAMER

One day Jacob sent Joseph, now about seventeen years old, off to a remote area to check on his brothers as they tended the flocks. When the brothers saw "that dreamer" coming from a distance, they plotted to kill him, thus setting in motion God's elaborate plan both to "reconstruct" Joseph's life and character, through great adversity, and eventually to rescue His people from famine. Reuben, the eldest brother, knew his father would hold him personally responsible for Joseph's welfare, and so he convinced his brothers not to kill Joseph. Instead, they threw Joseph into a deep, empty well. Reuben planned to secretly return later and rescue the young man. But before Reuben could carry out this plan, the other brothers sold Joseph as a slave to a caravan of Ishmaelite traders. Then, to cover their own sin, the brothers drenched their young brother's beautiful coat in goat's blood and allowed their father to assume Joseph had been torn to pieces by some wild animal. Upon seeing the bloody garment, Jacob went into a paroxysm of grief. He refused all of their attempts to comfort him, pledging to grieve for his beloved Joseph to the end of his days.

Instead of repenting for this horrible deed, Jacob's sons watched silently as years of grief ravaged and slowly devoured their father. It is difficult to imagine how these men, all co-conspirators in a heartless, vicious act, could subsequently stand idly by year after year as their father continued to mourn for a "dead son," while they knew the truth of the matter. Their hardness in the face of such sorrow reveals just how much jealousy and hatred can sear the souls and consciences of unrepentant men.

ALONE WITH GOD

Joseph's terror and confusion, first in that dark pit as he listened to his brothers cold-bloodedly discuss how to get rid of him and then during his forced march as a slave to a far-off land, are hard to imagine. Within the space of minutes he had gone from being the pampered, favored son of wealthy Jacob to a lowly slave. In Egypt, the Ishmaelites sold Joseph to Potiphar, one of Pharaoh's court officials. All of Joseph's idyllic boyhood security had utterly vanished. He had nothing left except his faith in the God of Abraham, Isaac, and Jacob.

Yet Joseph did not give in to fear and despair. Instead, he focused his strengths and abilities into doing well whatever tasks were set before him. Potiphar soon realized that the Lord was with Joseph because everything Joseph did prospered. Joseph was an able and successful manager, and he brought great abundance and prosperity to Potiphar's house (Genesis 39:5). Soon Potiphar entrusted the entire household to Joseph's care.

Trouble, however, was looming. Day after day Potiphar's wife attempted to lure this handsome, well-built slave into an affair. It would have been easy for Joseph, a lonely young man far from home, to have succumbed to her advances. But Jacob's teaching about God's holiness and faithfulness proved stronger than this woman's repeated sexual overtures. Joseph thus was able to resist her, not because he feared being caught, but because he would not sin against God (Genesis 39:9). Potiphar's wife refused to give up, however, and she made one last-ditch plan to seduce this young servant. One day, when the house was empty, she pleaded with Joseph to come to her bed. Instead of trying to argue the point with her, Joseph simply ran out of the house. The scorned and insulted woman then accused Joseph of rape. It seems likely that Potiphar didn't believe her accusation, since instead of having Joseph executed for what was a capital crime in that society, Potiphar only had Joseph imprisoned.

BEHIND BARS

Once more, Joseph fell from a place of authority, power, and relative comfort into yet another pit of hardship and despair. He had been sold as a slave because of the undeserved hatred of his brothers. Now he was in prison because he had acted rightly and refused to commit the sin of adultery. Joseph was once again trapped and alone, with nothing to cling to but the teachings of his father Jacob about the promises and great power of his God.

So powerful was the effect of God's presence in Joseph—in Joseph's remarkable peace, his sense of assurance, his abilities—that, in contrast to the general desolation and hopelessness of that prison, Joseph stood out like a bright light in the darkness. The warden noticed that Joseph was unusual, even gifted, and he soon put Joseph in charge of all that was done in the prison. Like Potiphar, the warden learned to rest easy regarding anything under Joseph's care because he could see that the Lord was with this amazing young man and gave him success in whatever he did (Genesis 39:23).

As with Joseph, God's presence in Christians still creates an oasis for others in the midst of various kinds of affliction.

Sharon's parents, Ralph and Eleanor Watts, for example, did not know that their faithfulness to Christ in the very mundane and ordinary tasks of raising seven children and building a successful construction company was preparing them to face long-term dramatic life changes. When a virus attacked Eleanor's heart, she was "sentenced" first to six months of absolute bed rest and then to years of one medical crisis after another. In those difficult days, this godly woman confronted daily her longing for the energy and good health she had always enjoyed in the past. Her weak heart forced her to give up lifelong traditions of body surfing, bike rides, camping, building autumn leaf forts, sledding, and many other motherly and grandmotherly activities that had built such a legacy of love and faith in her family. Her active "spiritual mothering" role in the lives of the young women of her church also appeared to be over. Fenced in by the physical weakness of her body, she was forced to choose carefully how to spend the little energy she had left.

Only in eternity will the Body of Christ know the impact of her daily choice to see her illness as yet another means to glorify God. Though bedridden, she continued to invest in the kingdom of God by sending cards and notes to hurting friends. Instead of dreading to spend time with a frail and sick woman, Eleanor's fifty grandchildren truly looked forward to laughing with her, hearing her stories, and playing games with her, and they often sought her godly advice. Women who had benefited from her involvement in a ministry to young girls frequently inquired about her health. Witnessing her authentic faith throughout this long-term illness has only strengthened their desire to pass on to their own children that same joy in living she once shared with them. And though she is now in His glorious presence, her influence continues in the lives of the many people she touched.

The "prison sentence" of long-term illness is not an easy one; it holds hostage entire families. It comes unbidden, unlooked for, and often by surprise; it is something we do not "deserve." And yet somehow God is building His kingdom through us, His people, in sick rooms and hospitals, from those in wheelchairs and those connected to life support machines, as the people around us observe the reality of our trust in the Lord. God can graciously use such "prison terms" in our lives, as He did with Joseph, as He did with Eleanor Watts, to accomplish His own great and bright purposes. And He will continue to work in this special way until that wonderful day, that day He comes to unlock the door and finally set us free.

FORGOTTEN AGAIN

Some time later when the cupbearer and the baker of the king of Egypt, the Pharaoh, were also imprisoned, the captain of the guard assigned them to Joseph's care. Joseph, because of a special gift God had given to him, was able to interpret the hidden meaning of the unusual dreams of these two prisoners. The cupbearer's dream, as revealed to and interpreted by Joseph, indicated that the man would soon be set free and would go back to work for Pharaoh. Joseph was so confident that his interpretation of this dream was true that he told the cupbearer his own life story and asked the man for his help, asking him to put in a good word for Joseph with Pharaoh. Joseph's words at this juncture give us a glimpse into his struggle to understand his difficult circumstances:

> But when all goes well with you, remember me and show me kindness; mention me to Pharaoh and get me out of this prison. For I was forcibly carried off from the land of the Hebrews, and even here I have done nothing to deserve being put in a dungeon. (Genesis 40:14–15)

Just as Joseph had predicted, the cupbearer was released within three days and went back to working for the king of

Egypt. The man, however, did not fulfill his promise to Joseph and in fact "did not remember Joseph; he forgot him" (v. 23).

Joseph's life appeared to be one long series of setbacks, disappointments, and personal disasters, but God's eternal plan was all the while being carried out with great precision. God was preparing Joseph to be placed, at just the right time, in an extraordinary, pivotal position of authority and power.

FROM PRISON TO PALACE

Joseph, of course, could not have known what God was planning, and one wonders whether he, on those nights when he could not sleep, remembered with sadness the long-ago days with his father and young brother Benjamin. What did he think when, day after day, month after month, year after year, he recalled the promises God had made to Abraham, Isaac, and Jacob? What doubts and questions arose whenever he thought of his father's stories about God's faithfulness? Had God abandoned Joseph to prison because of some sin? Later, after the cupbearer returned to Pharaoh's service, how agonizing it must have been for Joseph every time he heard a door being unlocked, every time some soldier or official entered the prison or the guards came marching by his cell; he must have thought a thousand times, "At last, the cupbearer has remembered me! Is this the day I'll be set free?" Finally, as he drifted off to sleep, did Joseph, once again, surrender his anguished questions and his loneliness to the sovereignty of God, a God whose ways are beyond understanding?

Whatever Joseph's doubts may have been, they surely led him into deeper and deeper fellowship with the Lord. Prison life, like the experience of slavery, sealed Joseph's trust in the God of his father, Jacob, much the way a hot iron might sear and close an open wound. With every difficult challenge he faced, Joseph repeatedly and remarkably gave credit and glory to God for his wisdom and behavior (Genesis 39:9; 40:8; 41:25, 28, 32, 50, 52). Again and again, Joseph reminds others, as he finally reminds Pharaoh, that "I cannot do it . . . but God will" (Genesis 41:16); this practice of constantly giving credit and glory to God is one of the hallmarks of this man's remarkable faith.

Two long years after Joseph had successfully interpreted the dreams of the cupbearer and the baker, Pharaoh himself had a strange and disturbing dream that no one in his court could interpret. It was only then that the cupbearer, now once again a servant of the king, finally remembered Joseph. Thus it was that Joseph, at long last, was summoned to the court of the great Pharaoh, king of Egypt.

Four times during his short conversation with Pharaoh, Joseph credited God as the source of his ability to interpret dreams. Joseph was able to tell Pharaoh the meaning of his mysterious dream: that seven years of plenty would be followed by seven years of terrible famine, a famine that would spread throughout the whole known world. Pharaoh decided that not only had Joseph interpreted the dream correctly but that Joseph was also the man most able to prepare Egypt for the coming crisis. It is interesting and significant that Pharaoh, too, was deeply impressed by Joseph's faith:

Can we find anyone like this man, *one in whom is the spirit of God*? (Genesis 41:37 [emphasis added])

At thirty years of age, Joseph became the Pharaoh's "second-in-command" over the entire nation of Egypt, and he immediately put into effect a masterful plan to save stores of grain and so prepare the nation for the coming hard years.

Stephen, the first martyr, would later say of Joseph,

But God was with him and rescued him from all his troubles. He gave Joseph wisdom and enabled him to gain the good will of Pharaoh king of Egypt; so he made him ruler over Egypt and all his palace. (Acts 7:9–10)

For seventeen years God had taught Joseph, through his father Jacob, about faith and obedience in the midst of a broken, troubled family. For another thirteen years, the Lord taught Joseph about Himself in the loneliness of his days first as a slave and then as a prisoner. God then set Joseph free, through a series of "remarkable providences" He had long ago ordained, to rise to great power and influence in Pharaoh's court. Those long years of slavery and imprisonment had not been wasted, for the loneliness had led Joseph into closer fellowship with God and had now, miraculously, put him in a position from which he could protect Israel and thus the entire covenant community from extinction.

Joseph's primary goal each day had always been to give the glory to God in and through his life. Joseph had made the most of his circumstances each step of the way, always making sure that the people around him—Potiphar, Potiphar's wife, the warden, the cupbearer, the other prisoners, Pharaoh—saw that he loved and worshiped God and would continue to honor God, no matter how grim and hopeless his circumstances might seem. Perhaps, from God's perspective, Joseph needed to learn the ways of a servant, serving others but most of all serving God, before he would be ready to lead; perhaps he needed to learn how to listen to God before he could speak for Him, how to serve faithfully in the lowliest of tasks before he could exercise the responsibility of royal authority.

Learning how to use his gifts unselfishly to serve others enabled Joseph to successfully lead a country headed for the severe crisis of a great famine. Joseph knew the terrible helplessness of being at the mercy of someone else. His own confidence in God's ability in turn helped him to care for these needy, famine-stricken people. Preparations for the famine required hard decisions and strong leadership. His plans would not work if the Egyptians did not trust him. Joseph's confidence in his Lord, strengthened by years of hardship and the close fellowship with God that only comes through such hardship, had forged Joseph into a man of great character and authentic faith. When the famine finally came, Joseph was prepared. In this man's life, as in so many others, suffering had produced perseverance, and perseverance had produced character, and character had produced hope—hope for one man, hope for a nation, hope for countless numbers of hurting people (Romans 5:1–5).

JOURNEY TO EGYPT

When the seven years of prosperity were in fact followed by seven years of famine, Joseph became a national hero. Word spread throughout the world that there was food to be found in the land of Egypt. Jacob and his family, like everyone else in Canaan, were hard hit by the famine, and so he sent his sons to Egypt to buy provisions for the family.

When Joseph's brothers arrived in Egypt, they came face to face with Joseph. But it had been many years since they had seen their younger brother, and they failed to recognize him. Joseph, however, recognized them, and although he would later forgive them for all they had done, Joseph first put his brothers through a series of difficult tests (Genesis 41–44).

First, before he would give them any food, Joseph insisted that these men bring back their youngest brother, Benjamin, and forced them to leave their brother Simeon in Egypt as "collateral." Joseph's brothers had little choice but to agree. Upon their return to Canaan, they told Jacob that they had to take Benjamin back to Egypt with them. But Jacob would have none of it. His passionate reply shows us his continuing despair and also that he suspected his sons might somehow be responsible for Joseph's "death":

You have deprived me of my children. Joseph is no more and Simeon is no more, and now you want to take Benjamin. Everything is against me! (Genesis 42:36)

Reuben then promised Jacob that he would put to death his very own sons should anything happened to Benjamin on this trip, and he begged his father to trust him. Jacob's response is a sad indication of how little regard he had for his other sons. It is both a revealing and a poignant statement, reflecting as it does Jacob's utter disdain for Judah, Reuben, and the other brothers, his misguided and destructive favoritism, and his yet-unhealed wounds resulting from Joseph's "death."

My son [Benjamin] will not go down there with you; his brother [Joseph] is dead and *he is the only one left.* If harm comes to him on the journey you are taking, you will bring my gray head down to the grave in sorrow. (Genesis 42:38 [emphasis added])

Clearly Jacob still held Benjamin's life more dearly than that of Simeon, or the rest of the family for that matter.

Jacob, however, was learning some of the same hard lessons God had been teaching Joseph. For Jacob, too, it appeared as though the promises of God would never come to pass. God had promised Jacob a land to call his own and a prospering, growing family. Instead it seemed to Jacob as though his family was already dwindling and that the land itself seemed to be dying due to the famine. The covenant promises, by all appearances, would never be realized in his lifetime and possibly were failing altogether. Jacob realized that he was not in control and could not manipulate his circumstances as he so often had—or thought he had—in the past. It is telling, then, that in grudgingly agreeing to his family's need for more food, Jacob evoked a covenant name of God, "El Shaddai," the All-Sufficient One, in his instructions to his sons:

Take your brother also and go back to the man [i.e., Joseph] at once. And may God Almighty [El Shaddai] grant you mercy before the man so that he will let your other brother and Benjamin come back with you. As for me, I am bereaved, I am bereaved. (Genesis 43:13–14)

FAMILY REUNION

Have you ever expressed inner emotion, whether laughter or tears, so intensely that your stomach actually hurt? When Joseph saw his brothers on their return trip to Egypt, this time with Benjamin, he was affected in this way. In a dramatic moment of great joy tinged also with overwhelming sorrow, Joseph told his dumbfounded brothers who he really was (Genesis 45:3). Later, he brought his father and entire family to live in peace and prosperity in Egypt. God had promised Abraham that from his old body a great nation would one day descend. Jacob's children, the early seeds of that great nation, needed a safe and sheltered place to grow; Egypt was the perfect location to do this. As with Joseph, God's work in our lives, though we often cannot see or understand it, is always intentional, always part of a greater plan, and always for our good.

Although the Egyptians despised the Israelites, they honored Joseph and treated Jacob and his family with great respect. Pharaoh gave the Israelites, i.e., the family of Jacob, the land of Goshen—the choicest, most fertile land in the country. For many years to follow, God's covenant people grew and prospered as a self-contained community in that protected environment. During and after Joseph's leadership as Pharaoh's chief assistant, the nation of Israel grew from a modest band of shepherds to a mighty force in the land.

God had told Abraham that the nation that would descend from him would be enslaved in a foreign country and be mistreated for four hundred years, but that, eventually, this people would return to Canaan (Genesis 15:13–16). Though as yet none of Abraham's descendants owned as much as one square foot of property in Canaan, Joseph's own pilgrimage with God had given him confidence that this promise, too, would come true. Even while his family was enjoying a good life in Egypt, Joseph knew that Egypt was not the land of promise and that they all would eventually return to Canaan.

GOD MEANT IT FOR GOOD

Joseph's childhood prophetic dreams, dreams that had so greatly angered his brothers, had in the end come true. His brothers, father, and mother had indeed bowed down before him. During Joseph's exalted and renowned period of service to the mighty Pharaoh for the next seventeen years, his family grew and prospered. But after Jacob's death, Joseph's brothers feared that Joseph would finally take his vengeance on them. God, however, had done an astounding, transforming work in Joseph's life. The man who had endured so much, so patiently, for so long had no desire for revenge. Joseph, indeed, took a much longer, more providential view of his life.

The brothers came to Joseph and "threw themselves down before him." Expressing their abject fear, they cried, "We are your slaves!" (Genesis 50:18).

In his gentle response to his worried and nervous siblings, Joseph shows that he was truly a man at peace with his God and totally yielded to the Lord's strange but miraculous ways. Surely here was a man who had "50:20 vision":

Don't be afraid. Am I in the place of God? You intended to harm me, but God intended it for good to accomplish what is now being done, the saving of many lives. (Genesis 50:20)

THE ONLY THING THAT COUNTS

Hebrews 11 is a record of the results of God's pursuit of intimacy with His children: Abel, Enoch, Noah, Abraham, Sarah, Isaac, Jacob, and now Joseph. For Joseph, in particular, it was his subjection to prolonged, unexplained suffering and injustice that drove this man to learn to accept and depend upon the living God. Joseph's dying request and his promise of God's comfort to his family revealed the peace he had learned to rest in during his remarkable and difficult life's journey (Genesis 50:24–25). God had used hardship upon hardship to prepare Joseph to be a blessing to his people, the covenant community, and to cultivate within his heart an almost "other-worldly" aura of trust and peace.

In preparing each of us to be a blessing, God will often allow us to undergo similar hardships. Prison doors may never slam shut behind us, as they did in Joseph's life. But prisons come in many shapes and sizes, and at times the very calling given to us by God can feel like "doing hard time." Peace under such circumstances only comes to us when we see, as Amy Carmichael did, that "the only thing that counts is that which is eternal."

Dave Tiberi thought God had called him to build His kingdom through winning the middleweight championship. But peace in his own life only came when he surrendered those goals for "success" to God's sovereign ways. "The privilege of ministering to hurting people has diluted the disappointment of that loss," Dave tells us. "What is a boxing loss compared to sitting at the bedside of a dying teenager and witnessing his living faith in Christ? Or seeing the tears in a father's eyes and comforting him as he speaks of his son's sudden, unexpected death—a boy I had had the great privilege of ministering to? One of God's greatest gifts to me was, strangely enough, that defeat. For through it, God has somehow opened doors for me into other people's lives to share with them the hope of Christ, doors that would never have opened otherwise."

There were several kinds of "thread" making up the fabric of Joseph's life. Some threads he could see, like the pain and loneliness of slavery and imprisonment, but could not understand. Still other threads, like the overall plan to rescue his family and indeed many families from the coming famine, were known only to God. Joseph's intimacy with God led not only to peace in his heart regarding all the threads he could see and had to endure but also trust in God for all the threads he could not see and was not yet ready to understand. Joseph is honored in Hebrews for how that "peace of God, which transcends all understanding" (Philippians 4:7), eventually opened his eyes to all the invisible plans of God. He knew that the God who had so faithfully prepared and protected him would one day do the same for his descendants.

In faith therefore, Joseph gave his children instructions concerning his eventual burial place: Canaan. In doing so, Joseph was affirming and surrendering to the promises of God given to his father Jacob regarding the land that would one day be theirs. At the very end of his life, Joseph did not rage against the painful parts of his journey but simply accepted them as part of his calling from the purposeful hand of God. Joseph is the link to the next great event of covenant history, the Exodus of the Israelites from Egypt into the land of promise.

Joseph never forgot his true home even amidst his pain and loneliness. He looked forward to the day his family, God's covenant people, would return to the land promised to them. Joseph thus becomes for us a wonderful archetype of the Messiah in the way he rescues his people from famine, fear, and death, the way he seeks reconciliation and shows forgiveness, and the way he, through his power and might, prepares the way for his people to enter the Promised Land.

Joseph had learned that the hand of God moves in mysterious and often painful ways in arranging the events and circumstances of our lives. But that hand also brings us peace, if we are but willing to accept it. As St. Augustine wrote in his *Confessions,* "Thou hast touched me . . . and I have been translated into Thy peace."

DIGGING DEEPER

Day One
- Read Genesis 37, 39–47, and 50. How would you have reacted to this sort of unfairness?

Day Two
- What do the following verses indicate about Joseph's relationship to God? Genesis 39:9; 40:8; 41:16, 25, 28, 32, 50, 52
- How do you respond when complimented for a job well done? Does your response indicate an intimacy with God?

Day Three
- Read Hebrews 12:1–3. What is God's special call in your life; what is "the race" marked out for you?
- What sacrifices does your calling require? Do you believe that the only thing that counts is eternal? How does this affect how you view those sacrifices?

Day Four
- Read Romans 5:1–5. How does believing God produce peace in your daily life?
- According to Romans 5:1–5, how does suffering produce hope? What part of your pilgrimage feels like a prison? How does this passage give you hope?

Day Five

- Read Psalm 91. How does the message of this psalm encourage you to view difficult times as opportunities to trust God?

- What circumstances in your own life are driving you into greater intimacy with God?

Day Six

- Read Romans 8:28. Joseph told his brothers that what they intended for evil, God intended for good. Consider a troubled time in your life, one that was not the result of your sin. Ask God to reveal ways He is using the pain of that hurtful time "for good." Consider how this experience has prepared you to help build God's kingdom.

- Joseph not only saw God's purposes; he surrendered to them and called them good because many people benefited from his suffering. One of the promises of the covenant is that the people of God would become a great nation and be a blessing to many. How did God keep that promise through Joseph? How is he keeping it through you?

Chapter 8

A SON OF THE KING—MOSES

By faith Moses' parents hid him for three months after
he was born, because they saw he was no ordinary child,
and they were not afraid of the king's edict.

By faith Moses, when he had grown up, refused to be known as
the son of Pharaoh's daughter. He chose to be mistreated along with
the people of God rather than to enjoy the pleasures of sin for
a short time. He regarded disgrace for the sake of Christ as of
greater value than the treasures of Egypt, because he was
looking ahead to his reward. By faith he left Egypt, not fearing
the king's anger; he persevered because he saw him who is invisible.
By faith he kept the Passover and the sprinkling of blood, so that
the destroyer of the firstborn would not touch the firstborn of Israel.

(Hebrews 11:23–28 [see also Exodus 1–15])

CHOOSING TO LIVE AS GOD'S CHILD—
SANDRA PRESSAU

My college boyfriend's marriage proposal had one troubling requirement: that I convert to Judaism. If I didn't convert, he told me, he would lose his family inheritance. Weighed against losing a man who had loved me through the traumatic separation and divorce of my parents, I found it fairly easy to push my Catholic upbringing and beliefs into the background. I loved this man very much, and I was prepared to do whatever I had to do to become his wife. Thus, I accepted his proposal and his conditions, and I converted to his faith.

Although I practiced Judaism and attempted to understand and observe Jewish customs, my husband's religion could not sufficiently meet my own spiritual needs. All of my attempts to be a faithful Jew only left me feeling empty and disappointed. I felt estranged from the very God I was trying so hard to know and please. Finally, as I sat in Temple on a Jewish holiday, I broke down in tears as I admitted to myself that I was practicing a religion I didn't really believe. I had turned away from Christ, and now I didn't know how to make things right in my life again. My deepening struggle to undo my mistake only intensified with the birth of my daughter. How could I raise this child in a faith I myself could not accept? Even though I felt estranged from God, still I pleaded with Him to help me figure out what to do.

To struggle along in silence, of course, would mean financial security and a life of ease for me and my daughter. But I just couldn't do this. I wanted to know Christ; I *needed* to know Christ. When I read about Moses I knew how hard it must have been for him, too, to leave the wealth and comfort of the Egyptian royal palace for a life of hardship and wandering with his true people. Choosing to follow Christ would mean that I, too, might lose everything, that I, too, would have a hard life. But it didn't matter. The longing in my heart to know God personally, as I could only do through His Son, proved greater than my fears of what the future might bring. So it was that I asked God to help me go back to the faith I knew was true, the faith my heart was really drawn to.

My husband could not understand my need, and he promptly left us, placing our home on the market. Instead of having financial security in a "perfect" little family, I was suddenly a single mother faced with scary, life-changing decisions. Where would I live? How would I survive? I was at my wits' end.

It was then that God sent Linda, a friend from my past, to help me through the next step in my spiritual odyssey. Linda listened carefully and lovingly as I shared my story with her one day over lunch. She wisely discerned the incompleteness of my own faith and told me very clearly and plainly that I needed to repent of the sin in my life and to ask Christ into my heart, and this I humbly did.

Though close to my own age, Linda proved to be a marvelous "spiritual mother" to me, someone who accepted me and my young daughter into her heart and home. Her congregation also welcomed us into their church family. Jesus' forgiveness and His presence in my heart really transformed me into a new person. I had been so hungry for God's Word, and I was so ready to start learning to trust His promises. Through the preaching and teaching in that fellowship, I learned solid scriptural truth, and I was, at long last, finally reunited with God. In a way, He became my new "husband" and was a loving "father" to my daughter. His compassion guided me through the difficult and confusing journey of single parenthood. His presence gave us bright direction and warm light during the dark days and shaded us from the burning sun of discouragement and lonely times. Instead of depending on people and circumstances for my security and wisdom, God's Word became a constant source of comfort and guidance for me. I was even able to accept my singleness unless or until God decided He had other plans for me.

Finally, after ten years as a single mother, I met and married a wonderful man, someone who loves me and who shares my faith in the Living God. The Lord has thus led me from darkness into His marvelous light; He has adopted me into His family and given me the desire to live for Christ. In sharing His compassion and mercy so freely with me, He has also given me a heart for finding and helping others who are now, as I was then, lost, lonely, and afraid.

Sandra Pressau

TIME TO GO HOME

God had used a divinely planned famine to bring His small band of people into Egypt, a safe place prepared just for them. Within barely a century, Jacob's relatively small family of seventy had multiplied into the thousands. Joseph's deathbed instructions had left this people with a strong warning that Egypt was not God's best place for them and that they would not be able to stay there forever. But the past protection of Pharaoh soon blinded them to the danger of viewing Egypt as their home. They did not see their trek into Egypt as only a temporary detour in God's eternal plan for them. Left to themselves, they would probably never have left that verdant, comfortable country. It would take the brutal oppression of slavery, which slowly began to descend over them like a net, to finally open their eyes.

The book of Genesis describes how God had arranged for this "insignificant" little family to make their way to Egypt; the book of Exodus describes God's rescue of this family from the death grip of that same country, which had gone from being a place of refuge to a prison house. After Joseph died, the new king and his descendants showed little regard for the debt owed to Joseph by the Egyptians and, in fact, the Egyptians actually began to fear the size and power of the Israelite presence in their country (Exodus 1:9). The new Pharaoh planned, in effect, to "get them before they get us":

> Come, we must deal shrewdly with them, or they will become even more numerous and, if war breaks out, will join our enemies, fight against us and leave the country. (v. 10)

Thus he enslaved them to contain that potential threat to his power. Yet the more he brutally oppressed these people, the more numerous they became (vv. 12–14). In his assault on the Israelites, Pharaoh had declared war on both them and their God.

Feeling ever more threatened by this "population explosion" among his slaves, Pharaoh ruthlessly ordered the execution of all Israelite baby boys by having them drowned in the Nile. At least one infant boy, however, would survive this ghastly slaughter: a baby boy born into the home of two ordinary slaves, Amram and Jochebed. Though no one could have foreseen it, this one small child represented the hope and salvation of God's people, a people oppressed, tormented, and in misery.

COURAGEOUS FAITH

Amram and Jochebed, simple, humble people yet gifted with extraordinary courage and faith, defied Pharaoh's murderous edict. By faith, they hid their baby boy from Pharaoh's soldiers for three months. At last, realizing the child could not be hidden from the Egyptians much longer, these loving parents did something incredibly brave and yet terribly painful for them. They literally committed their precious little boy into God's keeping to save him from the Egyptians. They built a little "ark," a small papyrus basket coated with tar and pitch, and then set the boy adrift on the Nile river to meet whatever destiny God had in mind for him. It is hard to imagine that moment as they kissed their beloved little son one last time. Then, with desperate, heart-wrenching prayers, they placed him in that basket and watched it drift away upon the very river where so many other little Hebrew boys had already died (Exodus 1:22).

Many parents believe their children are extraordinary. But for Amram and Jochebed, parental love was not their only driving force. They hid Moses *by faith*. Faith produced a hope that in turn produced courage. They did not know what God would do or even if He would prevent the death of their precious child. But they certainly believed God existed and that He rewards those who earnestly seek Him (Hebrews 11:6). Their love for God compelled them to protect the child God had given to them in the only way they knew. Their loyalty to God was far greater than their fear of the king of Egypt. Amram and Jochebed were trusting God for a miraculous intervention.

These two faithful parents certainly could not have known that the daughter of Pharaoh himself would find their son along the riverbank, or that this woman would have such compassion as to take the boy into her own heart and home, knowing of her father's horrific edict, knowing full well that this child was a Hebrew slave. Amram and Jochebed could also not have prepared the child's sister, Miriam, who had followed along after the basket, to step forward as she did, offering the services of the boy's own mother to be his wet nurse. Amram and Jochebed only could see what lay directly in front of them; they had to do what they could to save their child, surrendering all "the rest," by faith, to God.

Pharaoh's daughter named the boy "Moses," and his birth mother, Jochebed, became his wet nurse until he was weaned. It is likely then that Jochebed nursed and mothered Moses until he was two to four years old and that she impressed upon his young mind all of the stories of his true family: stories of Abraham, Isaac, Jacob, and Joseph.

COLLABORATIVE FAITH

In an extraordinary act of faith, Amram and Jochebed thus unknowingly collaborated with God. They knew their son was no ordinary child. But they did not know their act of faith would be the channel through which God would begin preparing their son to deliver the Israelites from bondage. Similarly our friend, Winnie, collaborated with God's eternal purposes when she sent her son, Ben, away for drug rehabilitation.

I seldom allow myself to remember the anguish of sending my only child far away to a place from which he could not escape. But giving in to my longing to have him with me would have exposed him to death. When I saw his friends succumbing to the temporary but destructive pleasures of drug abuse, I was terrified for his life. His outward behavior revealed an inward heartache caused by broken family relationships. In desperation, I reluctantly agreed to place our troubled teenager in a local boarding school, but the availability of drugs and the temptation to use them were still just too great.

Friends then recommended a Christian drug rehabilitation school located outside of the United States. Ben's father and counselor vehemently objected, and their understandable concerns at first weakened my own resolve and fueled my own fears. However, I knew God loved my son even more than I did. I trusted Him to open and close all the right doors. When both of these men finally agreed that this school was the best place for my Ben, I knew it was time to surrender him to God's purposes.

I put him on that plane, pleading that God had prepared a safe place in which to repair this wounded boy's shattered heart. Only God could convince Ben of the love that drove me to send him away. Only God's love could wash away his terror of abandonment and homesickness and fill the emptiness he had tried so hard to satisfy with drugs.

If not drugs, then what would satisfy his wounded soul? Loving houseparents and staff members showed him the love of Christ. Their intimacy with Christ exposed the futility of pouring drugs and alcohol into a vacuum that only Jesus could really fill.

I finally knew that the long, torturous journey was worth all the pain when, after his college graduation, Ben and his lovely new wife returned to the rehabilitation school to serve as houseparents. God redeemed Ben's past by sending him back to help rescue other broken youngsters like himself.

My knees remain callused—not from begging God to save my son, but from thanking Him for being a Father to a broken boy and for transforming that troubled boy into a faithful man of God.

These stories challenge us to consider every act of obedience, no matter how mundane or difficult it may seem at the time, as building blocks in God's kingdom, and perhaps most especially in our dealings with our own children. Extending godly love guided by biblical faith might not reap much immediate benefit and may even seem futile and a waste of effort, but faithfulness in even the smallest things can yield unimaginable eternal rewards.

If Amram and Jochebed were still alive the day Moses murdered an Egyptian and fled into the desert, they may have been heartbroken and dismayed, but we suspect that they continued to remember their lost son in prayer. Similarly, Ben's mother did not know that, during his long journey back to spiritual wholeness, her son would one day actually be used by God to help other emotionally broken children. God continues to "do immeasurably more than all we ask or imagine" (Ephesians 3:20)—and oftentimes more than we will ever see within our own lifetimes.

THE CALL OF FAITH

Moses was born in poverty but came to live in a palace. He was the child of slaves yet became the grandson of the mighty king of Egypt. Having experienced all of this comfort and grandeur, Moses nevertheless chose to be identified as an Israelite, as a son of God, rather than continue to enjoy a secure and pampered life in Pharaoh's palace. He weighed all of that temporal security, wealth, and power against the suffering and poverty but also the eternal hope of following God, and by faith he chose the latter. Moses learned early on a lesson King Solomon, years later, would put into words:

> [God] has made everything beautiful in its time. He has also set eternity in the hearts of men; yet they cannot fathom what God has done from beginning to end. (Ecclesiastes 3:11)

With his eyes wide open to the risks involved, Moses identified himself with the covenant community of God in spite of the deep hatred of his Egyptian family for the Israelites. But his own people rejected his initial attempts at leadership (Acts 7:23–29), and his first rash response to the brutality of slavery, the murder of an abusive Egyptian overseer, accomplished nothing. Instead, Moses was forced to flee Egypt to save his own life from a vengeful Pharaoh. Clearly, before Moses would be able to lead his people out of Egypt, God had much more work to do in his heart.

COMMISSIONED BY GOD

Just as God had used imprisonment to shape Joseph into a strong and disciplined leader, He used exile to remove Moses from the distractions and political intrigues of Egypt.

God, in effect, hid Moses away for the next forty years in the wilderness, in Midian, a place where he would be trained to do the work of a spiritual leader. Moses had learned how to fight during his reign as a prince in Egypt. The battle that lay ahead of him, however, would be unlike any fight he had ever experienced. This would be a battle that could only be won in close collaboration with the God of Israel.

After forty years in the desert, Moses met God in the form of a burning bush. God called Moses to a painful, difficult task: to confront Pharaoh and lead the Israelites out of Egypt. Moses, awestruck, did not feel up to this task. His fall from power and his ignominious flight from Egypt had left him filled with unanswered questions and self-doubt. Who was he, really? A nobody, to his way of thinking. And how could God use such a loser to rescue His people? The task just seemed too big to Moses, and he wanted no part of it.

Shortly after Chuck's graduation from seminary, an elderly retired pastor, a member of our inner-city church, asked Chuck to share his testimony. Chuck told the man how God had used Chuck's relationship with Sharon to confront him with his own need for Christ. In the tumultuous "dating years" before we were eventually married, God forced us both to come to grips with the fundamental issues of our faith— Chuck a devout Catholic, Sharon a "lukewarm Presbyterian." Finally, God literally stopped Chuck in his tracks: on the landing between the first and second floors of a university dormitory! Right then and there, in the stairwell, the Lord convicted Chuck of his sin, and he committed his life to Jesus Christ as his Lord and Savior.

After listening closely to the dramatic details of Chuck's conversion, the wise old pastor told Chuck, kindly, that "whenever the demands of the ministry are so great that you want to quit, remember how God saved you. Sometimes a conversion is dramatic because the calling will be very difficult. I believe God has called you, Chuck, to a hard ministry journey that will be filled with great pain. Remember the glory of the moment you met Christ; it will carry you through the dark times."

Many of us have not had a dramatic conversion experience or a "burning bush" encounter with God's presence. But we have all heard the wails of our own self-doubt or have felt our wills balk at the work laid out before us; we've all felt inadequate when ministry opportunities require us to move out of our comfort zones and take "risks." Sharon's attempts to write a book on the ministry of encouragement were hampered by her initial lack of confidence that God had really called her to this project. She decided she could not fulfill her obligations to those who had asked her to write it, and she wanted "out." She cried, she prayed, and she argued with God about her inability to write, finally concluding that someone else would do a much better job. Like Moses, she doubted herself: "Who am I to write such a book? Why would anyone listen to me?"

Sharon continued to rail against this ministry opportunity; it was really *too much,* she was *too busy,* and the whole thing was just *way beyond* her gifts and abilities. One day, stopped at a traffic light, in tears and at the end of her tether, Sharon watched, frustrated and angry, as two large dump trucks laboriously pulled out in front of her. Late for a meeting and frankly annoyed about that daunting book project, Sharon waited impatiently as these two huge, lumbering "land turtles" crawled out and slowly took their place. The two trucks, however, carried a message directly addressing Sharon's doubts and fears. On the back of each vehicle was painted in huge letters: "If the challenge is too big, your God is too small."

Sharon saw this message as a direct and gentle rebuke from God, and she realized that her eyes were looking more at her own limitations than on His enabling grace. As a believer, she knew, but had forgotten, that God had promised to be with her and that *Treasures of Encouragement* was not even her book—it was His. Chastened, Sharon recommitted herself to the task before her, believing anew that God also equips those He calls.

Moses, when given the task of leading the Israelites out of Egypt, objected strenuously (Exodus 3:1–4:17).

First, Moses questioned, "Who am I, that I should go to Pharaoh and bring the Israelites out of Egypt?"

God responded, "I will be with you," the very promise He had made to Abraham.

Moses objected. "Suppose I go to the Israelites and say to them, 'The God of your fathers has sent me to you,' and they ask me, 'What is his name?' Then what shall I tell them?"

God responded, in effect, "Tell them that Jehovah, the faithful and trustworthy God of their fathers, has sent you."

Moses doubted. "What if they do not believe me or listen to me and say, 'The LORD did not appear to you'?" Moses probably remembered his earlier rejection by his people and questioned why this time would be any different.

God responded that Moses should throw down his staff, the symbol of his identity as a working shepherd. Without this staff he could not take care of the sheep or protect himself. God changed the staff into a snake, the national symbol of Pharaoh's alleged sovereign power. God changed it back into a staff when Moses obediently picked it up. This was no magic trick; it underscored God's power and authority over Pharaoh. Moses had to surrender his shepherd's calling in order to accept God's commissioning. Though Moses carried the simple staff of a shepherd, God had invested it, as indeed He had invested Moses, with a power far beyond its humble appearance.

Moses continued to object, claiming he was not a man of words. "O LORD," he complained, "I have never been eloquent, neither in the past nor since you have spoken to your servant. I am slow of speech and tongue."

God responded, reassuring Moses and promising him that the Lord Himself would help him speak and teach him what to say. As with Moses, God also promises to give us the strength and abilities we need. As it says in the book of Ephesians, every child of God is "created in Christ Jesus to do good works, which God prepared in advance for us to do" (2:10).

Moses decided he wasn't the best man for the job. God's promise of His presence, power, and authority was apparently not enough for Moses. He desperately exclaimed, "O LORD, please send someone else to do it" (Exodus 4:13). This is the first time during this encounter that God actually became angry with Moses. He bluntly told Moses that his eloquent brother Aaron would serve as Moses' spokesman.

Moses at last acquiesced and obeyed. On his long journey back to Egypt and into the jaws of his enemy, however, Moses did not travel alone, for God was with him.

> Since then no prophet has risen in Israel like Moses, whom the LORD knew face to face, who did all those miraculous signs and wonders the LORD sent him to do in Egypt—to Pharaoh and to all his officials and to his whole land. For no one has ever shown the mighty power or performed the awesome deeds that Moses did in the sight of all Israel. (Deuteronomy 34:10–12)

Everyone who answers God's call to know Him intimately must confront His call to courageously serve as Moses did.

YOUR PART OF THE PUZZLE

Sharon's mother loved jigsaw puzzles; she loved solving the mystery, and she always appreciated seeing the completed picture. But, while she loved her puzzles, Chuck also loved to tease her. So it was that, as this patient and meticulous woman carefully assembled an extremely challenging puzzle, "Snow White Without the Seven Dwarfs" (a circular, completely white puzzle with well over a thousand pieces), Chuck mischievously hid one small piece of the puzzle in his pocket. Imagine her disappointment when she discovered she could not complete the puzzle and have the satisfaction of seeing her project really finished. The first question of everyone who saw her puzzle was, "Where's the missing piece?" Chuck finally sheepishly confessed to his little crime and handed over the missing piece. The picture, so hard to assemble, was now finally complete.

How many "incomplete puzzles" are there today in the ministry of local churches because the children of God refuse to bring their "puzzle pieces," their special gifts and abilities, to the table of ministry? Instead, they hide them in their pockets and then join the chorus of critics who ask, "Why isn't this church meeting those needs?"—when all the while they themselves are holding the missing pieces. Like Moses, they ask the same questions. But, unlike Moses, they never actually trust God to provide them with the wisdom and ability to do what He's called them to do.

FAITH IN THE TRENCHES: GOD VERSUS THE GODS

Hebrews 11 commends the faith Moses demonstrated through his celebration of the Passover. We cannot really appreciate the powerful significance of the Passover without considering for just a moment the mighty plagues God brought down upon the Egyptians. When Moses chose to be mistreated with the people of God, he also was repudiating the pantheon of Egyptian deities: a group of more than eighty false gods and goddesses that were worshiped and honored throughout that pagan nation.

At first we might think the plagues were simply a creative way to harry Pharaoh until he finally relented and set the Israelites free. However, each plague was an intentional, specific affront to a particular Egyptian god or goddess. This was no mere battle between Pharaoh and Moses. It was a spiritual war between the One God, Yahweh, and the false gods of this world. With each new plague, God challenged and mocked the Egyptian gods, proclaiming His sovereign right to rule over all things. These battles prepared Israel to believe in His protection in the midst of the tenth and ultimate plague: the coming of the angel of death. For 430 years the Jews had been assimilated into Egyptian culture and now they were enslaved by Pharaoh. But in just one year, Israel's God systematically exposed the barrenness of Egypt's entire religious system.

Throughout the early plagues Pharaoh hardened his heart. During the latter plagues, as Pharaoh grew ever more resolute in his defiance of Moses and his God, the Lord delivered Pharaoh over to his own evil desires and thus prepared him and his worthless gods for the ultimate judgment: a plague of death among the firstborn of Egypt. Even as God did this, He also prepared the people of Israel for what was to become the centerpiece tradition of Old Testament faith, the Passover. During the ninth plague of darkness God gave Moses His instructions concerning the Passover and how it was to be observed (Exodus 11:1–3; 12:1–28).

THE PASSOVER

By faith [Moses] kept the Passover and the sprinkling of blood, so that the destroyer of the firstborn would not touch the firstborn of Israel. (Hebrews 11:28)

On that terrible day of the last plague, tormented wails and anguished screams filled the air as Egyptian parents helplessly watched their firstborn sons die. The previous nine plagues had already convinced them that the gods of Egypt were powerless and that their priests would not be able to heal their children. Even the firstborn son of Pharaoh died. Meanwhile, the people of Israel worshiped God in awestruck fear and reverent silence as the angel of death slowly moved through the land. Forever engraved on every Israelite's soul was the terror of that night. What was God doing? What was happening to their Egyptian masters? Why did God choose this way, this plague? Would they really be spared God's wrath by the blood sprinkled on their doorposts?

As these people waited through that long, terrible night—listening, praying, worshiping—they learned to trust God despite their questions, their fears. The blood of the lamb had marked them as belonging to the Lord God, protecting them from His wrath and holy judgment. Just as the blood of Christ now covers the sins of God's people, the blood on those doors forever marked out those who trusted in the one and only God.

Throughout the rest of the Old Testament, the Passover became the rite that would continually reaffirm Israel's unique identity as God's special people and a light to the rest of the nations on earth. God gave instructions to build temples and to keep written records to preserve and remember the significance of that one amazing night. The Passover pointed to the coming of Jesus Christ, God's sacrificial lamb, the One who would provide full and final provision for our sins—and protect us forever from the angel of death.

THE STRENGTH WE NEED

God called. Moses, aware of the danger and more than a little afraid, nevertheless surrendered and obeyed. Even his wildest imagination could not have prepared him for the painful realities of the extraordinary days that lay ahead. A careful study of Moses' friendship with God reveals a man who frequently asked God "Why?" and "How?"—a man who doubted his own abilities but who soon learned that God was more than able to meet his needs. Being God's messenger and servant was a high-risk, lonely, humbling assignment.

Choosing to be identified not as the son of a king, Pharaoh, but as a son of *the* King, the Lord God of Hosts, placed Moses right in the center of the spiritual war being fought for the lives and souls of God's chosen people. In a way we cannot fully understand or appreciate, Moses' life of sacrifice was also actually driven by his belief in Christ, the final and great Deliverer of God's people, the Messiah who was yet to come.

> [Moses] regarded disgrace *for the sake of Christ* as of greater value than the treasures of Egypt, because he was looking ahead to his reward. (Hebrews 11:26 [emphasis added])

We must not miss the significance of these words, chosen so carefully by the writer of Hebrews, regarding Moses' willingness to serve God. Moses, like the other godly men and women of his day, as well as those before him, trusted in God and in the fulfillment of God's promise to bless and deliver them in whatever way He chose. These people trusted in the ultimate salvation they knew God would bring them, a salvation that still lay many centuries in the future, a salvation that would not be a miraculous *act* so much as a miraculous *Person:* God's own Son, the Lord Jesus Christ.

Thus Moses could obey God "for the sake of Christ" long centuries before Jesus was born in Bethlehem, trusting God for a faraway future he couldn't see. God promised Moses, as He promises us, "I will help you. Do you trust Me?" When we answer yes, we too are trusting Him for help we cannot see and perhaps can't even imagine. Isn't this the very essence of "being sure of what we hope for and certain of what we do not see"? Moses was asked to obey God for the present and to trust Him for the future, a scary future at that, a future yet unseen. It is the same question God is asking us today, indeed this very moment. And how shall we answer Him?

The story of Moses' choice to give up earthly security and join with his people struck a chord in Sandra Pressau's life. She too had to make hard choices. Who would provide for her and her daughter? How would she survive? Could she give up her comfortable, well-provisioned life to face an uncertain financial future? Would she believe God's promise to be with her even when her outward circumstances looked hopeless and grim? Every day presented new hard choices for Sandra, testing her faith in the power of her Savior, Jesus Christ.

Although our lives may not be quite so stark and challenging, every Christian is faced with similar difficult choices. Choosing to trust God for what we cannot see and think we cannot do first requires humility and a recognition of God's almighty power; it is also important to remember that God really does care deeply for each of us (1 Peter 5:6–9). Will we then draw near to God (James 4:4–10), ready to enter His presence, ready to hear what He would have us do? Will we believe His Word (Ephesians 5:19; 6:17) and obey His commands even when those commands are hard and the goals seem impossible?

You may not see a dazzling bush filled with bright flames before you, but be sure that God is present, that He is speaking to you now. He is promising to give you *everything* you need for life and godliness, for the growth of your faith; He will give you the strength for the days ahead and all the "provisions" for the journey that your heart will need: the goodness, the knowledge, the self-control, the perseverance, the godliness, the kindness, and—perhaps most of all—the love (2 Peter 1:3–8).

The question is: Will you trust Him? Will you?

DIGGING DEEPER

Day One

- The writer of Hebrews assumed his readers knew Old Testament history. Your understanding of his examples of faith will be incomplete unless you, too, know this history. Try to read Exodus 1–15 in one sitting. What strikes you about God's character throughout this passage?

Day Two

- Hebrews 11 showcases the results of Moses' decision to identify himself as an Israelite. How does understanding our identity as God's children equip us for the tasks God gives us?
- Read Ephesians 1:3–14. What are some of the gifts that God has given to you? How do those gifts enable you to persevere when life is difficult?

Day Three

- Conflict characterized Moses' life from the moment he identified himself with God and His people. How does being openly identified as a Christian separate you from unbelievers?
- How does God want us to prepare for the daily battles of life? Find your answer in 1 Peter 5:6–9, James 4:4–10, Ephesians 5:19, and 6:10–18.

Day Four

- Review your answers for Day Three in light of a specific struggle in your daily life. Which piece of "armor" do you need the most? How will that armor enable you to show God's compassion to others?

Day Five

- Read Exodus 3 and 4. What excuses did Moses give for rejecting God's call?

◆ Compare God's response to Moses to God's promises to Abraham in Genesis 12:1–3 and Genesis 15:1, to Isaac in Genesis 26:23–24, to Jacob in Genesis 28:13–15, and to Joseph in Genesis 48:21–22. What promise did God make to all of these men?

Day Six

◆ Review your answers for Day 5. How does Galatians 3:29 confirm that the same promise of God's presence is also made to you? How does understanding this promise to be with you encourage you to "take chances" in serving Him?

◆ In what specific way will you respond to God's desire that you serve Him wherever He calls you?

Chapter 9

CHOOSING RIGHTLY—
JOSHUA AND THE
ISRAELITES

```
FAITH PRINCIPLE #9
BIBLICAL FAITH ENABLES US TO MAKE THE RIGHT DECISIONS.
```

By faith the people passed through the Red Sea as on dry land;

but when the Egyptians tried to do so, they were drowned.

By faith the walls of Jericho fell, after the people had marched around them

for seven days. (*Hebrews 11:29–30 [see also Exodus 13:17–15:21]*)

I CHOOSE YOU, ANA—RALPH WATTS

As I walked across the hard tile floor of our kitchen, my cowboy boots made a distinctive hard clomping sound that my daughter Ana always associates with her father. She immediately dropped her favorite blanket and began flailing her one good arm about, reaching for my hand. At the same time, she started making those characteristic happy and excited sounds she makes with her mouth, and her sightless brown eyes began to sparkle with joyful anticipation. I reached for and held Ana's hand. She immediately pulled me closer (almost into the wheelchair with her). She then let go of me and moved her hand up my arm and shoulder until she found the back of my neck. She pulled my face down toward the side of her face, turned her face toward mine and formed her lips for me to give her a kiss. She held me there for a while as I tousled her hair and talked to her. Finally I said, "Okay, Ana." While smiling and making her happy noises, she released my neck, reached for her blanket, and settled back into her wheelchair.

Ana, now twenty-four years old, is one of our seventeen children. Our adopted daughter was born whole and healthy but a terrible beating she received when she was only two weeks old changed her future forever. The brain damage resulting from the beating ultimately left her profoundly mentally retarded, unable to walk, talk, or take care of herself in any way. She lived in an institution for nine years, where she was also abused. At age nine she weighed only twenty-five pounds, was drawn up in the fetal position (when not in her wheelchair), and was extremely self-abusive, scratching and clawing savagely at her legs, arms, and face. Her caregivers at the institution insisted that we not adopt her because she could never give or respond to love. According to them, she was totally withdrawn from the world, a lost cause.

They were wrong. Through our struggles and her struggles, God faithfully worked at breaking down the walls that kept us "out" until, over the years, Ana was finally free to experience and to give love, and she is today a wonderful and affectionate young lady. In our house the last sound at night is Ana's laughter, and the first sounds in the morning are her happy clicks and chirps.

When our four natural sons were approaching the time when they would begin leaving the nest, the Lord laid upon our hearts the plight of "special needs" children. God first led us to nine-year-old Ana, a tiny, severely handicapped child hidden away in an institution. After adopting two more special-needs children and acting as foster parents for thirty-five other special kids, we believed the Lord wanted us to leave the comfort of our successful pastorate in the suburbs to start a home for special-needs children in the inner city. We had no money, but we had already experienced a lot of God-given love through our special kids, and we had faith that God wanted us in the city, that He would be there with us. Through a series of miracles, God provided a hundred-year-old city house, and soon it was filled with our thirteen special kids. Sometimes I think God gave us that big old house as one more means to teach us how to love our kids. By the time our newly adopted children moved into our home, we realized that, just as it will take years to renovate this old house, it will take a lifetime of God's redeeming love to transform and heal the wounded souls of these children.

Each one of our special children has come to us with a history of heartache and pain; these precious kids have been cast aside by a society that has decided their lives are hopeless and useless. As we look back over the years and at each of the children the Lord has given to our family, we are amazed at the way God has so wonderfully directed us and provided for us at each step of the way. Whether the miracle was providing the exact amount of money we needed to purchase a big-enough house or "nudging" a believer to give us a fifty-pound bag of potatoes for our dinner, the Lord has taught us to call Him *Jehovah Jireh*—the "God Who Provides."

What we are doing does not seem wonderfully special to us, it just seems natural. To others it may seem crazy to start adopting special-needs children when our lives were just beginning to get a little less complicated. But to us it would have been somehow unnatural *not* to start adopting these kids. We knew this wouldn't be easy, but we also knew this is where God wanted us to go.

God has led us to this place in our lives, and we chose to serve Him in this way. His love led us to open our hearts and home to these broken children. We have learned to depend on Him daily for wisdom and direction and He, for His part, has given us a new awareness of His presence and His love. Surely God has given us some very special kids, children who have touched our lives with a very special love.

Ralph V. Watts, Jr.

SEARCHING FOR SHORTCUTS

Most of us like shortcuts. Book titles promise quick solutions to our problems—"Perfection in Five Minutes a Day!" and "Three Easy Steps to Success and Happiness!"—and we can't get enough of such materials. We eagerly latch onto surefire, money-back-guaranteed schemes for fast-track Christian growth: the Seven Secret Steps to Win Your Husband to Christ, the Ten Guaranteed Rules for Effective Parenting, or the Oh-So-Simple Solution for Conquering Serious Sins . . . *now for only $29.95*! Although there may be real truth hidden away in many of these books and seminars and tape series, the biblical road to maturity is *not* quick and easy, but is instead long and often strewn with suffering.

This is a hard lesson the Israelites, freshly escaped from Egypt, were about to learn. The people of Israel still needed to understand that the only way to get to the Promised Land was God's way, by putting into practice a faith-driven, faith-guided obedience empowered by the strength and grace of Jehovah God.

Trusting God thus means that we very often must obey Him in spite of what "common sense" would have us do. The writer of Hebrews reminds us, in recalling the crossing of the Red Sea, that the walk of faith requires a wholehearted commitment to God's call even when outward appearances would seem to spell defeat.

God had led the Israelites on a circuitous route along the desert road from the heart of Egypt to the edge of the Red Sea. He assured His people that He was with them, visibly and dramatically, by the presence of a pillar of cloud by day and a pillar of fire by night that traveled with them. How reassuring these ever-present signs of God's power and care must have been for these people, as they in turn reassured their children of God's presence. What a relief and a comfort the shade must have been in the burning heat of the day, the bright flames in

the darkness and cold of the desert night. The people obediently followed Moses as he led them to a place called Pi Hahiroth, near the Red Sea.

Meanwhile Pharaoh, the king of Egypt, had again
changed his fickle and evil mind; he now regretted his decision to let the Israelites go free. Believing them to be confused, lost, and vulnerable, Pharaoh attempted to catch them
all in a deadly trap. He planned to pin them in, trapping them
between the surrounding mountains and the Red Sea at Pi
Hahiroth. His armies would enter the area through a pass in
the mountains, thereby blocking the only escape route with
his chariots and infantry. Realizing their peril as the trap
slowly closed around them, the Israelites' joy at being free
quickly turned to abject fear and a longing to return to the
"security" of their former days of slavery.

Every Christian faces similar crisis points, places in our
lives that require serious, deliberate, and courageous faith-
based decisions.

KATHY'S FORK IN THE ROAD

We will never forget the night a friend of ours, Vince, a
young husband and father, was murdered. Vince and his wife,
Kathy, had recently accepted Christ into their hearts and lives.
Vince's terrible and brutal death threatened to completely overwhelm Kathy with grief, bitterness, and a terrible rage against
God. But in the midst of her grief and pain was a pure and radiant faith in the Lord Jesus. Kathy's attitude four years later toward her husband's killer at a resentencing trial was astonishing,
so astonishing in fact that the story was carried on the front page
of the state newspaper, *The News Journal.* The reporter wrote,

> The widow of a store employee slain in 1980 told the
> convicted killer Friday that she had overcome her grief

through religious beliefs and urged him to seek help from the same source. . . .

"I reread my journal last night trying to recall my emotions of four years ago and I came across this entry," she began. "I found out that David Rush got the death penalty and all I could say was, 'Oh, my God.' I felt so heavy I started to cry—for the Rushes, for Vince, for the fact that this guy had to die because he killed Vince." . . .

A few days later, she wrote, "I hate what this guy has done—sometimes I imagine killing him myself with slow torture. It just shows me that if I did not have Christ, I would be no different than he is. . . . Yet in the midst of indescribable grief, there was Jesus Christ. So I had this grief and I had this joy, both emotions at the same time." She said that now she is "healed and happy. Christ in me used this tragedy to teach me compassion and to not wallow in self-pity, and to be strong, and to know what real pain is, and to forgive someone I wanted to hate."

Reciting a prayer, she turned toward Rush. "Remember that prayer, Dave. Someday you may decide to pray one like it. You can have meaning in life even in prison."

Even as Kathy stood on the edge of a grief and bitterness she knew she could never pass through in her own strength, God made a way for her through the darkness (Colossians 1:13–14). As a result, this young, brokenhearted mother struggled to answer God's call to be kind, compassionate, and forgiving, just as she knew Christ had forgiven her (Ephesians 4:32). Kathy not only believed God's Word, she obeyed it. She knew that her young son needed to breathe the sweet air of God's love rather than to be raised in the stench of bitterness and spite. Kathy's eyes saw the eternal ramifications of each one of her daily steps, and she trusted God to keep her feet on dry and solid ground, certain that nothing would separate her from His love.

Kathy concluded her courtroom remarks with the words, "You can consider me a fool, or an emotional cripple for believing in Jesus, or you can consider that I have an anchor that is so firm even life's worst sorrows can't drown me. I invite you to grab hold of that anchor—Christ." Her husband's killer, whose death sentence was commuted to life, will spend the rest of his life in prison, but there are no bars of bitterness imprisoning Kathy.

BEATING THE ODDS

Six hundred massive war chariots, along with crack troops and still other chariots, suddenly bore down on thousands of Israeli men, women, and children. The Israelites, though not outnumbered, were certainly outmatched. It was as though an armada of tanks was descending upon a huge mass of weary and ill-prepared civilians. The Israelites, weak from years of deprivation and slavery as well as a long desert trek on foot and quite inexperienced in battle, were understandably terrified.

Instead of looking to God for help, however, they promptly forgot their true Deliverer and, in a frenzy of fear and panic, accused Moses of reckless leadership. They actually blamed him for this apparent looming disaster, saying, in effect, "This is all *your* fault! We're right back where we started. . . . No, this is far worse! What kind of God makes a mistake like this?"

Moses, however, had seen too much, had experienced too much, to doubt the Lord in this situation. Moses didn't argue with his countrymen, nor was he swayed by their fears. Instead, he exhorted them all to be still and to wait for God's deliverance. As Moses obediently raised his staff toward heaven,

the panic-stricken Israelites gathered beside the Red Sea. The
pillar of cloud and fire moved to stand between them and the
coming armies of Egypt, providing light and protection for
the Israelites, while at the same time blocking the Egyptians
with swirling darkness and confusion (Exodus 14:19–20).

What must it have been like to watch as those dark waters
of the great Red Sea divided, rising up into two huge, spectacular walls? At last, someone must have been the first to step
onto that dry sea bed, crying out, "Follow me! The way is dry
and safe!" The people demonstrated their corporate faith
through their obedience. Throughout the night men, women,
and children by the thousands put their lives in God's hands
as they crossed the sea floor, between two massive cliffs of dark
water, to reach safety on the other side.

The Egyptians, now no longer held back by the miraculous cloud, surged forward to pursue the Israelites across the
sea bottom. God then released those towering walls of water to
fall back down upon the enemy army and their chariots. The
waters crashed down upon them, destroying all of the Egyptian army with a deafening roar. The historian Josephus would
later report that not only did the bodies of these soldiers wash
up on shore, but so also did much of their equipment, thereby
providing the Israelites with the weapons they would need in
the days ahead.

By faith, therefore, the Israelites crossed through the
Red Sea as on dry land. They had trusted God to hold back
the water until they safely reached the other side, and God
had, as always, proved faithful to His Word. God asks from us
the same kind of obedience. Whether His command is that we
submit, *by faith*, to an unbelieving husband, or that we confess
and renounce a sin, *by faith*, knowing that we cannot possibly
break free from it in our own strength, or that we refuse, *by
faith*, to compromise our walk even if it should cost us our
jobs, the Christian must enter those parted and ominous waters by faith and cross over to the other side. God's directions

to Kathy that she forgive her husband's killer were just as difficult to obey as His command for the Israelites to walk through two thundering walls of water to the other side of the sea. But they obeyed, and so must we.

PERSEVERING IN THE DESERT

After their amazing deliverance through the Red Sea, the Israelites gave God all the glory for their escape. But their "spiritual high point" was, alas, short-lived. Indeed, it is stunning how quickly their joy and gratitude turned to grumbling.

God had promised them daily provisions for the journey, and He fed them miraculously with His divine bread, "manna." Yet even this great gift became a test of their faith, for they soon began to take this blessing for granted. Instead of choosing to be thankful to God for His daily provision, they began to complain. "What? Not manna *again*? After all," they moaned, "how many different ways can you prepare manna before you tire of the same old thing?"

What an accurate picture of human nature this is! We want excitement, we want change. We want to experience new heights of faith and new horizons of opportunity. But the walk of faith often requires just the opposite—an ability to endure and just keep plodding onward, across a sometimes dull and drab desert terrain, with only the basic necessities to sustain us. What God requires of us, as one author has so aptly put it, is "a long obedience in the same direction." We need to be willing to trust, to obey, and to persevere even when we don't get exactly what we want, when we want it. A spectacular deliverance is a wondrous thing, but to *expect* clouds of fire, miraculous partings of seas, the instant annihilation of every obstacle that stands in our way, this is not what the Christian life is all about. Jesus Himself warned against a faith built upon "signs and wonders"—or even just enough miracles to keep our bellies full (John 6:26–29). Faith demands contentment in the midst of routine. Certainly, God delights in surprising us with the unexpected. But it is a weak faith—and perhaps even a dead faith—that just withers away to nothing during every "dry spell."

In their constant complaining and doubting, the Israelites demonstrated that they had not really learned to endure, to persevere in all circumstances. Nor had they learned to trust God. They proved faithless and ungrateful in the ordinary things of life, adamantly refusing to be content and grateful for the miracles of God just because those miracles weren't coming fast and furiously enough to suit them. Moreover, when it came time to enter the new land, they trembled with doubt and fear—this in spite of all they had seen the Lord God already do for them. And so God judged them.

> How long will this wicked community grumble against me? I have heard the complaints of these grumbling Israelites. . . . In this desert your bodies will fall—every one of you twenty years old or more who was counted in the census and who has grumbled against me. Not one of you will enter the land I swore with uplifted hand to make your home, except Caleb son of Jephunneh and Joshua son of Nun. (Numbers 14:27, 29–30)

Thus did an entire generation of men and women, except for only Joshua and Caleb, pass away without ever entering the Promised Land.

STANDING ON THE EDGE AGAIN—FORTY YEARS LATER

Whereas the rebellious Israelites of Moses' day were ready to stone him for trying to lead them into Canaan, their sons and daughters, some forty years later, now chastened and trusting the Lord, were ready and willing to go. They obediently promised their new leader, Joshua, "Whatever you have commanded us we will do, and wherever you send us we will go" (Joshua 1:16).

Joshua, who had succeeded Moses, had been present when the Israelites stood on the edge of the Red Sea just after they had left Egypt. By faith, he, along with his fellow Israelites, had crossed through the Red Sea to reach the safety of the other shore. Thus Joshua understood, as well as anyone, what the prophet Isaiah would later proclaim—that this deliverance was not due to the faith of the Israelites but to the great faithfulness and grace of God.

> Was it not you [O, LORD] who dried up the sea, the waters of the great deep, who made a road in the depths of the sea so that the redeemed might cross over? (Isaiah 51:10)

Now, forty years later, a new generation of Israelites stood poised on the edge of the Promised Land. To get there they, too, had to cross over a body of water: the Jordan River. Moses was now dead, and Joshua was God's anointed leader. God's call to Joshua linked him to all those who had come before him. Just as God had promised Abraham, Isaac, Jacob, Joseph, and Moses that He would never leave them, the great "I AM," Jehovah God of Israel, promised Joshua,

> I will give you every place where you set your foot, as I promised Moses. . . . No one will be able to stand up against you all the days of your life. As I was with Moses, so I will be with you; I will never leave you nor forsake you. (Joshua 1:3, 5)

Three times in this conversation God reassured Joshua and exhorted him to "be strong and courageous" (Joshua 1:6,

7, 9). Joshua's God was about to fulfill the covenantal promise He had made to Abraham hundreds of years earlier:

> The whole land of Canaan, where you are now an alien, I will give as an everlasting possession to you and your descendants after you; and I will be their God. (Genesis 17:8)

In preparation for the invasion of Canaan, Joshua secretly sent men into the great fortress city of Jericho to spy out the land and its people. In that heavily walled city, a prostitute, Rahab, would confirm for them what God had already promised would happen, that "all the people are melting in fear" (Joshua 2:24 [for more about Rahab, see chapter 10]).

Between the Israelites and Jericho stood the Jordan River. Unless God intervened as He had at the Red Sea, the Israelites would have to wait until the flood season passed. But God used this very obstacle to establish Joshua as their anointed leader (Joshua 3:7) and to prepare them for the even more difficult challenges ahead (vv. 9–13).

CROSSING OVER: NO GOING BACK

The Christian life is marked by innumerable big and little "decision points," places in our lives where we cannot stand still but where we're also almost too afraid to move forward. The future looks bleak, and we know that once we set foot upon a particular course of action there will no going back—not ever.

For each of us, first coming to faith in Christ is like this, but so also are the thousands of decisions that come afterward. Once you "go public" about your faith in Christ with a friend, for example, you are somehow even more obligated to live out your faith boldly and consistently before that person. You recognize intuitively that sharing Christ openly commits you to a course of action that will forever change your relationship to that friend. It can be a scary and intimidating thing, and many of us try to hang back, waiting, perhaps, for some easier way. We may know what is right and what God wants us to do in a given situation, but the way ahead seems, as it did to the Israelites of Moses' generation, populated with "giants," and we lose our nerve.

Looking back, it is easy for us to say glibly that God was with the Israelites and that everything turned out just fine for them in the end, so what did they have to be worried about? But these people were not looking back; they were looking *forward*—into an unknown and pretty scary future—and yet they trusted God. Surely, this is living faith.

What then will we need in order to cross the "rivers" that stand before us?

CROSSING OVER: RELYING ON THE WORD

A commitment to "cross over" requires clear direction from the Word of God.

When God transferred leadership from Moses to Joshua, He tied His promise to go with the people to a command that Joshua and his fellow Israelites must study and meditate *daily* on God's Word, God's Law, as given to them through Moses. Moreover, Joshua and the people were not just to read the Word, but they were commanded to obey it:

> Do not let this Book of the Law depart from your mouth; meditate on it day and night, so that you may be careful to do everything written in it. Then you will be prosperous and successful. Have I not commanded you? Be strong and courageous. Do not be

terrified; do not be discouraged, for the LORD your God will go with you wherever you go. (Joshua 1:8–9)

Joshua took this command to heart. God gave His people very specific instructions, and they obeyed each one. In crossing the Jordan, the Ark of the Covenant, containing the stone tablets of God's Law and carried by the priests, was to come first; behind the Ark, the leaders and then the rest of the people followed. God was thus showing them (and us) that, by His Word, He leads us. As the priests carrying the Ark stepped into the surging river, the waters suddenly and miraculously stopped—standing up "in a heap" (Joshua 3:16)—and the people were able to cross the Jordan on dry ground.

Many others, at great personal risk, have stepped into dangerous waters following steadfastly the truth of God's Word. Martin Luther, an Augustinian monk in sixteenth-century Germany, was deeply troubled over the heresies he saw practiced by the church of his day. When God revealed to him the real meaning of "justification by faith," he took his stand at great personal risk. John and Charles Wesley and George Whitefield crisscrossed America and England, preaching the truths of Scripture against the backdrop of heretical religious practices. The rallying cry of the followers of John Knox in Scotland was "For Christ's Crown and Covenant!"—even as these Scottish Reformers were tortured and murdered for refusing to bow to any king but Christ.

The heart cry of the Reformers was *sola fide, sola gratia,* and *sola scriptura* (faith alone, grace alone, Scripture alone). These were risky and dangerous truths in that day; standing up for them cost many of these believers their lives. Yet their faithful willingness to stand against the raging waters of heresy paved the way for others to follow. God's call for us to cross over may not be as dramatic as it was for these courageous believers, but each act of faith-driven obedience, however small, is yet another significant part in the building of the kingdom of God.

CROSSING OVER: READY TO SUFFER

A commitment to "cross over" requires a readiness to undergo suffering and loss in serving the Lord.

Before crossing the Jordan, Joshua also called the people to set themselves apart in preparation for God's mighty work (Joshua 3:5). The very act of consecration reminded them that the coming campaign was not for their own glory, but for God's glory alone.

Several days after Mark's death, God led Sharon to review her most recent journal entries. She wept as she realized that in the months before the accident, God had led her to repeatedly surrender our son to God's protection and sovereign plans. Although she had also written prayers for our other children, Mark's name appeared more frequently, even in the context of possibly losing him in a car accident. Coupled with her fears was the written conclusion, in one entry, that "if Mark were killed in a car accident, I know You would give me the grace to not only survive but to also experience joy once again." On days when torrents of grief threatened to wash her away, the memory of this Spirit-led consecration gave her enough strength to trust God and to withstand the discouraging whispers of the Enemy, who always wants us to turn back, to give up, at the water's edge.

Though God had promised the Israelites victory in Canaan, they were still about to face the fear and horror of hand-to-hand combat. There would be moments when they would wonder if He had abandoned them altogether. At those moments the memory of their solemn consecration—of their possessions, their loved ones, their own lives—would give them the strength they needed to stay the course, to continue choosing to serve God.

CROSSING OVER: TRUSTING IN GOD'S LEADERSHIP

A commitment to "cross over" is founded on a confidence that God will lead the way.

God does not send us; He leads us. The priests actually touched the water's edge before the water stood up in a heap. As God had commanded, they stood with the Ark in the middle of the river until every Israelite had crossed over the Jordan and reached the other side. The Ark is mentioned eleven times in this passage and was the focus of their obedience; it represented the very presence of God. He dried up the Jordan River not just to get His people to the other side but also so "that all the peoples of the earth might know that the hand of the LORD is powerful and so that you might always fear the LORD your God" (Joshua 4:24).

By faith, our friend Dominic left the safe shore of a secure job and crossed over to a new ministry to teenagers. Daily he helps organize and lead Bible studies in public and private schools. He mentors students and equips them to share Christ with their classmates. Dominic and the ministry staff have built up such a reputation of integrity that school officials now call on them to help other counselors when their students are facing severe personal crises. But this ministry, like so many others, runs on a shoestring. Dominic never knows if he will receive a paycheck in any given month, since his salary depends on the faithful giving of other believers. Some of Dominic's friends see this as a crazy, foolish existence. But Dominic himself is certain that God has His own eternal purposes—even for the "lean months" when the money is scarce. Dominic understands that his journey is not about finding personal comfort, but about trusting in God's glory and power, God's own eternal purposes.

SHUT UP, THEY WERE SHUT UP

The inhabitants of Jericho were terrified. They had not only heard the stories of this God who miraculously protected His people, they had seen the miracle of the crossing of the Jordan River with their own eyes—or rather through the eyes of their own scouts and spies. Now they were holed up in their city. The literal meaning of "Jericho was tightly shut up" (Joshua 6:1) in the original Hebrew is "Jericho was shut up, it was shut up." The people of Jericho may have felt reasonably safe behind their high, thick walls. Yet they must have peered over the tops of those massive walls with great unease, wondering just what action these strange invaders and their "one God" might take against them.

Our eagerness to know God better will lead us to study His Word, to pray, to spend time with other believers, and to consecrate our lives to His service. In this way God prepares us to face each "Jericho" in our own lives—someone who might be making our lives difficult, some grudge we are nursing, or some pet sin we refuse to forsake; perhaps it is a friend who needs the Lord but who is locked away behind high walls of distrust and anger. We go to church with our Bibles in hand, hoping, perhaps, to find some easy way to topple those walls and move on to our next triumph. Meanwhile, the world tells us such battles cannot even be won, that prayer and witnessing and repentance and God's Word are all pointless and a waste of time.

God, however, calls upon us to trust Him in spite of the obstacles, the difficulties, the scoffing and doubt and opposition of the culture we live in. God's directions for moving forward are specific and direct and clear. They may also sometimes even seem a little ridiculous: Love your enemies? Turn from sin? Pray without ceasing? Rejoice always? What? *Are you kidding, Lord?*

The Lord, of course, is not kidding, although, sadly, we often act as though He is. God's instructions to the Israelites must have seemed preposterous at the time, but they couldn't have been clearer. He commanded the Israelites,

> March around the city once with all the armed men. Do this for six days. Have seven priests carry trumpets of rams' horns in front of the ark. On the seventh day, march around the city seven times, with the priests blowing the trumpets. When you hear them sound a long blast on the trumpets, have all the people give a loud shout; then the wall of the city will collapse and the people will go up, every man straight in. (Joshua 6:3–5)

The Israelites were apparently ready for anything, because they marched exactly as they had been ordered. The people of Jericho must have wondered at this; perhaps they even mocked the Israelites. But, in the end, the walls fell with a great crash, and the city was destroyed.

FREE TO CHOOSE RIGHTLY

God's instructions require trust and discipline. His answers to our prayers for help and guidance—whether these answers come through our circumstances or through the clear teaching in His Word or through the godly counsel of a friend or pastor—will often confuse or surprise us.

Will the Christian employee, asked to compromise biblical values in order to keep his job, "cross over" and remain faithful to God no matter what? Will the father, who must demonstrate "tough love" to rescue his child from some life-destroying sin, "cross over"? Will the busy family answer God's call to extend His mercy to the homeless and the hurting; will they, too, "cross over"?

Many of God's directives appear to defy what we consider to be reasonable and normal behavior. As we consider these commands, we are, in a sense, poised on the brink of the River Jordan. "Can I trust God to keep His promise to be there with me, to protect me? Can I trust God with the results of my obedience?" The answer is certainly "yes"—you *can* trust God for all of this and more. The harder question, of course, is this: *"Will* you?" The foot will not move toward the water until the heart is willing to move it.

The story of Ana at the beginning of this chapter is an example of such a special calling—and of the special people who answered that calling. Ralph and Karen Watts, with four grown sons of their own, had a special heart for severely handicapped children. Having observed Karen's parents' care for her own mentally challenged sister, this couple knew full well that adopting such needy children would be a difficult task. Nevertheless, they sought God's guidance and asked Him to lead them to the child or children He wanted them to love and care for.

Ralph and Karen found Ana's name listed in a national catalog of children available for adoption. She was in an institution on the other side of the country. All of the experts urged them to invest their time in a child who would really benefit from their home, essentially writing off Ana as a lost cause. But Ralph and Karen were confident that God wanted Ana in their home. She was the first of thirteen adopted special-needs children to eventually find love and acceptance with the Watts family. Numerous foster children have also found this home, dubbed "The Eagle's Nest," to be a place of love and refuge.

For the Watts, the days are jam-packed with doctor's appointments and medical crises; they also struggle to keep up with the pastoral needs of their inner-city church. The way is difficult, certainly, but Ralph and Karen see God building His kingdom every time a child cast aside as hopeless and worthless confounds the experts: some who would "never walk" have learned to walk; others, beyond all expectations, have learned to feed themselves or can reach up and give their adoptive father a kiss. Small victories, perhaps, but not for these children, not for Ralph and Karen, and not for the Most High, who is doing greater things than this, though our eyes may not see it, not yet. These weary parents remind one another constantly of Amy Carmichael's theme, "The only thing that counts is that which is eternal. Some day these children will have new bodies and new minds and will joyfully dance in the streets of heaven—and we will be there to see it."

RIVERS LEFT TO CROSS

Joshua had begun his term as the leader of God's people by a strong and faithful decision to follow God wherever He might lead. At the end of his life, Joshua was able to make the same deliberate and God-honoring decision: "As for me and my household," proclaimed Joshua, "we *will* serve the LORD" (Joshua 24:15 [emphasis added]). Joshua's life was thus characterized by a lifelong pattern of choosing to follow God, and the people followed along with him. God, in turn, honored and upheld His covenantal people.

Why? Joshua knew. He never forgot who gave them the victories—or the reason God gave them. He had reminded the people,

> The LORD your God dried up the Jordan before you until you had crossed over. The LORD your God did to the Jordan just what he had done to the Red Sea when he dried it up before us until we had crossed over. He did this so that all the peoples of the earth might know that the hand of the LORD is powerful and so that you might always fear the LORD your God. (Joshua 4:23–24)

It was by God's grace that the Israelites were chosen from among the nations of the earth to glorify Him and make

His name known so that others might fear Him. It was by
grace that they crossed over the River Jordan and entered the
land of promise. It was by grace that they were able, at long
last, to fight and finally defeat their adversaries. Joshua later
noted,

> So the LORD gave Israel all the land he had sworn to
> give their forefathers, and they took possession of it
> and settled there. The LORD gave them rest on every
> side, just as he had sworn to their forefathers. Not one
> of their enemies withstood them; the LORD handed all
> their enemies over to them. Not one of all the LORD's
> good promises to the house of Israel failed; every one
> was fulfilled. (Joshua 21:43–45)

Joshua had trusted God to fulfill His promises just as He
had done for Abraham, Isaac, and Jacob. It is by the grace of
God, not the frailty of human reason, that we choose daily to
cross over our own rivers and fight our own battles—to do
whatever God has called us to do, and count not the cost.
The Day is coming and, indeed, will be here sooner than we
imagine, when we stand at the edge of one last river to cross.
Only then will the battle be truly over, and all the choices
made.

> Then said he, "I am going to my Father's, and though
> with great difficulty I am got hither, yet now I do not
> repent me of all the trouble I have been at to arrive
> where I am. My sword I give to him that shall succeed
> me in my pilgrimage, and my courage and skill to him
> that can get it. My marks and scars I carry with me, to
> be a witness for me that I have fought His battles who
> now will be my Rewarder."
> When the day that he must go hence was come,
> many accompanied him to the river-side, into which,

as he went, he said, "Death, where is thy sting?" And as he went down deeper, he said, "Grave, where is thy victory?" So he passed over, and all the trumpets sounded for him . . . on the other side. (John Bunyan, *The Pilgrim's Progress*)

DIGGING DEEPER

Day One

♦ Read Joshua 4:23–24. Why is it important to remember the goals of God's miracles? How does His purpose differ from the "worthwhile goals" of modern culture?

♦ How does knowing God's purpose to conform us to the image of His Son (Romans 8:29) help you rest in Him when His commands seem to be "out in left field"—or just too difficult to obey?

Day Two

♦ Review Exodus 13:17–14:31. Why didn't God take the Israelites directly to the Red Sea? How did their frightening circumstances affect their faith?

♦ How does seeing God's character in this story help you to trust Him with your own circumstances?

Day Three

♦ Faith requires action that sometimes appears ludicrous. Review the story of Ana Watts (pp. 175–78) and the authors' comments about Ralph and Karen Watts (pp. 194–95). What sacrifices are these two people making in order to obey God's calling?

♦ What action does God require of you today that others may not understand? What sacrifice will you need to make in order to obey?

Day Four

♦ Read Joshua 3 and 4. Note each time the Ark is mentioned. Why does Joshua emphasize the Ark so strongly in this passage?

♦ How did the Ark encourage the Israelites to keep walking across the previously flooded Jordan River? How does the promise of God's presence encourage you to act against your own natural inclinations in order to obey God's specific instructions for you?

Day Five

♦ How did the miracle at the Jordan River "equip" the Israelites to take the city of Jericho?

♦ What kind of "Jericho" are you facing in your life? How does God's faithfulness to the Israelites give you hope in your own circumstances?

♦ Review past "scorch marks" in your life and focus on one in which you clearly experienced God's faithfulness. How does remembering this event give you the courage to "cross over" whatever you are facing today?

Day Six

♦ How did the Israelites prepare to cross over the Red Sea and then the Jordan River to take the city of Jericho? Consider these accounts in light of the specific elements of "crossing over" as discussed in this chapter.

♦ In response to God's specific instructions, consecrate yourself for obedience to Him and act with confidence in His presence and leading.

Chapter 10

BECOMING NEW—
RAHAB

FAITH PRINCIPLE #10
BIBLICAL FAITH MAKES US NEW.

By faith the prostitute Rahab, because she welcomed the spies,

was not killed with those who were disobedient.

(Hebrews 11:31 [see also Joshua 2–6])

DAUGHTER OF A KING—HILDA MARTIN

As a child I was subjected to daily physical, mental, and sexual abuse from numerous family members. Even the spiritual world was frightening to me because my relatives practiced witchcraft within their religion. I knew that we were different, but there was nothing I could do about it, and so I inhabited a lonely and bewildering world. Our move to America from Costa Rica only deepened that loneliness. I felt as if I was destined to always be an outsider; my inability to speak or understand English was like a high wall cutting me off from the rest of the world. Even as a child I would wonder why everybody in my life seemed to want to hurt and use me. I would wonder, too, if I would ever break free, ever find some-place safe.

In my search for love and security, I made a lot of bad choices. Hoping to escape a painful family situation and thinking that I had finally found that "safe place" I had longed for, I got married at the age of sixteen to a man who proved to be every bit as cruel and abusive as my own family had been. More troubling still, I became pregnant almost imme-diately. Certain I wasn't yet ready to love and care for a child, I planned to get an abortion. Looking back, I can see now that it was God who stopped me from destroying my unborn baby. I did not know it then, but this child would be one of only two children who would survive my six pregnancies. Over the years I would lose four babies because of the physical abuse of the men in my life.

My marriage came to a bitter end, and I was left alone as a desperate, struggling single mother. I wanted to die and I even tried to commit suicide. Yet God did not give up on me, and He graciously sent a woman into my life who understood my background and yet who did not judge me for my past sins. This woman invited me to her church, where I met Jesus in 1968. Life still wasn't easy, but I no longer felt like I was all alone.

I soon remarried, thinking I had found safety with a man who was a leader in his church. When he, too, began to physi-cally abuse me, I turned to the church leaders for help. They didn't believe me and instead insisted that I learn how to be a "submissive wife." That marriage, too, came to a messy, painful end. Once again I was a homeless, single mother with no place to go. Hopeless and desperate, I again considered suicide my only option. But God was holding me tightly in His grip, and He reminded me of that friend who had loved me before so un-conditionally. I got in touch with her, and she helped me get back on my feet. God led me to a church that taught me how to respond biblically to my past and how to trust His people again.

Even though I had asked Jesus to forgive my sins, it was a long time before I could fully understand just how special I am to God, how much He loves me. I also still struggle to believe that other people really do care about me. It is God's love and forgiveness that gives me the courage to honestly tell my story today. His great power has changed me from wanting to end my life to wanting to live—*for Him*. He is the reason I am alive today, and I know now where I belong. The Lord is giving me the confidence and strength I need to reach out to others with His love—to the women in my church, to teenagers who feel like misfits, and to women at several nearby prisons.

All of my life I had hoped to find someone to love me as I truly am, in spite of all the wrong things I had done and the things that had been done to me, someone who would treat me kindly and lovingly, someone who would *really* care for me. Then, one wonderful day, my Father found me at last. When I repented of my sins and His Son's precious blood washed them all away, I felt clean and new for the first time in my life. I learned who I truly was, the daughter of a wise, loving, and mighty King.

No matter what challenges come my way now, I know I can trust Him to see me through them all.

Hilda Martin

BAGGAGE FROM THE PAST

The Scriptures promise that those who wait on God will rise up with the wings of an eagle (Isaiah 40:31). Many believers, however, remain earthbound, held down by the heavy "baggage" still strapped to their backs. These people accept unsettled issues of the past as a way of life. Bitterness, self-imposed guilt, regret, and unresolved conflict are their daily bread. Instead of enjoying the transforming power of God's forgiveness and His promises of restoration, they are being crushed by the burdens they carry. They can never move forward, let alone take flight on eagles' wings. They are seemingly unable to follow God's counsel: "Forget the former things; do not dwell on the past" (Isaiah 43:18).

Rahab is the only character in the list of godly men and women in Hebrews 11 who is identified by her evil past. Clearly, the sinful lives of the other people mentioned here in Hebrews could also have been described. Why then is only Rahab portrayed as a sinner, as "the prostitute"? We believe that the author of Hebrews, by his deliberate use of these words, was reminding his readers, through Rahab, that *all* believers can know and demonstrate saving faith, leaving behind the sins of the past and going on to serve Christ by the power of His Spirit.

By referring to Rahab's past sin in this way the writer does not seek to glorify it, nor is he trying to define this woman by what she used to be. Rahab's glory was not in the wrongful things she had done but in the way God, through His great grace, saved her and gave her a new identity, a new life.

In the early church, especially in this primarily Jewish congregation, this would have been a significant issue. The church needed to be a safe haven. The Hebrew church was hard pressed by persecution from the outside and the potential for strife within. They needed to pull together and rise above deeply rooted prejudice, the age-old tensions between "good people" and "bad people," tax collectors and Pharisees.

In such a group of believers, as in the church today, there would have been many people familiar with and already abiding by God's commandments, God's moral requirements. Some of these people had been raised in strict Jewish homes, while others had been brought up in God-fearing gentile homes. But there were also many in this church who had been delivered by the power of Christ directly from pagan immorality and the worship of false gods. This passage in Hebrews was written to encourage believers sorely tempted to condemn one another or to abandon the hard life of the Christian altogether, returning to their old lives and former lifestyles.

The redemption of Rahab, who was not only a prostitute but a Gentile, was thus a memorable object lesson about God's grace. The Lord transcends our past, no matter what it might be, and redeems us from it, leading us to safety and refuge within the covenant community. If the Lord God, Maker of Heaven and Earth, can see past our differences and sins to show us His marvelous grace, then surely, in our dealings with one another, so can we. The church, therefore, must be a place of refuge, a place open to anyone, with any background.

WHO WAS RAHAB?

God had promised Abraham that He would bless those who blessed him and his descendants (Genesis 12:3). We see the continuing fulfillment of that promise in the story of Rahab. In order to prepare for the coming battle, Joshua sent two spies to infiltrate the mighty walled city of Jericho. These two men found refuge in the house of Rahab, a brothel built right into the thick wall surrounding the city. If discovered, they probably planned to escape the city by climbing down from a window and hiding in one of the hundreds of caves scattered throughout the nearby hills. The king of Jericho somehow learned about the spies and that they were staying at Rahab's house; he immediately sent soldiers to seize them (Joshua 2:1–3).

With no time for them to escape, Rahab hid the two men under a pile of flax on her rooftop. The men must have prayed as Rahab spoke at the door with the king's soldiers. For long, tense moments they waited. Did they fear that Rahab, a pagan woman, a prostitute they hardly knew, might betray them? All we know for certain is that Rahab displayed great bravery in the face of danger; her courage reminds us of Jochebed, the mother of Moses. These two men were compelled by circumstances beyond their control to entrust their lives to this remarkable woman—a prostitute, a Canaanite, the "enemy"—and yet, somehow, now their only hope.

Rahab's inclusion in Hebrews 11, along with Abraham, Isaac, and Jacob, is a heartening indication of God's unconditional love for His people. The choice of a figure with three great strikes against her—her sex, her profession, and her nationality—gives gentle affirmation and encouragement for every believer who feels ruined and worthless because of an ugly past. Moreover, Rahab's example here, commended by the writer of Hebrews, makes it clear (should there be any doubt) that membership in God's family is not based on our own "goodness" but on God's amazing, redeeming grace.

FAITH IN ACTION

Doubtless, the spies held their breath and kept their hands on their swords, prepared to fight to the death should Rahab betray them. Instead, in Joshua 2:4–5, we read that Rahab, the harlot and Canaanite, lied three times in order to protect the two Israelites hiding in her home:

[1] Yes, the men came to me, but I did not know where they had come from. [2] At dusk, when it was time to close the city gate, the men left. [3] I don't know which way they went.

The two men must have been tense with fear, and their hearts must have been pounding when they finally heard the front door slam shut. Then they listened, sick with relief, as the sound of the soldier's voices faded off down the street. Though temporarily safe, the spies realized that their lives still lay in the hands of a Canaanite prostitute, one of the very people whose sin had reached its full measure (Genesis 15:16) and whose city they had been sent to spy upon and which they planned, eventually, to utterly destroy. How could they trust her? What was her game? What did she really want?

Rahab, however, must have completely astonished them by what she said to them next. "I know that the LORD has given this land to you," she said, "and that a great fear has fallen on us, so that all who live in this country are melting in fear because of you" (Joshua 2:9).

And how did this woman know about the God of Israel?

We have heard how the LORD dried up the water of the Red Sea for you when you came out of Egypt, and what you did to Sihon and Og, the two kings of the Amorites east of the Jordan, whom you completely destroyed. (v. 10)

Her next few words were even more surprising. Rahab confessed to a strong and genuine faith in the Lord God, and then she made a daring offer to the two spies:

When we heard of it, our hearts melted and everyone's courage failed because of you, for the LORD your God is God in heaven above and on the earth below. Now

then, please swear to me by the LORD that you will
show kindness to my family, because I have shown
kindness to you. Give me a sure sign that you will spare
the lives of my father and mother, my brothers and sisters, and all who belong to them, and that you will save
us from death. (vv. 11–13)

God had clearly opened the eyes of the people of Jericho
to His might and power. They were terrified of the Israelites
and their God. But God had done a greater work than this in
the heart of Rahab. This unusual woman did not know the
Ten Commandments; she could not have known the stories of
Abraham, Isaac, and Jacob. All Rahab had was the inner conviction of God's existence and His power. Yet, based on that,
she put her own life and the lives of her family at great risk,
entrusting them all to a God she barely knew. She hadn't been
to seminary; she hadn't even completed the most basic "Bible
study." She only knew that God *is*—and that she wanted to give
herself and all she had into His care. Many years later James
would commend this woman's remarkable, active faith.

In the same way, was not even Rahab the prostitute
considered righteous for what she did when she gave
lodging to the spies and sent them off in a different direction? As the body without the spirit is dead, so faith
without deeds is dead. (James 2:25–26)

RAHAB'S FAITH

Merchants and other travelers, bringing with them colorful stories of this strange God and His wandering people,
must have frequented Rahab's brothel. She must have listened
carefully to the amazing stories of waters parting and great victories won. She also must have wondered many times how that

ragtag mass of Israelites had become such a formidable fighting machine, destroying any enemy that stood in its way. These Israelites had only one God and anyone who challenged either them or their God lived to regret it.

Rahab not only listened to these stories but, surprisingly, was also moved to adopt a believing faith as she came to identify herself with the people of God. Perhaps she, too, felt like an outsider, a wanderer, among her own people. Perhaps her worship of false gods left her feeling empty, or perhaps she was so cynical by that time about human nature and religion in general that she had already abandoned the pantheism of her corrupt culture. But somehow Rahab concluded that God was different and that He had already given the land—her own homeland—to these Israelites. Her faith was incomplete, to be sure, but she wanted to follow this new God, and she risked everything she held dear to do it.

Just as God had planned, the Canaanites were terrified (Joshua 4:23–24), though they still refused to bow to God or honor Him, thus continuing to be "disobedient" (Hebrews 11:31). Their eventual destruction is a warning to all of us that it is possible to hear and know and even believe all the Scripture stories to be true, to be familiar with the many promises and warnings of God, and yet still reject Him. Hearing alone is not enough; it must be accompanied by faith (Romans 10:11–14).

Throughout all our years in ministry, we have worked with many people who have said they believe in Christ, and yet our hearts have ached as some of these same people chose to reject God's commands rather than to repent and walk in holiness. A pastor friend of ours listened carefully as Chuck described for him the scriptural warnings against adultery. Chuck pleaded with this man to consider the effect his infidelity would have on his children and his wife. Chuck challenged this pastor to fear God, the very God he claimed to love and serve. But a terrible spiritual darkness had walled him in, and the man answered coldly, "I know what the Scriptures teach. I've taught them to others. But I don't love my wife anymore. I'm leaving her and the children, and that's that. I need to be with this other woman."

This man thought he had saving faith and that it really didn't matter how he lived. Real, saving faith, however, is more than mere intellectual ascent to a creed or a thorough knowledge of the Bible. Genuine faith is borne out by how we live, the choices we make, as it was in the life of Rahab.

WHAT ABOUT HER LIES?

Rahab lied to protect the spies. Some of the ancient rabbis believed in a situational ethic when it came to the issue of lying. That is, these scholars believed there are times when it is not only necessary to lie for the greater good but quite right and proper to do so. Thus, they reasoned, Rahab must not be faulted for her lies to the king's soldiers.

The Old Testament, however, makes it clear that all lying is sin. It records the lies of Abraham, Jacob, and others and shows plainly the hard and grim consequences of those lies. Because Rahab's lie protected the two Israelites, we may be tempted to rationalize her behavior as the appropriate thing to do under difficult circumstances. Most people, in fact, when asked if they think Rahab was justified in her lying, will say she most certainly was. Under similar circumstances, most of us will admit that we'd probably do the same thing Rahab did (assuming, of course, that we even had the courage to hide those two spies in the first place!).

Nevertheless, two very important things should be kept in mind with regard to Rahab's lies. First, this woman's faith was incomplete, really only just beginning. She almost certainly wasn't aware of the specific commandment of God against bearing false witness (Exodus 20:16). Second, *nowhere* in Scripture is Rahab ever commended for her lies—only for her willingness to take her stand with the people of God. We believe that Rahab's lies, like all lies, were offensive to God since God is Truth. God did not need for Rahab to lie to protect the spies but, as He so often does, He used the faith—and even the sin—of this woman to accomplish His own good purposes.

Rahab was thus a liar and a sinner, and therefore not very different from any one of us. God is gracious, however; this woman's past sins and present failures did not disqualify her from joining God's family or serving Him.

GETTING "CLEANED UP" FIRST

The couple before us, Jerry and Rose, nervously began to explain why they had waited so long before meeting with us. Their stumbling words hinted at a story we had heard many times before. These two people needed to unload the "dirty laundry" they had been lugging around with them. Their past sins were forgiven, perhaps, but not forgotten. Like so many people who have come to Christ, this couple continued to be haunted by their own past behavior, always fearing that someone would find them out.

"Well, you see . . . you keep telling us that God forgives. But we are just so ashamed of our past. The people at our church are all so nice, but if they ever heard about what we did, well, they would never let us close to them. We want to get involved in the ministries at church, but we feel so . . . unworthy."

Too many people in the church today feel this way. Such people feel as though they have to get "all cleaned up" first, somehow completely erasing the past, or they will never experience God's forgiveness or be able to serve Him effectively. They don't understand that, by God's grace, we are already "made perfect" in His sight and that living in holiness is a life-time, ongoing process (Hebrews 10:11–18).

We shared with our friends the story of Rahab, assuring both of them that "every person sitting in our church on any given Sunday is a 'Rahab' of one kind or another. Their sins may be different from yours and perhaps the consequences of your sins are more serious. But we all start out as Rahab the prostitute. That is the meaning of *grace*. The love of Christ covers over the sordidness of our past and gives us a brand new life in Him."

If anyone understood that burden of guilt, it was the apostle Paul. He had personally directed the murders and vicious persecution of many of the first followers of Christ (Acts 8:1; 9:1–2), a sin that would remind him to the day of his death of the meaning of the word grace. It is probable that Paul was later able to minister to some of the same families of those he had wronged. Paul's subsequent letters to the early church teach us what God had taught him: that we, His sons and daughters, can trust God to redeem the pain of the past.

Consider some of the following remarks written by Paul regarding the whole issue of dealing with the past:

> Therefore, there is now no condemnation for those who are in Christ Jesus, because through Christ Jesus the law of the Spirit of life set me free from the law of sin and death. (Romans 8:1–2)

> For you did not receive a spirit that makes you a slave again to fear, but you received the Spirit of sonship. And by him we cry, "Abba, Father." The Spirit himself testifies with our spirit that we are God's children. Now if we are children, then we are heirs—heirs of God and co-heirs with Christ, if indeed we share in his sufferings in order that we may also share in his glory. (Romans 8:15–17)

For you were once darkness, but now you are light in
the Lord. Live as children of light. (Ephesians 5:8)

Perhaps most encouraging of all were Paul's words, written from prison, to the believers at Philippi:

Not that I have already obtained all this, or have already been made perfect, but I press on to take hold
of that for which Christ Jesus took hold of me. Brothers, I do not consider myself yet to have taken hold of
it. But one thing I do: *Forgetting what is behind and
straining toward what is ahead,* I press on toward the
goal to win the prize for which God has called me
heavenward in Christ Jesus. (Philippians 3:12–14 [em-
phasis added])

The more baggage you carry, the more difficult it will be
for you to strain toward what is ahead and press on toward the
goal, to win the prize Paul alludes to above. God promises us,
however, that "he is faithful and just . . . [and will] cleanse us
from all unrighteousness" (1 John 1:9 KJV)—in other words,
all that "baggage" we tend to haul around with us. We obvi-
ously cannot change what is past, but we can, by God's grace,
be made new, continuing to press on, continuing to look
ahead.

A New Identity, A New Life

In 1998, Honduras endured the full force of Hurricane
Mitch, a storm in which some ten thousand people perished.
One local newscaster commented as he saw the approaching
storm, "May God have mercy on our souls." Rahab must have
felt something akin to this as she and her neighbors anxiously
watched the Israelites move into position around the city of

Jericho. Rahab understood that the only safe place for her and her family was with the covenant community—the people of Israel. Thus, she had cut all ties with her past when she chose to identify herself with the people of God.

Rahab knew this act of faith put her family at great risk. What if she were wrong? The penalty for treason, in that day and age, was dire. Yet, God had given Rahab eyes to see what others could not see. Abraham confidently looked forward to the city whose architect was God. Rahab embraced in faith the same God of Israel, naming Him as her only hope for deliverance.

The spies had told her to hang from her window, the one built into the perimeter wall of the city, a scarlet rope by which they would climb down the wall and make their escape. They instructed her to hang that same cord from her window a few days later, when the Israelites returned to take the city. Her house would be identified by that scarlet cord and she and the people within her home would be spared.

THE SCARLET ROPE

The spies' instructions to Rahab are reminiscent of God's warning to the Israelites on the eve of the last and most terrible of the ten plagues. In that day, the angel of death had visited every home in Egypt that was not marked by the blood of a sacrificial lamb. As it had in Egypt, death was now about to strike the people of Jericho.

Rahab's family huddled together in her house for the following week, a seeming eternity, as the Israelites marched around the city walls every day, carrying the Ark of the Covenant, in utter, eerie silence. What pressure must have built up inside that city; what strained, nervous laughter there must have been among the people as they observed the Israelites' strange behavior! Meanwhile, the scarlet rope was hung from the window, marking Rahab's house and indicating that her hope was in the God of Israel. Finally, on the seventh day, the shouts of the Israelites joined the blare of the trumpets and the great walls of Jericho suddenly began to crack and crumble. Only one part of the massive city wall was left standing: the section where Rahab's house was, the bright red rope still hanging from her window.

The Israelites destroyed everything and everyone in the city. One can only imagine how it was for the members of Rahab's household as they hugged each other and listened to the blood-curdling screams just outside the house, chaos followed by an ominous, terrible silence.

Rahab had made a faith decision; she was no doubt afraid, but she had made her stand and she would not back down. When the Israelite soldiers suddenly burst through her doors, imagine Rahab's relief upon seeing the two spies she had sheltered. When she could catch her breath, she would have been grateful to God to be alive, for surely He had saved her and her family. It was a moment she would never forget as long as she lived, a turning point, a "scorch mark"—at once both terrible and wonderful—forever etched upon her soul.

PERSEVERANCE IN THE DARKNESS

Knowing the right thing to do is fairly easy. Doing the right thing is much harder. Not long ago God convicted a good friend of ours, Ellen, about her hateful behavior toward her husband. In spite of his claim to Christianity, he was unloving, impatient, and sometimes even cruel to her and to their children. She had begun screaming right back at him and using her own forms of mental and emotional attack to "get him back."

Ellen realized this was wrong, and so she asked an older, wiser woman in the church to teach her how to love her husband in a way that would honor God. In their very first meeting, the two women agreed their discussions would focus on the wife's behavior, not her husband's sins. In each session Ellen renewed her commitment to respond to her husband in a godly manner. The older woman warned Ellen that obedience would require faith in God's love and presence and that the power to obey would come through God's enabling grace.

Ellen soon learned that making a commitment to love her husband was far easier than actually *loving* her husband, day in and day out. Sometimes loving him meant she had to suffer in silence. At other times, loving him meant praying and then speaking quietly, in courage and strength, when she needed to confront him about his ungodly behavior. Ellen learned that her life would probably get much tougher for a while, but that by faith she must stay the course of obedience and trust God to supply grace for each moment.

This young woman wanted to honor God in her marriage, but betrayal, pettiness, and downright hatred had turned their home into a kind of prison, one in which she, her husband, and her children were all trapped. The only way to break down those walls was faithful obedience on her part. While still not sure how "the story will end," Ellen has committed herself to God, His people, and His Word, trusting Him to rescue her family from a situation that seems—to everyone else—all but hopeless. God will not fail her.

STARTING ALL OVER AGAIN

Rahab's story of coming to faith is a familiar one. She was initially drawn to the Lord by learning of His mighty and transforming work in the lives of His people. She was drawn to them and came to know Him through them.

Today, people just like Rahab are still drawn to believers who are experiencing God's power in their daily lives. Rahab came from a clearly sinful and immoral past. Such people may seem strange and "out of place" to the traditional church-goers. Those coming from unchurched backgrounds may not be familiar with Bible stories or know how to build Christian relationships. They may also bring with them their own "baggage"—shabby reputations or the consequences of past or present sin. As He did with Rahab, God will move many of these people from mere curiosity to genuine, saving faith. Finally, like Rahab, they will bring others into the family of God as well. The lesson for the church today, as when the book of Hebrews was written, is clear. We must welcome such people into the church with open arms.

Rahab had much to learn about this God to whom she had committed her life. How would the women of Israel respond to this tainted woman? It is interesting to see that the Israelites didn't seem to know quite what to do with their Canaanite heroine. "They brought out her entire family and put them in a place outside the camp of Israel" (Joshua 6:23). We suspect that at least one woman in the Israelite camp, perhaps the mother of one of the two spies, accepted Rahab as a sister. We imagine this woman insisting that Rahab, who had so bravely welcomed and protected those two men, should not remain "outside the camp" but should become a full member of the covenant community.

Earlier in the letter to the Hebrews, the writer had exhorted his readers to seek solace and encouragement within the community of believers (Hebrews 10:25) as they persevered together. Rahab is a dramatic example of God's desire for the local church to be a safe place for His children. Indeed, Jesus tells us that the way we treat the "stranger" reveals the way we feel about Him (Matthew 25:35–40). Rahab's act of faith identified her with the people of God; she knew that her only hope lay in journeying with them, since she had literally lost all her possessions and would have to begin life over again. Is our church a safe haven for Rahab? Is yours? What risks are we willing to take to make our churches safe places for people who want, by God's grace, to start over, to build a new life?

Among God's people Rahab found a safe place in which to learn the ways of Yahweh and His people. Rahab was given a second chance; she was able to put her past behind her and enjoy a whole new life. She was eventually brought into the family of no less a person than Nahshon, head of the entire clan of Judah (Numbers 1:7, 16; 7:10–17; Matthew 1:4–5). His son, Salmon, would eventually marry Rahab; their son Boaz, in turn, would marry another "outsider," the incomparable Ruth. Their family line would continue unbroken on to King David and, eventually, to Christ Jesus Himself. What a marvelous demonstration of the transforming grace of God! We watch with awe the rise of a woman who overcame, by faith, a sordid and ugly past to become royalty, a forebear of the very King of Kings.

Certainly there are consequences for our behavior. There may be certain types of service for which we are not qualified because of past sin. But, instead of focusing on what we cannot do, we must invest every part of our lives in what we can do in service to our God.

The story at the beginning of this chapter is a dramatic example of how a lonely, broken woman was transformed into a daughter of the King. Today, Hilda Martin is absolutely radiant in her faith and she does not hide that radiance. However, she is also wary of sharing the details of her past. Hilda does so only after much prayer. She is not afraid of the judgment of others because she is confident that the blood of Christ has cleansed her from all sin and the abuse of others. But she wants to be sure her listeners focus only on the glory of Christ, not the details of her own past. God's overpowering love has left her no choice but to "declare the praises of him who called [her] out of darkness into his wonderful light" (1 Peter 2:9–11). She now ministers to women who feel forsaken and thrown away, reminding them daily of God's unconditional love for them.

Have you considered that even your past must be offered back to God to advance His kingdom? Is there failure and great sin in your past? Offer God your experiences. In grace, He may give you an opportunity to help someone else find her way out of a similar situation or protect her from making the same mistakes. Be very careful, however, to use your experiences for God's glory and not your own. Seek wise counsel about what in your past is appropriate to share, with whom, and for what purpose. The church today errs whenever we glorify a sordid past or encourage people who are immature in their faith to share publicly every detail about their lives. Such candor can sometimes harm innocent parties or make reconciliation with others more difficult. Only a humble testimony will exalt the Lord and draw others to Christ. The focus of our words must always be only on "what is helpful for building others up according to their needs, that it may benefit those who listen" (Ephesians 4:29).

The past can be a burden we carry with us all our days, or it can provide a basis for ministry, giving us a special and unique perspective on the great grace and love of God. We can spend our lives always looking backward with either longing or regret and, like Lot's wife, be destroyed in the process, burdened forever by things we can never undo or transfixed by a nostalgia about the "good old days" that is so paralyzing we are rendered useless. By His grace, God allows us to slip free of the icy, deadly grip of all that is past, all those things that we cannot change, thus allowing us to become new, to start over, to move on—indeed, to take to the very air on eagles' wings.

Do you not know?
Have you not heard?
The LORD is the everlasting God,
the Creator of the ends of the earth.
He will not grow tired or weary,
and his understanding no one can fathom.

He gives strength to the weary
    and increases the power of the weak.
Even youths grow tired and weary,
    and young men stumble and fall;
but those who hope in the LORD
    will renew their strength.
They will soar on wings like eagles;
    they will run and not grow weary,
    they will walk and not be faint. (Isaiah 40:28–31)

DIGGING DEEPER

Day One

- Read Joshua 2, Joshua 6:1–27, and Matthew 1:5. Describe Rahab's journey from misery to experiencing God's mercy and from there into ministry. How does her story give you hope?

Day Two

- Read Romans 8:1–2, 15–17; Ephesians 5:8; and Philippians 3:12–14.
- Ask God to show you areas of your life where you have refused to believe He has really forgiven you, and allow Him to show you the truth of these verses to remind you that as His child, you are clean before Him.

Day Three

- Rahab realized that her only way of escape was with the people of God. God expects sinners redeemed by His Son to find safety within the covenant community (the local church). Would a "Rahab" find safety, acceptance, and help in your congregation? Why or why not?
- What kind of ministries identify your church as a safe place for broken people like Rahab?

Day Four

- As a Christian, you are also the church (1 Corinthians 3:16; 6:19–20). Would a Rahab find safety and acceptance with you? Why or why not?

- Read Galatians 6:5. Identify one person in your life to whom you find it difficult to extend God's mercy. Seek forgiveness for your lack of love and ask God to show you one specific way you can express your faith by showing His love to that person.

Day Five

- Read Genesis 15:6 and Romans 4:1–5. Why did God call Abraham "righteous"?

- Read James 1:22–27 and 2:20–26. What is the evidence of true faith? How do these passages teach us that genuine faith does not end with salvation but instead equips us to be a blessing to others?

- What should be our motivation when we extend God's mercy by meeting practical needs?

Day Six

- Spend time praying about what you have learned from Rahab. Specifically ask God to give you a heart that intentionally extends His mercy to people you might once have considered unlovely and unreachable.

Chapter 11

CIRCUMCISED HEARTS—
FIVE MEN OF FAITH

FAITH PRINCIPLE #11

BIBLICAL FAITH, CHARACTERIZED BY GENUINE REPENTANCE,
GIVES ORDINARY PEOPLE EXTRAORDINARY POWER.

And what more shall I say? I do not have time to tell about Gideon, Barak,

Samson, Jephthah, David, Samuel and the prophets, who through faith

conquered kingdoms, administered justice, and gained what was promised;

who shut the mouths of lions, quenched the fury of the flames, and escaped

the edge of the sword; whose weakness was turned to strength; and who

became powerful in battle and routed foreign armies. (*Hebrews 11:32–34*

[see also Judges 4–8, 10–16; 1 Samuel 16–31; 2 Samuel])

THE HEALING OF GENUINE REPENTANCE—
TOM GRAY

My eyes slowly adjusted to the darkness inside the plush adult club. I had driven fifty miles out of state to hide my shameful deed. I was acting as if I were not married, not a father, not a Christian, not a pastor—but I was all of those things. Every time I entered a dark and evil place like this one, I was sick with remorse and guilt, but at the same time the sinful desires of my own heart had me in a kind of death grip. I could not break free; I just could not. For thirty-five years, I remained deeply involved with various forms of pornography.

My family, of course, knew nothing about my life-dominating love of pornography. I had convinced myself I could remain close to God, my wife, my children, and other Christians, all without ever letting go of my secret sin. What a fool I was! Those living in my house began to realize that something was wrong, that my outward, spiritual façade was nothing but a sham. Finally, hesitantly, my son and daughter asked me to spend a weekend alone with God to discover why I was so half-hearted toward Him—and them. I knew their suggestion made sense, offering a possible lifeline out of the muck and garbage of my secret life.

I realized during that weekend that I would never overcome this sin by myself, in my own strength. I also knew that I was going to have to confess my sin to the people I had betrayed, especially my wife. Layer by ugly layer, God showed me the utter deceitfulness of my own wicked heart. I had robbed God of the glory due His name. I had robbed my family of the godly husband and father they deserved. And I had robbed myself of my own identity, squandering my life, my strength, and the sense of fulfillment that comes with serving God faithfully. Until that weekend, I had never been entirely open and repentant before God without dodging the real issue or making excuses for my sin, as though I could somehow "hide" from Him what I was doing.

My sin was a monstrous stumbling block in our marriage. Before I repented, I could not have real intimacy with my wife because I was so consumed by my own sin. Instead of loving her with the love of Christ (Ephesians 5:25), I condemned and criticized and crushed her spirit. I couldn't really see her, nor would I let her get near enough to see the real me. I effectively kept her *out*, successfully fighting off every attempt she made to "connect" with me.

When I returned from my life-changing weekend, I was forced to confront my deepest fear that she would leave me after I confessed to her. Only God's gracious mercy could prepare her to hear the terrible things I had to tell her. Only in His strength could we ever recover what my involvement in pornography had stolen from us.

Pornography is not a victimless act. It is an affair of the mind that compromises and damages everyone involved; it also deadens and destroys the God-created, God-honoring desire we should have to love other people more than ourselves. God, in His mercy, has broken its stranglehold on my soul, but now the work of restoring relationships with those I love looms before me.

Ephesians 4:17–5:21 spells out God's specific strategy for building homes that will display His redeeming love to fellow broken believers. God mercifully gave my wife the willingness to forgive me and to welcome me back into her life as her best friend. Every day I am learning how to put off the ravages of a thirty-five–year pattern of sin and put on instead the strength and righteousness of God. I will never be the same as a result of God's purifying work through His Word.

I have learned through painful and difficult personal experience that sin is life-destroying and that there is only one way to break its hold: through sincere repentance. Biblically defined, such repentance involves change that puts off the sin habit and puts on holiness (Colossians 3). It's been a difficult, pain-filled road for me and my family but one that, finally, has led from darkness to light, back into the joy of being in His presence.

I have also learned, however, that when Jesus sets you free, "you will be free indeed" (John 8:36).

Tom Gray (a pseudonym)

LEARNING FROM THE PAST

In the days after Joshua, God's people knew that they had been set apart by Him to serve as a model nation under His sovereign rule. In our own faith journeys, we will face the same temptations and spiritual choices that Israel faced, and we may well make some of the same mistakes they did when confronted by our enemies—or *the* Enemy, Satan—or any of the other challenges we face.

There is benefit, therefore, in reviewing the lives and choices of some of the judges, these chosen leaders of Israel. This is clearly what the author of Hebrews had in mind in recalling such figures as Gideon and Samson, as well as King David. In this chapter we will not only study the lives of some of these men, we will learn from them.

The author of Hebrews first takes us on a whirlwind tour through one of the darkest eras in Old Testament history—the period of the judges. In their struggle to "get along in this world," the tribes of Israel again and again lapsed into apostasy and idol worship. In response, God used their enemies as agents of discipline to drive His people to call upon Him for mercy and restoration. Hearing their cries for help, God in grace raised up the judges, great men of His choosing, to lead the Israelites to spiritual renewal and revival. Four of these judges are mentioned in Hebrews 11: Gideon, Barak, Samson, and Jephthah.[1] Perhaps no other Old Testament book better captures the special relationship between faith and repentance than the book of Judges.

---

[1] These same four men, interestingly enough, are also mentioned by the prophet Samuel in a speech he gave to the Israelites after they chose Saul to be their king (1 Samuel 12:11).

THE DECLINE AND FALL

One significant verse from the book of Deuteronomy characterizes God's primary desire for His people and provides a thematic basis for the judges epoch:

> The LORD your God will circumcise your hearts and the hearts of your descendants, so that you may love him with all your heart and with all your soul, and live. (Deuteronomy 30:6)

After the battle of Jericho, the Israelites were poised to possess the Promised Land and face their remaining enemies with God's promise and Joshua's military strategy still ringing in their ears (Joshua 23–24). Following Joshua's death, God commissioned Judah, the tribe from which the Messiah would come, to lead the army (Judges 1:1–2).

The stage was set for a great spiritual and military victory. The Israelites settled in Gilgal where they worshiped God. But instead of taking what God had given them, they decided they were content with the status quo. The people were tired of fighting and had enough land and money, and so they broke off claiming the land in order to "take it easy" for a while, leaving the job of conquest half done. Thus, they failed to seize all of the Promised Land as God had directed, especially in the lowlands where the strongholds of the enemy were still significant.

Canaan was heavily populated with the Edomite descendants of Esau, as well as Phoenicians, Babylonians, and Assyrians. All of these people would eventually grow into such powerful enemies of Israel that their names became synonymous with evil. The people of Israel had wrongly concluded that these Canaanites were not so bad as long they stayed in their valleys. But the close proximity of these unbelieving peoples and their pagan culture continued to be a problem for the people of Israel, appealing to their basest lusts and clouding their spiritual vision. At first they only tolerated the worship of Baal, a lewd nature religion. But eventually they began to blend the worship of Yahweh with their neighbors' worship of many gods and goddesses, including Asherah, the wife of Baal, and others—in direct defiance of the First Commandment. The covenant community of Israel became corrupt and compromised, bringing dishonor upon the Lord God.

> After that whole generation had been gathered to their fathers, another generation grew up, who knew neither the LORD nor what he had done for Israel. Then the Israelites did evil in the eyes of the LORD and served the Baals. They forsook the LORD, the God of their fathers, who had brought them out of Egypt. They followed and worshiped various gods of the people around them.
>
> They provoked the LORD to anger because they forsook him and served Baal and the Ashtoreths. In his anger against Israel the LORD handed them over to raiders who plundered them. He sold them to their enemies all around, whom they were no longer able to resist. Whenever Israel went out to fight, the hand of the LORD was against them to defeat them, just as he had sworn to them. They were in great distress. (Judges 2:10–15)

THE RESCUE

In response to the cries of His people God would raise up, over the next 350 years, twelve judges (thirteen including Deborah, a prophetess, who also judged Israel [Judges 4:4]) to rescue His people as they waded through numerous cycles of sinful behavior: disobedience, followed by judgment, followed by repentance, followed by God's rescue, followed by still more disobedience and apostasy (Judges 2:16–19).

These judges acted as counselors and at times as military leaders. They were the channels of God's grace; their task was to call the people of God to "circumcise their hearts"—that is, to forsake their sins in genuine repentance, turn to God in faith, and recommit their lives to Him—and pray for revival. Over the first 253 years of the period of the judges, God sent different oppressors into the land to act as rods of discipline. He also sent five different judges (six including Deborah), heroes of the faith who would lead Israel into true repentance and restoration that was followed by years of peace. But their commitment to holiness was so fragile that seven of the twelve judges actually came and went during the final ninety-seven years of this period, as the moral bondage of the people intensified.

TRUE REPENTANCE

It is *by faith* that we confess and turn from our sins, *believing* that God "is faithful and just and will forgive us our sins and purify us from all unrighteousness" (1 John 1:9). Faith and repentance cannot be separated from one another. The early believers, in hearing of the judges, were reminded that only a circumcised heart, one created by an intricate interaction between an individual's broken, contrite heart and a marvelous, heart-renewing God—could experience true intimacy with Him. Such repentance, joined inseparably to genuine faith, would mark these Hebrew Christians as true sons and daughters of God.

Four of the judges—Gideon, Barak, Jephthah, and Samson—are listed as examples of great faith in Hebrews 11. Why were these four men, all greatly flawed, selected for this great honor? Uncertain Gideon, weak Barak, foolhardy Jephthah, impetuous Samson—this unlikely team seems to show us instead the entire range of human weakness, sin, and frailty. How did such men demonstrate repentance, that their hearts had truly been circumcised by God?

A MAN WITH EMPTY HANDS—GIDEON

Gideon is the first of the judges mentioned by the author of Hebrews. How does this man's life and leadership illustrate a circumcised heart, a heart characterized by faith and repentance?

In Gideon's day, God used the Midianites, the Amalekites, the Philistines, and other Eastern peoples to discipline Israel. These marauding forces had devastated the crops and sacked towns and cities, leaving the Israelites starving and destitute. In response to their earnest prayers for help, God sent a prophet who admonished the people to repent and turn away from the false gods they had been worshiping (Judges 6:7–10). God also sent an angel to Gideon, a simple and fearful farmer. The angel told Gideon he was God's choice to lead His people against the Midianites. Gideon's terrified responses to God's call might leave us wondering how this man could rescue anyone (Judges 6:13, 27; 7:10).

God explained to Gideon that the coming battle would be fought as none other so that the Lord alone would be credited for the victory. He gave specific instructions that eventually reduced Gideon's army to a mere three hundred men, warriors who would have to engage an army of thousands of Midianites. Since the enemy numbered some 135,000 men, this meant that each of the three hundred Jewish warriors was outnumbered 450 to one!

How was Gideon able to face such odds? Through a series of encounters with God, Gideon's character was shaped, instructed, and humbled. The Lord met him in his need, strengthened him in his doubts, and made it clear to Gideon that the victory would belong solely to God. In other words, Gideon's heart was permanently marked—circumcised—as a result of his encounters with his Lord. He was forced to set aside his own ideas and his own pride, and confess his complete inability to save himself or lead the people. He came into God's service, as it were, with "empty hands": no excuses, no blame shifting, no self-assured swagger. And because of that, God was able to use him.

We live in a world where sinful behavior is often excused so as to remove any personal responsibility. We've all heard such excuses (some of us have even used them).

- "I was born this way."
- "It's only natural."
- "Everybody does it."

Any confession of sin that admits to wrongdoing but then quickly excuses that sin by blaming it on some other person or life circumstance is false repentance, a total sham. True repentance requires coming to God with empty hands. We must set aside all such excuses before God; we must grieve, mourn, and wail over our sins, in faith recognizing that God blesses those who mourn and promises comfort (James 4:6–10).

Pastors and congregations sometimes ask Chuck to help them resolve internal church conflicts. The first step toward resolution of these problems and effecting reconciliation is a willingness to put aside personal agendas for the greater purpose of building up the kingdom of God. Sadly, men and women often make being "right"—and making sure everybody knows it—the first order of business. Proud, defiant words, sometimes laden with scriptural proof texts, are hurled back and forth like grenades. Ignoring the wise and godly counsel of James, such churches often split, the people are scattered, and reputations go down in flames. How such behavior must grieve the Lord!

James advises us to first humble ourselves. Only then will He "lift you up." Thus, a circumcised heart, one like Gideon's, is characterized by *humility*.

A MAN OF THE WORD—BARAK

If we come to God with nothing of our own to bring, as Gideon did, except our lives and hearts, what then will God put in our outstretched, empty hands? He will give us something "living and active," something mightier and far more effective than anything we might slap together in our own strength; He gives us His Word (Hebrews 4:12). People who are genuinely repentant submit to God's Word. The Bible is where we learn the godly behaviors that must replace our patterns of sinfulness.

Barak, the second Judge of Hebrews 11, was unwilling to take on the evil enemy leaders of his day, the Canaanite king Jabin and his mighty general Sisera. Instead Barak insisted that the prophetess Deborah be at his side to guide and lead him in battle.

Deborah agreed, answering God's call (and Barak's pleas) and leading the people in repentance and faith against King Jabin and his minions. It was rare, if not unheard of, for a woman to lead in battle in that culture; any man who relied upon or was defeated by a woman endured great humiliation (Judges 9:54). Why, then, is Barak commended for his faith in Hebrews 11? Barak, according to the traditional view, is considered dishonorable because of his refusal to go into battle without Deborah.

> Barak said to her, "If you go with me, I will go; but if you don't go with me, I won't go."

"Very well," Deborah said, "I will go with you. But because of the way you are going about this, the honor will not be yours, for the LORD will hand Sisera over to a woman." So Deborah went with Barak to Kedesh. (Judges 4:8–9)

Clearly, this passage shows us that Barak would not receive the glory for the impending military victory, and he didn't. But his inclusion in this remarkable listing of faith heroes in Hebrews led us to look at Barak's life more closely. Deborah was a prophetess (Judges 4:4), and Barak clearly recognized her as such. He believed she spoke God's truth, and he obeyed God's commands given through Deborah (vv. 6, 10, 14). While the Israelites had ignored or abandoned God's Word, this is a sin Barak was determined not to repeat.

Barak thus regarded Deborah as someone who proclaimed God's Word truly, as she most surely was. By insisting on her presence with him, Barak is making it clear that he *would not move forward* unless accompanied by the Word of God, in the person of Deborah. Barak's obedience did not depend on public affirmation, nor did he fear the snickers and joking that would inevitably follow his decision to defer to a woman. It would seem that Barak cared more about gaining the victory than about his own personal honor and glory, his own "male ego." He was willing to sacrifice the laurels of fame and glory for the greater good. This is why Barak is honored in the book of Hebrews.

Elsewhere in Hebrews, the writer places tremendous emphasis on the astonishing, unique power of God's Word.

For the word of God is living and active. Sharper than any double-edged sword, it penetrates even to dividing soul and spirit, joints and marrow; it judges the thoughts and attitudes of the heart. (Hebrews 4:12)

Barak set aside his reputation to adhere to and uphold God's Word; it mattered more to him than the praise of men and women, and it gave him a power far beyond that of any weapon or army. And so it is that a circumcised heart, one like Barak's, is characterized by *trusting and upholding God's Word.*

A MAN BLOODIED AND BOWED—SAMSON

At the turn of the century, the well-known agnostic and writer W. E. Henley wrote his now famous poem *Invictus.* The first two stanzas describe well the kinds of traits we so admire in our culture:

> Out of the night that covers me,
> Black as the pit from pole to pole,
> I thank whatever gods may be,
> For my unconquerable soul.

> In the fell clutch of circumstance,
> I have winced but not cried aloud.
> Under the bludgeonings of chance,
> My head is bloodied but unbowed.

Sadly, the "unconquerable soul" Henley refers to here is one that stands in opposition to God and all other comers. Those of us who choose to remain aloof, unconquered, will never know God, for the key to knowing Him lies in just the opposite direction. As David said, what God seeks from us is "a broken spirit; a broken and contrite heart, O God, you will not despise" (Psalm 51:17).

Samson, the next man listed in this great faith chapter of Hebrews, a long-haired, muscle-bound, charismatic leader and judge of Israel, started out confident, impulsive, and proud. His life, unfortunately, reflected too well the moral degradation and compromise of his nation. Instead of living a life of holiness, he repeatedly compromised his faith and allowed his "animal instincts" to get the best of him. Finally, beguiled and betrayed by the vixen Delilah, he fell hard—a victim of his own lust and foolishness. Captured, blinded, and imprisoned, Samson's sin led him to slavery and humiliation.

Samson was chained to a grinding wheel by his enemies, the Philistines, to live out the remainder of his days. One is reminded of David's lament for King Saul: "How the mighty have fallen!" (2 Samuel 1:19). Through this pain and suffering, Samson's heart was purged of all its former pride and self-sufficiency. Samson's repentance, as well as his life, was nearing completion. When given one last opportunity to again display his God-given strength, he prayed, humbly and contritely, for God's help, even though what he planned would cost him his own life. In the huge pagan temple of the god Dagon, amid the taunts and jeers of the thousands of Philistines who had gathered to mock and belittle him, Samson "performed" for them. The big man confidently and prayerfully placed his large hands on the support pillars of the temple (Judges 16:28) and brought that entire great structure down upon them all.

Our God is an awesome God. He reigns over heaven and earth. He desires that we see our sins in the light of the cross—and hate them for their ugliness. But He also desires that we bow in our failures, recognizing that apart from Him we can do nothing.

Samson ended his life with a broken, a contrite heart. He was, at the end of his days, a man both bloodied *and* bowed. Through his pain and his terrible suffering, he came back into close fellowship with his God; his heart was marked and renewed, made truly alive for perhaps the first time in his life. A circumcised heart, one like Samson's, is always characterized by *brokenness*.

A MAN WHO DIDN'T BELONG—JEPHTHAH

Jephthah's father was Gilead, a very prestigious man, but his mother was a prostitute. And so Jephthah's half-brothers considered him, the bastard son, a disgrace and an embarrassment. Because of this he had no inheritance, was ostracized from society, and was cut off from his family. He was alone except for God. Jephthah ended up leading an armed band of misfits who acted as an unofficial police force. For a price, he became a sort of Robin Hood. He did not seem to fit into any prescribed role for doing God's work. Nevertheless, Jephthah, a born survivor, would eventually use what he had learned in his checkered past to lead the nation of Israel into genuine revival.

God has a way of taking those who appear worthless and somehow transforming them into instruments of hope. Jephthah knew rejection (Judges 11:1–3). Like Joseph, who also was rejected by his brothers, Jephthah found himself isolated and alone, just the sort of situation in which we are most likely to turn to God for help.

When Israel faced the wrath of the Ammonites, the people recruited Jephthah to lead them into battle (vv. 4–11). The king of the Ammonites had gathered a great army against Israel, demanding the return of lands he claimed were his. Jephthah sent a message to the pagan Ammonite king, reminding him of God's history of faithfully protecting His people. Jephthah then challenged the king to a battle between the armies of his god and those of the God of Israel. In doing so, Jephthah was relying upon God's great record of faithfulness to His covenant people, and God gave him great victories.

The actions of Jephthah and the faith he demonstrated illustrate yet another mark of a circumcised heart: getting beyond a hurtful past. We are often the victims of the sinful behavior of others. Sometimes we are wrongly accused, injured, or harmed through no fault of our own. As a result, we may suffer severely. At other times we may suffer as a result of our own sinful failures. Regardless of the cause, the result of genuine repentance is still the same. God restores the years the locust have eaten (Joel 2:25–26). It is just too easy to play the victim—always blaming others, or the environment, or something in the past, or society in general—instead of taking responsibility for our own lives, our own spiritual condition.

There is nothing we can do to change our past. We can seek to understand it, of course, and grow from our mistakes. But we certainly cannot change it. Anyone who genuinely repents in faith, however, will be able to use the lessons learned through past suffering for their own good and for the good of the church. God's grace knows no social or religious barriers or stigma. Faith that produces genuine repentance will give us the courage to face—and overcome—the trials and suffering of our past.

The Israelites of Jephthah's day, in dire straits, had endured the terrible crushing weight of God's discipline. When they cried out to God, He responded, "Go and cry out to the gods you have chosen. Let them save you when you are in trouble!" (Judges 10:14). This may sound surprisingly harsh. What follows, however, gives us tremendous insight into what the heart of God is really after:

> But the Israelites said to the LORD, "We have sinned. Do with us whatever you think best, but please rescue us now." Then they got rid of the foreign gods among them and served the LORD. And he could bear Israel's misery no longer. (vv. 15–16)

These people accepted full responsibility for their sin. "We have sinned," they confessed, and then they did just what God had asked. They got rid of the foreign gods and served the Lord. In doing this, they also accepted the full consequences of their sin and surrendered to God's sovereign will: "Do with us whatever you think best, but please rescue us now."

Jephthah, the outsider, the man who didn't belong with his family or his people, is listed among the exemplary men and women of Hebrews 11 because he followed the Lord faithfully, despite the hardships of his youth. He could have spent his life railing at God and wailing to anyone who would listen about his hard life, but he didn't. He simply obeyed. God, in turn, was able to accomplish great things though him. Jephthah led a nation into genuine repentance when he could have easily wallowed in self-pity, anger, or bitterness.

A circumcised heart then, one like Jephthah's, is characterized by *overcoming past circumstances.*

A MAN LIKE US—DAVID

The first four men we have discussed were judges of Israel. The book of Judges focuses on repentance, both that of a nation and that of the men and women who led it. The next figure in the Hebrews Hall of Faith is not a judge, but a king of Israel.

It is the human condition that our hearts, even when aware of the truth about God, are still prone to wander. In Judges the lives of the leaders and of the nation itself were characterized by repeating cycles of faithful obedience, followed by spiritual malaise, then disobedience, and compromise. This, in turn, was inevitably followed by God's discipline and judgment, which in turn led men and women to repent, crying out to God for relief and rescue.

Even as the book of Judges describes this ongoing process in the history of a nation and its leaders, the life of David shows us this same cycle in the context of a single human heart. David's high and low points are striking because they are so extreme; he was a man who succumbed to great sin—including the murder of Uriah and adultery with Bathsheba—and yet God in His mercy bore David up. How was a man whose sin was so great, whose personal life was such a mess, to become perhaps the single most remarkable—and yet most human—of all Old Testament figures?

Caught dead to rights in the midst of his terrible sin, David was completely undone, left without excuse. He prostrated himself before God and admitted plainly his own sin. The extraordinary Psalm 51 was David's prayer of confession. It gives us insight into why this man, guilty of such evil, could still be called "a man after God's own heart." Here is a man ready to accept full responsibility for what he had done, recommitting himself to obedience, and pleading for renewed intimacy with God—an intimacy he knew he did not deserve.

> Have mercy on me, O God,
>   according to your unfailing love. . . .
> Wash away all my iniquity
>   and cleanse me from my sin.
> For I know my transgressions,
>   and my sin is always before me.
> Against you, you only, have I sinned
>   and done what is evil in your sight,
> so that you are proved right when you speak
>   and justified when you judge. . . .
> Create in me a pure heart, O God,
>   and renew a steadfast spirit within me.
> Do not cast me from your presence
>   or take your Holy Spirit from me.
> Restore to me the joy of your salvation
>   and grant me a willing spirit, to sustain me. (vv. 1a,
>   2–4, 10–12)

Broken and contrite, King David renewed his commitment to his sovereign King and Lord. David's intimacy with

God had been nurtured in the lonely Bethlehem fields as he tended the sheep of his father, as he opened his young heart to the majesty and wonder of his Lord.

Though David sinned severely as an adult and a leader, his kingship was a model of righteous rule for other kings. Under David's reign, God fulfilled His promise to Abraham and expanded the borders of the Israelite nation from Egypt to the Euphrates River. By God's strength and presence Israel defeated her enemies and continued to prosper. At the end of his life David, like his forefathers, Abraham, Isaac, and Jacob, had absolute confidence in God's covenantal promises.

David's many psalms reflect the longings of his heart. He was a man who sinned, yes, but he was also a man who knew the destructive power of sin. What David most longed for was to know the joy of God's presence, and he knew that his sin isolated him from that joy. To be separated from God was more than he could endure.

> Man is a mere phantom as he goes to and fro:
>   He bustles about, but only in vain;
>   he heaps up wealth, not knowing who will get it.
> But now, Lord, what do I look for?
>   My hope is in you. (Psalm 39:6–7)

David's sins were great, but his God was far greater. In the end, David counted fellowship with God as his greatest privilege. A circumcised heart, one like David's, is thus characterized by *a longing to be in God's presence.*

BIND MY WANDERING HEART

In this chapter, we have met five outstanding, though struggling, believers. Each of them led the nation of Israel into a period of national repentance and revival. They each demonstrated the characteristics of a circumcised heart, one etched by genuine faith and repentance, hearts sealed forever as belonging to God. As we have seen, such a heart is characterized by:

- humility,
- trusting God's Word,
- brokenness,
- overcoming past circumstances, and
- a longing to be in God's presence.

We cannot simply avoid the consequences of our sins. Real repentance is often painful because we must acknowledge before God how we have dishonored Him and hurt those around us. But God's "grace upon grace" heals our hearts, and His forgiveness restores us. That grace, accessed only through the channels of a genuine repentance rooted in faith, transforms us, giving hope, strength, and joy not only to us but to others through us.

These characteristics of a circumcised heart are evident in Tom Gray's story (see the beginning of this chapter), a story that is not yet ended, for it will be a process of healing that will take years. Tom's wife wrote to us describing her own reaction to his confession and the start of their spiritual recovery together:

> I see Tom cry often. He now realizes he poured filth all over himself and kept God's Glory from shining through. He sees that he threw away blessings by the bucketful hoping to snatch one moment of cheapened pleasure. All the masculine energy of Christ that should have blessed his wife, children, family, church, and community had been suppressed for years.
>
> Tom values me now like he never did before. I always felt excommunicated from his prayers. Yet, as his

repentance grows, my forgiveness deepens. And, as he feels that, his repentance also deepens.

My husband was bleeding spiritually. We were two devastated bodies on the battlefield who couldn't help ourselves without the body of Christ. I am amazed at God's goodness in how He brought specific events and people to perfectly promote healing. I saw in myself the conflicting desires both to embrace Tom in sorrow for his loneliness and to hurt him for so cheapening me and his own family. That set up an enormous battle within me. I had to choose between loving Tom and embracing the hurt, or running from it like crazy with the energy of hatred and fear of blame. I was hurting so badly, I didn't even care to do what I knew was right. The devastating sight of my own struggle made me face my own shame, turn to God, find His grace, and finally "put on" what He required of me at that moment: to love Tom no matter what.

What I needed was more of Christ, and I took my anger and hurt to Him, sometimes with fasting and prayers lasting all night long. My anger was just *so deep*. In His calm presence He settled my rage and gave me more grace to forgive Tom. I'm grateful to finally see Tom's real heart. A wife longs for that kind of intimacy. We are struggling to experience the kind of marriage God desires for us. Digging through the garbage is excruciatingly painful and sometimes feels endless. But His grace is deep, and I am slowly learning how to trust Tom again.

Like Gideon, Tom came to Christ humbly, with empty hands. Like Barak, he submitted his life and marriage to the Word of God. His experiences and shame have beaten him down and left him broken, like Samson. Tom is recovering from the past, like Jephthah, and looking to the future—for Tom, like David, desires more than anything else to be back in close fellowship with his Lord. He continues to claim the promises of God to redeem the past and teach him how to cherish, protect, and provide for his wife. Through his genuine repentance, the healing process has begun.

These men all stumbled and fell, as we do. They wandered, they sinned; they succumbed to rage, to foolishness, to hate. But their "weakness was turned to strength" (Hebrews 11:34). How? For them as for us, the way is open, the way of repentance. It is a path awash with our tears, perhaps, but it is the way home, the *only* way home, the only way back into the loving arms of a Father who forgives.

> O to grace how great a debtor
> daily I'm constrained to be.
> Let that grace now, like a fetter,
> bind my wand'ring heart to thee.
> Prone to wander—Lord, I feel it—
> prone to leave the God I love.
> Here's my heart, O take and seal it,
> seal it for thy courts above.
> *Robert Robinson (1758)*

DIGGING DEEPER

Day One

♦ Read Joshua 2 and note how God used the enemies of Israel as agents of discipline in order to drive His people to call upon Him.

♦ Read Hebrews 12:3–11. What is the difference between discipline and punishment?

Day Two

♦ Read Hebrews 12:3–11 and Psalm 119:67, 68, 71, and 75. Whom does God discipline? How do these verses

help you see God's response to your sin as evidence of
His love for you?

Day Three

♦ Review the five characteristics of genuine repentance
discussed in this chapter.

♦ Examine your most recent response to conviction of a
specific sin in your life in terms of these five characteristics. If you did not respond with genuine repentance, ask God to help you to see your sin as He does
and then commit yourself to obey Him and truly repent.

Day Four

♦ Read Psalm 38 carefully. What does sin produce in the
believer?

♦ Ask God to open your eyes to the damage unconfessed
sin has caused in your life. Write out a prayer of repentance. Be specific about what behavior(s) you must
"put off."

Day Five

♦ Review your prayer of Day Four. Read Ephesians
4:17–32.

♦ Add to your prayer of repentance the behavior you will
now "put on" to replace the sinful behavior you have
renounced. Be specific.

Day Six

♦ Your repentance of a specific sin may put you on a difficult path. You may stumble as you learn to walk in
Christ's righteousness. Read Psalm 103 and be comforted and encouraged by the compassionate forgiveness and love of God.

Chapter 12

FURNACE, HAMMER, AND FIRE—THE PROPHETS

And what more shall I say? I do not have time to tell about Gideon, Barak,
Samson, Jephthah, David, Samuel and the prophets, who through faith
conquered kingdoms, administered justice, and gained what was promised;
who shut the mouths of lions, quenched the fury of the flames, and escaped
the edge of the sword; whose weakness was turned to strength; and
who became powerful in battle and routed foreign armies.

Women received back their dead, raised to life again. Others were tortured
and refused to be released, so that they might gain a better resurrection.
Some faced jeers and flogging, while still others were chained and put in prison.
They were stoned; they were sawed in two; they were put to death by the sword.
They went about in sheepskins and goatskins, destitute, persecuted and
mistreated—the world was not worthy of them. They wandered in deserts
and mountains, and in caves and holes in the ground. (Hebrews 11:32–38)

Through the Flames of Affliction—
Fritz Manampiring

Fritz Manampiring has been pastoring in Bantargebang, Bekasi, in Indonesia since 1987. On November 27, 1997, Fritz and his wife were attacked by radical Muslims. The small mob surrounded his church with rocks in each hand, clapping the stones together furiously. They were like madmen carrying out a holy pilgrimage of terror.

A policeman implored him, "Pastor, please hold no service here today. This is what the Muslim leaders want. They have become mad!"

Not desiring to stir up any additional trouble, Fritz assured the police officer that he would turn away the congregation. He also tried to reason with Haji Dudung, who was leading the mob. As members of the congregation arrived for the service, Fritz shouted at them to leave. But before the church members could respond, the mob's fury erupted, their stones flying. As the Muslims attacked the church, which is also Fritz's home, they chanted, "Allah-u-Akbar!" (Allah is mighty!)

Like Saul in the New Testament, they believed they were serving God in persecuting Christian believers. In their eyes, they were punishing an "infidel," someone who had blasphemed. The police tried to stop the mob, but with little success. These Muslims were intent on persecuting the followers of Jesus.

The mob dragged Fritz's wife outside, beating and kicking her. If the security officers hadn't stopped them, Fritz and his wife would have been killed.

The officers took the pastor and his wife to the military office in Bekasi for their safety. Fritz filed a report, but no arrests were made. No one would have blamed Fritz or his wife if they had fled their town, if they had ceased their church services altogether. But they didn't. Despite their home being ransacked and the threat of imminent persecution, they remained in the area to minister the gospel to their brothers and sisters.

Later that year, on December 12, a security officer warned Fritz of another planned attack by radical Muslims. This time the mob had grown in anger and in size, and they were ready for *jihad* (holy war).

That evening the mob arrived. Again they surrounded the church and began to throw stones yelling, "Attack! Attack!" But this time, the police did not show up to protect Fritz's family. It didn't take the mob long to enter the church, ransacking everything in sight. They cut off the electricity, leaving the rooms in darkness. Before Fritz and his wife could escape, a club came down across the back of his wife's head, and Fritz also was clubbed until his face was drenched in blood.

As they tied Fritz with steel wire and continued to beat him, Fritz cried out, "Lord Jesus, help!" One of the attackers forced his burning cigarette into Fritz's mouth. Laughing and jeering, he told Fritz, "Eat your Jesus!"

A hood was placed over the pastor's head, and he was taken outside and stripped bare. Attackers beat him, burned him with cigarettes, and rolled him through the broken glass from the church window. Others continued to ransack their home and church. The chants of the attackers echoed in his ears, "Allah-u-Akbar! Allah-u-Akbar!" Eventually, Fritz fell unconscious; a final blow to his jaw was more than he could bear.

When he came to, he found himself lying on a pile of wood from the church ruins, with his attackers throwing shattered furniture on top of him. He was soon choking from smoke as flames emerged around him. Fritz prayed what he thought to be his final prayer before meeting his Lord face to face: *Lord, I give my soul and spirit to you.*

Fritz doesn't remember how it happened, but he suddenly found himself being lifted from the blaze. As with

Shadrach, Meshach, and Abednego (Daniel 3), God had spared him from the flames. After Fritz escaped the fire, he was tied to a pole, stoned, and left for dead. In addition to his other injuries, his jaw had been smashed, the nerves in his eyes were irreparably damaged, and he had suffered a severe concussion.

Fritz and his wife are now staying with friends less than two miles from where their church and home were destroyed. Not surprisingly, this courageous minister continues to pastor his flock.

Voice of the Martyrs, Canada[1]

---

[1] This story is adapted with permission from an article appearing in the July 1998 issue of *The Voice of the Martyrs* newsletter (Voice of the Martyrs, Canada, P.O. Box 117, Port Credit, Mississauga, ON L5G 4L5, Canada), p. 3. Readers are encouraged to visit their website (www.persecution.net) or the U.S. Voice of the Martyrs website (www.vom.org) to learn more about the persecuted church.

MORE LOVE TO THEE

When government officials in Communist North Korea discovered thirty Christians living in caves and tunnels underground, they brought these believers out before the people for a public execution. For years these Korean Christians had lived in hand-dug tunnels beneath the earth. Outraged by their refusal to subscribe to official Communist party ideology, dictator Kim Jung Il was adamant that these Christians must publicly renounce their faith. They steadfastly refused. The dictator then ordered their children seized and threatened to kill them. Yet even when faced with the death of their own children, not one of these faithful Korean Christians would deny his or her faith in Jesus. Then this godless, vicious leader had a steamroller brought in and, as these Christians lay on the ground, ordered that all of them be crushed to death. Even as they died, however, these courageous believers found strength in a hymn they had often sung together:

> More love to Thee, O Christ, more love to Thee.
> Then shall my latest breath whisper Thy praise;
> This be the parting cry my heart shall raise,
> This still its prayer shall be.
> More love, O Christ, to Thee.[2]

These modern-day believers were following in the footsteps of the men and women whose faith remained strong, even unto death, described in Hebrews 11:32–38. As the writer of Hebrews moves here from specific to more general depictions of faith, he acknowledges that his list is only a sampling of the many who "through faith" faced terrible opposition with uncommon courage. In Chapter 11 we saw how the author of Hebrews, by his inclusion of Gideon, Barak, Samson,

---

[2] July 1998 issue of *The Voice of the Martyrs* newsletter (U.S. edition).

and Jephthah, focused on the era of the Judges. These men were certainly flawed, and each one "came up short" in some way, and yet their faith was characterized by and renewed through genuine repentance. Such a faith empowered ordinary, sinful men to accomplish extraordinary things: to conquer kingdoms, administer justice, become powerful in battle, and rout great armies (vv. 32–34).

Similarly, David represented the kings who followed the period of the Judges. Among these kings—some godly, some very evil—David was remarkable, unique, and despite his many failings he found favor and grace in God's eyes. The Lord describes David as a man "who kept my commands and followed me with all his heart, doing only what was right in my eyes" (1 Kings 14:8). Because of David's sincere sorrow for his sins and because he forsook those sins in genuine repentance, God forgave him. The leadership of this remarkable "shepherd king" proved, in fact, to set the standard of righteous rule for all other kings (2 Kings 18:3; 22:2).

SPEAKERS OF THE WORD—THE PROPHETS

The writer of Hebrews goes on from listing these five men to describe the era and ministry of the prophets, the upholders and proclaimers of the truth of God's Word. Though only Samuel is mentioned here by name, we believe that the focus of much of the ensuing passage of Hebrews 11 refers to the lives and sacrifices of these valiant men of God, now remembered collectively as the prophets.

The era represented by Samuel and the prophets overlaps the era of the kings. Samuel, like all of the true prophets, boldly proclaimed God's Word to great rulers and common people alike. When God spoke, Samuel listened (1 Samuel 3:9), and when Samuel spoke, he spoke with the authority of the living God. The prophets were God's messengers; their role was to call the people back to covenant loyalty as God's special people.[3] The prophets thus faithfully received, proclaimed, and upheld God's Word.

Though they are sometimes viewed as a kind of bludgeon in God's hands, one that He used to hammer the people into submission, the prophets actually were a reflection of God's great grace and mercy. In keeping with His covenant promises, blessing inevitably followed obedience. Throughout the period of the prophets, as well as during and after the exile to Babylon, God continued to raise up prophets to warn and admonish, to encourage and enlighten His people. Sadly, however, the people often chose to ignore God's warning, sometimes responding with indifference and ridicule, at other times reacting with outright violence and hatred.

The writer of Hebrews provides, in dramatic, panoramic language, an overview of the remarkable lives and testimonies of these faithful men of the Word. The prophets . . .

- conquered kingdoms,
- administered justice,
- gained what was promised,
- shut the mouths of lions,
- quenched the fury of the flames,
- escaped the edge of the sword,
- experienced weakness turned to strength,
- were powerful in battle,
- routed foreign armies, and even
- raised the dead to life again.

All of these things did occur during this period. It isn't difficult to see here allusions to the faith-characterized lives of Daniel, Samuel, Elijah, Elisha, Isaiah, and many others. These

---

[3] For a description of God's view of the church and its covenantal responsibilities, see Deuteronomy 7:6–9 and 36:18–19.

men of faith refused to bow to any king but Jehovah God of Israel. At times, God protected and enabled these men in miraculous ways; at other times, however, obedience to God and the faithful proclamation of His Word led these individuals down difficult paths of hardship, loneliness, and martyrdom.

If God Is Willing

The story of Shadrach, Meshach, and Abednego (Daniel 3), for example, shows us three men who remained faithful but who did not presume upon God to provide a miraculous deliverance. These men refused to bow to the image of King Nebuchadnezzar of Babylon, claiming they would bow only to Jehovah. They knew the punishment for such a refusal would be death in a blazing furnace. The furious and arrogant king of Babylon then dared the three men to trust their God in that furnace. Their godly reply foreshadows the faithful surrender to God of thousands of persecuted believers through the ages who have followed in their footsteps:

> O Nebuchadnezzar, we do not need to defend ourselves before you in this matter. If we are thrown into the blazing furnace, the God we serve is able to save us from it, and he will rescue us from your hand, O king. *But even if he does not,* we want you to know, O king, that we will not serve your gods or worship the image of gold you have set up. (Daniel 3:16–18 [emphasis added])

These three courageous young men knew that God *was able* to save them from the fire, but they also recognized that God was *not obligated* to save them, that indeed their deaths might serve some other, greater purpose of their true Lord and King. Thus, even knowing full well that they might suffer a horrible and painful death, they remained faithful—even unto death. God *would* save them in due time; but they left it to Him whether that deliverance would be in this life or in the life to come.

By God's miraculous power and grace, He did indeed rescue the three men from the wrath of the king, allowing them to pass through the fire without harm. The only thing that burned inside that fiery furnace were the ropes that had tightly bound their arms. Nebuchadnezzar, awed by this deliverance, looked on in wonder. To his amazement, he saw among the flames not three men but four, the fourth man "like a son of the gods" (Daniel 3:25). The king believed that this mysterious fourth man was an emissary of God. This fourth man may even have been a vision of the preincarnate Christ. Nebuchadnezzar was greatly affected and moved by this demonstration of human faith and God's almighty power.

God promises to protect every believer from such "fires" of this life:

> When you pass through the waters, I will be with you; and when you pass through the rivers, they will not sweep over you. When you walk through the fire, you will not be burned; the flames will not set you ablaze. For I am the LORD, your God, the Holy One of Israel, your Savior. (Isaiah 43:2–3)

We can be certain that God will love and sustain us, though we cannot know whether His protection will include our physical lives and bodies, nor can we always expect that our enemies will experience a miraculous change of heart. Yet while our bodies may perish by sword or flame or gunfire, our souls can never be touched. Nothing, indeed, can ever snatch them from His hand (John 10:28).

FAITH-BASED ENDURANCE

It is probable that the letter to the Hebrews was first read aloud to a small group of believers in a house church hidden away somewhere in the first-century Roman world. The pastor of that struggling, fearful little congregation must have paused in his reading of this letter after speaking the words: "Women received back their dead, raised to life again" (Hebrews 11:35a). Perhaps he looked up at that point, taking in the faces of the people gathered around him, while a deep, expectant stillness filled the room. This pastor would have sympathized with the fears and sorrows of these dear people. He knew that the fires of persecution were growing fiercer and getting closer all the time. Surely it was an encouragement for this congregation to recall the mighty deeds achieved through ordinary men—men such as Barak, Samson, and David—and to consider for a blessed moment how the prophets of former days had "quenched the fury of the flames and escaped the edge of the sword" (v. 34).

Daily, these people were being threatened with flames and swords and worse. It is likely that the Roman persecution of Christians was by this time in full sway. If so, perhaps many of their loved ones had already died in the arenas or as human torches for the amusement of the Emperor Nero and his guests. How it must have encouraged them to remember how the prophet Elisha had, through God's great power, actually brought a young boy back from death to life again (v. 39 [see also 2 Kings 4:8–37]).

Yet the way of faith is not always easy or paved with such mighty victories, and often God, for His own reasons, seems to stand at a distance as His children perish in the flames of affliction. Although the history of God's people was certainly full of marvelous stories of great triumphs and mighty miracles, this is not the whole story of faith. God has never guaranteed that we would have only peace and safety in this life. And so the passage goes on, in painful, chilling detail, to give the "other side" of faith:

> Others were tortured[4] and refused to be released, so that they might gain a better resurrection. Some faced jeers and flogging, while still others were chained and put in prison. They were stoned; they were sawed in two; they were put to death by the sword. They went about in sheepskins and goatskins; being destitute, persecuted and mistreated—the world was not worthy of them. They wandered in deserts and mountains, and in caves and holes in the ground. (Hebrews 11:35b–38)

The people mentioned or alluded to in Hebrews 11 had suffered for their faith, for their steadfast belief that God would one day send a Redeemer for His people. Yet they continued to trust God that "something better" was coming (v. 40). Rather than compromise God's truth by bowing to any other king or ideology, these faithful people endured prejudice, torture, and death.

Scattered throughout the Old Testament are the stories of prophets such as Zechariah, the son of Jehoiada the priest, who was executed "by order of the king" simply because he called the people of Israel to repent of their disobedience against God (2 Chronicles 24:20–22). Jewish tradition teaches that the prophet Jeremiah was stoned to death after a lifetime of intense personal struggle and unswerving commitment to God's honor and God's Word. His nation and his own family rejected his warnings of God's judgment and his call to re-

---

[4] The Greek word for "tortured" here, *tympanizo*, is used only once in the New Testament. It refers to a "drum"-like torture wheel upon which a person would be stretched and then beaten to death.

pentance. The prophet Isaiah, also according to Jewish tradition, may actually have been sawn in two. What enabled these people to persevere on such a terrifying journey? And what does their example have to do with us?

THE ENEMIES OF THE WORD

Throughout history, there has always been opposition to the Word of God. The sinful, stubborn hearts of men and women continue to reject the call to repentance. Like Cain, most people, in their heart of hearts, believe God exists but do not wish to submit to Him. Most religions simply invent a vague mystical "force" to believe in, a belief system whose standards are far less demanding and which certainly does not require sorrow for sin and humble submission and obedience.

Such religions ultimately do not satisfy, nor do they stand on solid ground. When Christians respond to these religions with the truth about God, when they share His holy and inerrant Word, the vain, evil, empty, and self-sufficient philosophies of this world cannot stand against it. But men and women would often rather suppress the truth about God, and it is that intense desire to suppress and extinguish the truth, by whatever means necessary, that leads to persecution.

The situation in North Korea today is a good example of this. The famine in that nation has been terribly severe. Perhaps as many as two million people have already died of starvation in that country. Yet the spiritual famine they endure is even more deadly.

Only two "official" churches in North Korea are permitted to minister to some 23 million people. The North Korean dictator, Kim Jung Il, refuses to relax this restriction, and he has instead tried to impose the Juche religion, a political invention, forcibly upon the people. Loudspeakers throughout North Korea blare out the same message every morning as dawn breaks, a message that goes something like this: "Our nation is under threat of foreign forces bent on destroying this, our paradise on earth." The people are told that their only hope lies with their "great leader" and to keep constant watch for anyone who strays from the party line. Such people must be regarded as potential traitors and spies. It is a situation tragically and eerily reminiscent of the days of King Nebuchadnezzar thousands of years ago.

THE POWER OF THE WORD

Yet the government of North Korea—and its dictator leaders—are actually afraid. They are afraid of the Word of God and of the people who believe it, and their fear is what underlies their cruel and desperate attempts to suppress the truth. This fear has led to intense persecution of the church in that nation. When the Communists came to power in North Korea in 1948, they would often question the children concerning their religious beliefs. If they were found to be "indoctrinated" by their Christian parents, they would be removed from their homes and enrolled in a strict government school, where they would be trained in Communist ideology in order to become "faithful" Communist leaders.

The depths to which the enemies of God will sink in order to suppress the Bible and those who believe it are appalling. Recently, a representative of the Christian ministry Voice of the Martyrs traveled to China, where he met a woman, a refugee from North Korea, who related the following story:

> One day our teacher told us that we would not have the normal homework today; rather, the students were asked to participate in a special game. We were delighted and cheered. School was strict and it was a special day not to have the usual homework.

The teacher went on to reveal the special homework she had for us. She began to whisper as she
walked among us, telling us about a special book that
our parents may have hidden in our homes. We were to
wait until Mommy and Daddy went to sleep and search
for this book and bring it to school the following day.

All of the children were excited because the
teacher said we would receive a special surprise if we
found this book. We asked her how we would know
what the book looked like. The teacher told us that the
book usually had a black cover and that our parents often read the book after we went to bed. We were not
to tell our parents about this homework or we would
forfeit our surprise.

I went home that afternoon and immediately began searching for a black-covered book. I couldn't wait
for my parents to go to bed. I was anxious to complete
my assignment.

The next day I was one of 14 children who
brought the black book, a Bible, to class. We were all
lined up at the front and had a bright red scarf placed
around our necks. All of the students clapped as the
teacher paraded us around the room.

I ran home that afternoon and yelled, "Mommy,
Mommy!" I was so excited to tell her how I had won
the red scarf at school.

My mother wasn't in the house, so I ran to the
barn, again yelling, "Mommy, Mommy!"

I waited for my mother to come home. Hours
passed and I didn't understand where she could be.
My father didn't come home either, and I was beginning to become afraid. I was hungry and it was quickly
becoming dark outside. I fell asleep in a chair, hoping
that, at any moment, my parents would come home
and carry me to bed. I began to feel sick inside.

The next day police officers were at my door and informed me that I was now in the care of the government and would be placed in a home with other children. I never saw my parents again.

This poor woman has not seen her mother or father in 40 years. She regrets the homework she did that day and has cursed herself ever since. After relating the story, she cried out in pain, "Why did I do this homework? What have I done?"[5]

Like the prophets, we too are entrusted with the Word. God expects us to share its truth with everyone we know. Are we doing this now, or are we too afraid of the consequences? The apostle Paul, no stranger to ridicule and jeering, to angry mobs and the fierce opposition of ungodly rulers, understood the great power of God's Word, the truth. He describes for us what "dynamite" we possess:

> The weapons we fight with are not the weapons of the world. On the contrary, they have divine power to demolish strongholds. We demolish arguments and every pretension that sets itself up against the knowledge of God, and we take captive every thought to make it obedient to Christ. (2 Corinthians 10:4–5)

It is well for us to remember that the Word of God is no ordinary book. It is living and powerful; it is like fire—or "a hammer that breaks a rock in pieces" (Hebrews 4:12; Jeremiah 23:29). Small wonder that its opponents fear it so. As Christians, we often fail to appreciate what a reservoir of power the Bible actually is, that it goes out into the world, into the lives of people, and it does not return to us empty (Isaiah

---

[5] This story and testimony are adapted with permission from the June 1998 issue of *The Voice of the Martyrs* newsletter (Canada edition), p. 3.

55:10–11). The principalities and powers of this world may try to suppress the Word with brutality and hate, *but they will fail.*

GUARDIANS OF THE WORD—GOD'S PEOPLE

In this amazing and poignant chapter of Hebrews, the cause for which each of these people of faith lived and died was founded upon God's covenant promise of the Redeemer, His Living Word. "Though none of them received what had been promised," God commended them for persevering through the hardship, with their eyes focused not upon their present trials and torments, but upon Him and Him alone. The lives of these courageous men and women demonstrated their absolute belief in the coming Redeemer. Today, we can look back and rejoice in the fulfillment of God's promise to redeem His people, to create a community, to dwell with us and in us, and to bring us into glory—all of which have been accomplished through the life, ministry, death, and resurrection of the Lord Jesus Christ.

God has promised again and again through the ages to be our God and that we, in turn, would be His people, sharing both a great privilege and a great responsibility. God has commissioned His people to worship Him, to build His kingdom, and to uphold and proclaim His truth. Louis Berkhof, in his work *Systematic Theology,* affirms the call of the church to be the keepers of the Word:

> By giving His Word to the Church, God constituted the Church the keeper of the precious deposit of the truth. While hostile forces are pitted against it and the power of error is everywhere apparent, the Church must see to it that the truth does not perish from the earth, that the inspired volume in which it is embodied be kept pure and unmutilated, in order that its

purpose may not be defeated, and that it be handed on faithfully from generation to generation. [The Church] has the great and responsible task of maintaining and defending the truth against all the forces of unbelief and error.

How can we, like those who have come before us, faithfully uphold and proclaim God's Word? Jesus taught that true discipleship often requires relinquishing our own wants and security for a greater purpose. In fact, He taught us that it is only in losing our lives for Him and for the gospel that we can experience eternal life (Mark 8:34–38). Too often we think of living for Christ in the context of the "big" crises, but it is just as important to demonstrate our faith in the simple, daily decisions of life.

As with Habakkuk (see chapter 1), the best way for faithful people to guard the integrity of God's Word is by the daily choices they make to obey Him, *especially* when that obedience is not the safest or easiest choice. By faith, we learn to leave the results of that obedience in God's hands, trusting Him for the outcome. Peter told the early church that we "prove" what we believe not just with our words but by our daily obedience to God's truth:

> But you are a chosen people, a royal priesthood, a holy nation, a people belonging to God, that you may declare the praises of him who called you out of darkness into his wonderful light. Once you were not a people, but now you are the people of God; once you had not received mercy, but now you have received mercy.
>
> Dear friends, I urge you, as aliens and strangers in the world, to abstain from sinful desires, which war against your soul. Live such good lives among the pagans that, though they accuse you of doing wrong,

they may see your good deeds and glorify God on the day he visits us. (1 Peter 2:9–12)

FOR CHRIST'S CROWN AND COVENANT

Countless thousands of men, women, and children have, like these early believers, accepted contempt, torture, and even death rather than compromise their belief in God's Word. In the 1600s a pitched and bloody battle raged in Scotland between those who saw Christ alone as King and those who supported the monarch, Charles I of England, as the "Head of the Church." Charles and his supporters were clearly Catholic in their religious sympathies and wanted to lead the nations of England and Scotland back into the Catholic fold. Many Scots, devout Christians, refused and resisted. They drafted a document now known as *The National Covenant of 1638.* This statement declared in no uncertain terms that these courageous people, thereafter known as the Covenanters, were determined to submit only to the claims of Christ, their Redeemer, and never to any king who sought to exercise his own sovereignty over that which rightfully belonged to God. Their rallying cry became "For Christ's Crown and Covenant," and they courageously resisted the king's efforts to wipe out the true church:

> The more they [i.e., the authorities] insisted on this inquisition, the more did the number of witnesses multiply, with a growing increase of undauntedness, so that the shed blood of the martyrs became the seed of the Church; and as, by hearing and seeing them so signally countenanced of the Lord, many were reclaimed from their courses of compliance, so others were daily more and more confirmed in the ways of the Lord and so strengthened by His grace that they chose rather to

endure all torture and embrace death in its most terrible aspect than to give the tyrant and his accomplices any acknowledgement, yea not so much as to say, "God save the King," which was offered as the price of their life.[6]

Both men and women shed blood to guard Christ's kingship and the supremacy of God's Word. Dragoon garrisons made barracks out of homes left vacant by fleeing believers. Marauding parties sent out by Sir William Bannatyne carried out terrible atrocities against anyone associated with the Covenanters:

> One, David McGill, in that parish, whom they came to apprehend, escaped . . . but dreadful was the way taken with his poor wife whom they alleged accessory to her husband's escape. They seized her and bound her, and put lighted matches between her fingers for several hours: the torture and the pain made her almost distracted. She lost one of her hands, and in a few days she died. They pillaged the country round about as they pleased. . . . Bannatyne in this country never refused to let his men rob and plunder wherever they pleased. His oppressions, murders, robberies, rapes, adulteries and so on, were so many and atrocious that the managers themselves were ashamed of them.

Hearing of such horror, we ask the question, "Why did they have to suffer so?" Historian Jock Purves explains:

---

[6] This and subsequent references to the Covenanters are from Jock Purves' *Fair Sunshine: Character Studies of the Scottish Covenanters* (Carlisle, Pa.: Banner of Truth, 1997). Purves is here quoting from Alexander Shields, *A Hind Let Loose* (1774).

In the ultimate issue the question at stake, in all its stark nakedness, was whether a temporal monarch or the Lord Jesus Christ was to be "Head over all things to the Church." To faithful Covenanters only one answer was possible, and whether their problems concerned individuals, families, conventicles, or general assemblies, they urged with fierce and unshakable tenacity that "Jesus Christ is Lord."

No suffering could be too great to endure in such a cause. The scaffold could not daunt them; instruments of torture could not make them quail; the sufferings and discomforts of cave or moor or prison-cell could not move them to act and speak against conscience. Behind and above covenants subscribed with their hands and witnessed to by their hearts, and in an even truer sense subscribed in their blood, was the everlasting Covenant, ordered in all things and sure, itself sealed with the blood of the Mediator, and itself the pattern of all lesser covenants.

Faith gave buoyancy to the Covenanters' resolution; hope was the Anchor of their souls; the love of Christ shed abroad in their hearts ever spurred them on to do and to suffer; "outside the camp" they bore His reproach; and before them ever loomed large "the recompense of the reward" and the gates of the city of God.

Their joyful surrender to Christ as King and their love for God's Word empowered them to remain faithful—even unto death. Hebrews 11 regularly impresses us with the nomadic existence of the early church. The phrase "so that they might gain a better resurrection" really summarizes for us the theology of every inhabitant of the Hall of Faith and of all genuine believers after them. The Scottish Covenanters shared Abraham's nomadic vision as well; for they too were strangers here, and they too looked forward to the city whose architect and builder is God (Hebrews 11:10). Their eyes were fixed on Jesus and on the enduring supremacy of His Word.

EVEN UNTO DEATH

Hebrews 11:38 indicates that the world was "not worthy" of these faithful people, men and women who demonstrated their absolute faith in God's promises by giving up lives of comfort and security in order to follow after God. It is clear that there is a growing intolerance and ridicule toward biblical Christianity in our culture. In such an environment, a life of faith and obedience to God will shine brightly. That light, however, may not be regarded as a beacon of hope since it will also expose all that is done in darkness. Many in this world, unwilling to acknowledge or renounce the sin in their own lives, will therefore do all that they can to extinguish that light. To such people godliness, faithfulness, and truth are an affront.

It may seem unlikely that anyone in our generation or our own country would be called upon to die as a martyr. Yet in 1999 the nation watched in horror as two hate-filled teenaged boys viciously gunned down their fellow students at Columbine High School in Colorado. These killers targeted, in particular, high school athletes, black students—and *committed Christians*. Cassie Bernall, a personable, cheerful seventeen-year-old girl, was well known in school for her faith in Christ. When one of these two boys held a gun to her head and asked her if she believed in God, Cassie replied without hesitation, "Yes, I believe in Jesus." The boy immediately shot and killed her.

Pastor Fritz Manampiring, in caring for his church family, daily faces danger, and yet to this day he persists in proclaiming the love and truth of Christ in a country—Indonesia—that is predominantly Muslim and where hostility against Christians is growing more intense every year. Even our own nation is becoming increasingly tolerant of every kind of behavior and belief system *except* for a righteousness and faith based on God's Word. We may not actually be martyred as we uphold God's truth in our present culture, but we will undoubtedly be mocked and ridiculed. Are we prepared to faithfully proclaim and live out the truth of His Word through the example of our lives and the words we speak each day? Are we prepared to face the ostracism and the ridicule?

The Hebrew church was a small group of believers hemmed in and beset by seemingly overwhelming opposition. The examples of persevering faith presented in the book of Hebrews were an encouraging reminder that God's church would prevail. This brief review in Hebrews 11 of their covenantal history served to remind these discouraged Christians that they did not need to fear Nero or any other power, for the church of God is eternal.

> For here we do not have an enduring city, but we are looking for the city that is to come. Through Jesus, therefore, let us continually offer to God a sacrifice of praise—the fruit of lips that confess his name. (Hebrews 13:14–15)

> Therefore, since we are receiving a kingdom that cannot be shaken, let us be thankful, and so worship God acceptably with reverence and awe. (Hebrews 12:28)

C. H. Spurgeon, as we have noted in an earlier chapter, gave glory to God for "the furnace, the hammer, and the fire." He went on to say that "Heaven shall be all the fuller of bliss because we have been filled with anguish here below, and earth shall be better tilled because of our training in the school of adversity." Spurgeon was simply affirming what the author of Hebrews also believed. Though the way may be dark and painful, God and His people will continue to shine through even the darkest of circumstances, against the bitterest and most vicious opponents. Though hard pressed and perhaps even in torment, we will nevertheless shine in this world, illuminating the hearts and lives of the people around us—those we love, surely, but even those who hate us.

Even at the moment of his death, the martyr Stephen forgave his enemies and gave his life over to Christ Jesus. Paul (then known as Saul), coldly standing by, looked on with "approval" (Acts 7:59–8:1). And yet who can say but that a seed of hope was planted in the one man's heart by the other man's death?

The disciple Peter, a man who himself eventually endured a brutal martyr's death, reminds us of our obligation, and he encourages us to take heart. "We have the word of the prophets made more certain, and you will do well to pay attention to it," he tells us, "as to a light shining in a dark place, until the day dawns and the morning star rises in your hearts" (2 Peter 1:19).

DIGGING DEEPER

Day One
- Read Psalm 19:7–11. How does your day-to-day behavior illustrate that your attitude toward God's Word is the same as the psalmist's? How does your conduct encourage others to trust God's Word as the truth?

Day Two
- Read Deuteronomy 6:6–7. What is the benefit of God's Word? In what ways do our lives reflect a love for God's Word? How does obedience "guard" God's Word?

Day Three

- List and define the uses for God's Word in 2 Timothy 3:16–17. How do you use the Word for correction, for reproof, and for instruction in your daily life?

Day Four

- Ask God to direct you to one specific area of your life that does not conform to His Word. Review your answer to Day Three and ask God to direct you to verses that will correct, reprove, and instruct you regarding that specific problem area.

Day Five

- The rallying cry of the Scottish Covenanters was "For Christ's Crown and Covenant!" What did they mean?
- Write out one specific way you will deliberately demonstrate today that Christ is your King and that His Word is your supreme guide for life.

Day Six

- Read James 1:22–27; 2:14–16; 1 Peter 2:11–12. Is it possible to love God's Word without reflecting that love by the way we live? Ask God to give you a love for His Word that compels you to connect with others in order to reflect His compassion.

Chapter 13

ON OUR WAY HOME

FAITH PRINCIPLE #13

BIBLICAL FAITH GIVES US CERTAIN HOPE
IN AN UNCERTAIN WORLD.

These were all commended for their faith, yet none of them received
what had been promised. God had planned something better for us so that
only together with us would they be made perfect.

Therefore, since we are surrounded by such a great cloud of witnesses,
let us throw off everything that hinders and the sin that so easily entangles,
and let us run with perseverance the race marked out for us. Let us fix
our eyes on Jesus, the author and perfecter of our faith, who for the joy
set before him endured the cross, scorning its shame, and sat down
at the right hand of the throne of God.

Consider him who endured such opposition from sinful men, so that you will not
grow weary and lose heart. (Hebrews 11:39–12:3 [see also Hebrews 10–12])

BEAUTY FOR ASHES—MARGIE MOORE

As we prepared to write a book about faith, one based on
Hebrews 11, we asked our close friend Margie if we could

share in this book some of her own difficult life experiences. We mentioned this woman and her young son, Eric, in our first chapter. Eric, Margie's oldest child, never fully recovered from the effects of a rare coma he experienced when he was almost four years old. He is now brain damaged and is no longer the lively and active little boy he used to be. For Margie, as for so many others in this book, walking in faith will never be an easy thing. Every day for her and her husband, Randy, is a struggle.

Margie, after reading through our first chapter, wrote to us:

> As I read through the chapter, tears rolled silently and uncontrollably down my face. Somehow, when I saw it there in black and white, as I read the paragraph about my own initial reaction to Eric's condition, it all seemed so immature, as though I just could not trust my God and my Lord. Yet I do know He loves my family, our sweet Eric, and me more than I can even imagine. There are times when I want other people to see that same raw grief, especially those who are undergoing similar trials, so they and I will both know that we are not alone in our sorrows. But seeing my doubts there in print still makes me feel vulnerable. Maybe that is why so many people do not want to share such painful moments. It is certainly easier to share the times of victory. Can I really allow myself to be that vulnerable in order, perhaps, to help someone else?
>
> I do miss my happy little son. That little boy whose joyful laughter used to light up our days and our hearts is gone. The boy left behind sits day after day in his wheelchair and stares out at life with empty eyes. But he still possesses our hearts. Sometimes Randy and I see the peace of Jesus in his sleeping face and his beauty overwhelms us.

For Eric's sixth birthday, I am having the Thomas the Tank Engine party that I had planned for his fourth birthday. We don't know what Eric feels or thinks except that lately he has started smiling a little. We are praying for Eric's complete healing. Medically, we realize that such a hope may not be realistic, but our God is all-powerful and merciful, so we continue to pray for this, the deepest desire of our hearts. We also pray that we will learn to be able to say, no matter what, "It is well, it is well with my soul."

We are taking seriously your counsel: "When you are going through a trial and the way is hard, go back to what you know." By faith, we are learning how to live out what we believe—that God's promises are true, that God is good, that we can trust Him, and that He loves us beyond anything we can comprehend. We know He will never leave us nor forsake us, that we are His children, and that He knows Eric *by name.* Although we may not know what Eric is thinking and feeling, God does, and He is accomplishing His eternal purposes even in this.

One day God will wipe away my tears, and Eric will be whole and healthy for all of eternity. I am trusting God to keep His promise: "To appoint unto them that mourn in Zion, to give unto them beauty for ashes, the oil of joy for mourning, the garment of praise for the spirit of heaviness; that they might be called trees of righteousness, the planting of the LORD, that he might be glorified" (Isaiah 61:3 KJV).

How grateful we are for those who have allowed this tragedy in our lives to become a part of their lives as well, as they share this burden with us. Every act of kindness has reminded us to find strength in our God. On a particularly difficult night at Mission Hospital during the first few days of Eric's three-month stay there, I left his side to take a short break. The soft light of the waiting room framed a few of the women from our church as they prayed there. What a precious reminder that Randy and I were not alone.

You told us that God's grace is not an anesthetic. It helps to remember that just because we feel excruciating pain right now does not mean that God isn't here with us. We are learning that we don't have to find "joy" in a trial by itself, but that God does ask and encourage us to find joy in Him, despite that trial. And I'm convinced that for joy and sorrow to occupy the same space at the same time is a miracle only God can perform.

Randy and I have actually learned to laugh again and enjoy the blessings God sends our way—one of the most special being our three-year-old daughter, Emily. We are finding His purpose and are learning to give to others the comfort He has given to us [2 Corinthians 1:4]. Every time we start to "drown," thinking about all the things we had hoped for and wanted for ourselves and for our Eric, we ask God to give us the grace to stay focused on the eternal. I keep repeating to myself the chorus, "Turn your eyes upon Jesus. Look full in His wonderful face, and the things of earth will grow strangely dim in the light of His glory and grace."

How we long to be in heaven with Jesus! How we long to see our son, restored and well, standing there with us!

By faith, we are trusting that the pathway God has placed us on will one day lead us Home.

Sharon Betters

A Better Resurrection

It is unfortunate that an uninspired chapter heading interrupts the flow of thought between chapters 11 and 12 in the book of Hebrews. The author has carefully illustrated how God has fulfilled all of His promises to His people, faithful men and women who, through the centuries, have entrusted their lives and all they had to His care and keeping. The writer builds up to a mighty crescendo, bringing to center stage the very culmination of this passage, the hope for the future, the city not seen, where we will dwell in the full and everlasting glory of Jesus Christ. Thus we believe that the first three verses of chapter 12 are essential to a proper understanding of Hebrews 11.

The author of Hebrews, with the conclusion of the main point of this passage at hand, brings the Hall of Faith in Hebrews 11 into sharp focus with a resounding "therefore" (Hebrews 12:1). *Therefore,* he concludes,

> . . . let us fix our eyes on Jesus, the author and perfecter of our faith, who for the joy set before him endured the cross, scorning its shame, and sat down at the right hand of God. Consider him who endured such opposition from sinful men, so that you will not grow weary and lose heart. (Hebrews 12:2–3)

The author here reminds us of the greatest suffering anyone has ever had to endure. In these verses the pivotal event of human history—the shame and agony of the cross—is brought into full view. For Jesus suffered more loneliness, more trials, more persecution, and more wrath than anyone else who has ever lived. He suffered the wrath of God the Father for the sins of men and women. He endured all that we deserved: He suffered for the lies of Abraham and of Jacob and of Rebekah. He suffered for the lusts of Samson, for the crimes of Jephthah, for the tainted life of Rahab, for the foul murder committed by David, for the vile persecutions carried out by Paul—and for the mean-spirited gossip you shared just this past week. Does it not grieve you? Does it not shake you? Jesus endured the punishment for every sin of every believer throughout history. He sacrificed Himself out of love for His people. There simply can be no greater demonstration of love than this.

It is significant that the first thing Jesus prayed in the Garden of Gethsemane, shortly before His arrest and crucifixion, was for the Father to glorify the Son (John 17:1). Jesus was prepared to endure the shame of Calvary for one reason: that through His death and subsequent glorification—by His resurrection triumph over death—He would open the way for His people to enter into glory. In order to vanquish death for His people, the death brought on by the sins of Adam and Eve and all of their descendants, Jesus had to undergo death Himself—not just bodily death but also spiritual death, complete and utter separation from God.

It was a prospect so agonizing for Jesus that He could scarcely bear to contemplate it. Great drops of blood dripped from His forehead (Luke 22:39–45) as He groaned in His spirit and imagined being alienated from His Father. We cannot even begin to comprehend the torment that Jesus suffered.

How could He endure this for us—*for us?*

Jesus did it out of His own great love for us. He knew that the only way back to His Father, the only way for us to get back home, was through the cross. Only the Most Perfect Sacrifice could satisfy the debt we owed. In this way Jesus obtained the "better resurrection" of Hebrews 11:35. It is "better," indeed, because it is the only way—*the only way*—back into fellowship with God. This teaching concerning the resurrection is vital to the Christian; it is the very basis for our faith and our certain hope, for "if Christ has not been raised, our preaching is useless and so is your faith" (1 Corinthians 15:14).

Embracing the truth of the resurrection means that we will be refugees and strangers in this world (1 Peter 2:11) because our true citizenship is in heaven (Philippians 3:20–21). Even as we live in the "already," the present world, where sin, pain, and suffering will test the faith of every believer, we also live in the "not yet," the life to come, where at last in His presence God will make sense of all that has confused and hurt us here.

THE ETERNAL CITY

Our lives on earth, the Bible tells us, are a mere wisp of breath on a cold winter day (James 4:14). So much more awaits us. The author of Hebrews seemingly cannot mention the life to come often enough. He refers variously to:

- a city with foundations (11:10),
- a country of our own (11:14),
- a better country—a heavenly one—a city for us (11:16),
- a better and lasting possession (10:34),
- a better resurrection (11:35),
- the heavenly Jerusalem, the city of the living God (12:22),
- the eternal presence of God (13:5),
- the city that is to come (13:14).

In the Old Testament, the belief of God's faithful people that the Messiah might come at any moment transformed their whole view of life. They believed the covenant, the promises made by God to Abraham, Isaac, Jacob, and to all who followed after them. Today, we live in the glow of those fulfilled promises. Jesus' resurrection from the dead has fulfilled the terms of the covenant and has sealed the promise of eternal life for every believer. We have been given the gift of the Holy Spirit, who lives within each one of us and who is the "deposit" guaranteeing the full inheritance yet to come (Ephesians 1:14). We no longer hope for the Messiah for He has already come. Indeed, He is here now, among us, and His resurrection transforms how we look at life.

We now must have a forward view, as Abraham did, toward the eternal city. As Joni Eareckson Tada explains, "I know what it's like to grab hold of memories, like bricks, and build a dyke against time. When I was first paralyzed in 1967 . . . time was an enemy in that it kept putting more distance between the past on my feet and the present in my wheelchair." What she really longs for, however, lies ahead of her, in the future:

> Our nostalgia for Eden is not just for another time, but another *kind* of time. Those who do not believe still feel the tug. Even those who do not hope for heaven still wrestle with this vexing enigma of "eternity" set in their heart.
>
> Most people have it backward.
>
> Unlike those who don't believe in God, our road is not back to the Garden of Eden, but forward. One should never look over one's shoulder on the road of hope. In Genesis, God sent the seraphim with the flaming sword to bar Adam and Eve from returning to Eden once they had fallen. "The road to God lies ahead, 'east of Eden,' through the world of time and history, struggle and suffering and death. Ejected from Eden's eastern gate, we travel through and around the world, from west to east, forever seeking the rising sun (the Rising Son!) and find Him standing at the western gate . . . saying 'I am the door.' "[1]

---

[1] Joni Eareckson Tada, *Heaven: Your Real Home* (Grand Rapids: Zondervan, 1995), 102–3. She also quotes here from another book (Peter Kreeft, *Heaven* [San Francisco: Ignatius Press, 1989]).

It is very easy to lose sight of what lies ahead because we are so prone, in our weakness, to look sadly and longingly behind us. Transfixed by the siren song of what was, of hurts that cannot be undone, of people we have loved but who, to our limited vision, never trusted in Christ and now it is too late, too late. "What about them?" we ask. "How can we ever be joyful again . . . even in heaven?"

But God says that we can and we will, and that we must trust Him for all we do not understand. Gently, with firm but loving hands, He turns our faces again toward the east, toward the Rising Son. And who can say what lies beyond that far and bright horizon? When your heart is breaking and the "winds and waves" threaten to drown you and you long for all that you have lost, speak softly to your own soul the words of Katharina von Schlegel's marvelous hymn:

> Be still, my soul: your God will undertake
> to guide the future as he has the past.
> Your hope, your confidence let nothing shake;
> all now mysterious shall be bright at last.
> Be still, my soul: the waves and winds still know
> his voice who ruled them while he dwelt below.
>
> Be still, my soul: when dearest friends depart,
> and all is darkened in the vale of tears,
> then shall you better know his love, his heart,
> who comes to soothe your sorrow and your fears.
> Be still, my soul: your Jesus can repay
> from his own fullness all he takes away.

MY HEART WILL GO ON . . . WON'T IT?

God has set eternity in *every* heart, a longing for the presence of God, and nothing else will truly satisfy (Ecclesiastes 3:11). Some people believe in a glorious afterlife, but mistakenly

275

believe it is open to all comers, regardless of behavior or belief. The popular movie *Titanic* is a classic reflection of this view. Though the two young lovers in this film are temporarily separated by death, the movie ends with gauzy, glowy scenes implying that they are eventually reunited in some lovely, ethereal plane of existence. The idea seemed to be that God doesn't care all that much about how we've lived or what choices we've made, that we'll all just float off to bliss on angel wings after living a "reasonably good life." But the Bible directly contradicts this view of human nature—and of God. Our lives in and of themselves are not nearly good enough. We need Christ, and we need Him desperately. Just as the Israelites sometimes attempted to blend their worship of God with the idols and the false religions of their neighbors, so the unbelieving world attempts to lay claim to the eternal privileges of Christ's resurrection without having to worship Him or even acknowledge who He is.

Perhaps even more disconcerting is the fact that this endless search for a "no restrictions, no obligations" type of religion is finding fertile soil among many believers. Instead of viewing life with eternity's values in view, oftentimes Christians, like the rich man of Jesus' parable (Luke 16:19–31), are busy filling up their "barns" with more and more things, more and more activities. As a result, they give little thought to the eternal consequences of their behavior. In stark contrast, the "scorch marks" of their lives taught the people portrayed in Hebrews 11 to keep their eyes fixed on God's covenant promise of an everlasting, eternal inheritance. These men and women were all heirs to a "better resurrection," a *true* resurrection, one that came not via cheap grace but by the precious blood of Jesus Christ.

LONGING TO GO HOME

The deaths of Mark and his friend Kelly left us shocked and bleeding as nothing else ever has. Now we long for heaven—we *long* for heaven. The death of your own son is something you will never get over in this life. *Never.* How could you? Would you even want to? When you lose a loved one, you lose a precious part of yourself, an extension of your own flesh and bone, like a part of your very own soul. Thus we feel Mark's absence keenly and painfully. It is an ache we bear each day like an old wound. We are reminded of him again and again and again and again in a thousand different ways. Sometimes we wince, sometimes we cry, sometimes we just hide our sorrow. Mark's death brought our previously dim and vague perception of heaven into bright and sudden focus as we began to realize that nothing—nothing, *nothing*—would ever really remove the ache from our souls except being in the blessed, healing presence of Jesus Christ. With Him there is no sadness, no night, no tears. How we long for that day, the day that is coming, the day God will restore to us all of the years that "the locusts" have eaten (Joel 2:25)!

Sometimes our waiting seems interminable; we want to hurry the day—like children impatient for something wonderful to happen. Thoughts of heaven consume us. We have even wondered if our longing is an obsession that might be displeasing to God. Paul's words to Timothy, however, assure us that while our suffering serves a purpose, it is normal and right to long for the return of Christ:

> For I am already being poured out like a drink offering, and the time has come for my departure. I have fought the good fight, I have finished the race, I have kept the faith. Now there is in store for me the crown of righteousness, which the Lord, the righteous Judge, will award to me on that day—and not only to me, but also to all who *have longed for his appearing.* (2 Timothy 4:6–8 [emphasis added]).

Do you ever get "homesick"? We do. We get tired and discouraged, and we want to go *home.* This is not an evil desire;

indeed, longing to be at home with our Lord pleases God and was a focal point of Jesus' teaching. To help them persevere after His death, Jesus encouraged the disciples to think often of the preparations being made in heaven for them:

> In my Father's house are many rooms. . . . I am going there to prepare a place for you. And if I go and prepare a place for you, I will come back and take you to be with me that you also may be where I am. (John 14:2–3)

Heaven is really more than we can imagine. It is a place of peace and beauty, a place radiant with the very presence of Christ. Paul wrote, "no eye has seen, no ear has heard, no mind has conceived what God has prepared for those who love him" (1 Corinthians 2:9). Heaven sounds almost too good to be true, except that it *is* true—for our hope is certain.

THAT GREAT AND GLORIOUS DAY

Not long ago Cal Ripken of the Baltimore Orioles was honored for breaking a record few imagined would ever be broken: Lou Gehrig's record for playing the most consecutive ball games. The game scheduled for that day was interrupted in order to honor the new "iron man" of baseball for his many years of devotion to the sport. Fans, players, and umpires screamed and yelled in unison when the new record became official in the fifth inning and Ripken was coaxed by his teammates and fans to circle the field. He jumped above the outfield wall and "high-fived" the fans. He was carried on the shoulders of his fellow players, who later prodded him out of the dugout for yet another "victory lap." Ripken waved from a convertible that circled the field. Even the members of the opposing team stood starry-eyed and applauded his every move; they too were pleased to honor this great ball player.

The cheering lasted for more than twenty minutes. It was impossible even to hear the announcers, who finally gave up, themselves overcome with emotion. Although we were moved by this celebration on television, we began to imagine another celebration, a far more significant one. We glanced at each other for a moment, just long enough to confirm the inner thoughts of our souls. In that passing glance we knew we were both thinking the same thing: If this moment in baseball history could move us in this way, what will the wonder and glory of Jesus' return be like? The incredible adulation for this one ballplayer was but a poor shadow of what awaits us in heaven when the wedding feast finally begins, when the Lord welcomes us home.

The remarkable men and women of Hebrews 11, people who pleased God by persevering in their faith, did not live to see the Messiah fulfill the promise of redemption, but they never gave up believing that He would one day come. Even the book of Job, believed by many scholars to be the oldest of all the books in the Bible, reveals an unswerving confidence in this great Redeemer and in the resurrection He would bring. Despite his terrible suffering and his questioning, Job was unshakable in his faith:

> For I *know* that my Redeemer lives, and that in the end he will stand upon the earth. And after my skin has been destroyed, *yet in my flesh I will see God;* I myself will see him with my own eyes—I, and not another. (Job 19:25–27 [emphasis added])

Now that the Messiah has come, we also wait to experience the promise of eternal life with the family of God. But the ultimate fulfillment of that promise will not come until the last child of God has come into fellowship with Christ. God will not begin the great celebration until all of His children have responded to the finished work of redemption.

We must remember, even in our pain, the greater vision. In our own grief for our son, it was difficult to see that greater vision. But God has taught us that His love for His people is even greater than our love for our son. He longs for His lost children to come home, too. It is left for us to bring His words of hope to lost and hurting and sometimes even defiant people. That difficult coworker beside you each day may be destined for heaven and perhaps, in some mysterious way known only to our Lord, *you* will be the one to tell that person about Christ. We often pray our loved ones will come to faith; yet too seldom do we think that we, in turn, might be part of the answer to someone else's prayer, someone who is hoping against hope that their friend or son or sister will meet a faithful believer, someone just like you. Are you yielded? Are your eyes open to the needs around you? Can God use you to help bring His lost children home?

ANTICIPATING THE NOT YET

In the darkness of our grief we longed for that indescribable celebration and often started the day thinking, "Lord Jesus, this would be a good day for you to come. Please come soon!" As we have walked through our own broken world and shared in the suffering of those close to us, we have often questioned why God has not yet sent Jesus to take us home. As Sharon prayed about this one day, she read Hebrews 11:39–40:

> These were all commended for their faith, yet none of them received what had been promised. God had planned something better for us so that only together with us would they be made perfect.

This Scripture gave us a new understanding of God's love for His children. It reminded us that the picture is not yet complete, that God has planned "something better" for us. One day the acute sense of loss we now feel will be gone forever because, together with our son Mark and all those who, by faith, came before us, we will finally be restored, "made perfect." This passage gave us a clearer vision of God's timing and His purposes and comforted us. We feel incomplete now, since we miss our son terribly, but this is only because the work God is doing is still in progress.

Thus it is that, for the moment, one of our children is missing from us. No matter how hard we try to recapture the joy of earlier years, there is always the shadow of sorrow and loss hovering near, a bittersweet aspect to every family gathering, every holiday. How we miss our son, how we miss our son!

Yet we are coming to understand that it is not really Mark who is missing, *it is we*. We are the ones who are still en route, still traveling to our Father's house. The empty place at the table is not in our house, but in His—the place He has reserved for us. Whenever our journey seems too long or too hard, we have found that just knowing our Father's table is already set, that the lamps are alight, helps us to keep moving forward. We are able to persevere because we know there will be no empty places at *His* table. No, no more empty places. For on that Day all of our loved ones, all of those who have trusted in the Lord, will be forever together, forever home—*home!*

So then, how should we live in this broken world, where thoughts of heaven so consume us? How does being "heavenly minded" help make us "earthly good"? Paul regularly encouraged hurting believers to persevere by focusing on the resurrection and on eternal life. His encouragement was always in the context of the kingdom work that must be completed by us as we journey homeward. He used strong verbs of action to describe how we are to walk in faith:

> Forgetting what is behind and straining toward what is
> ahead, I press on toward the goal to win the prize for

which God has called me heavenward in Christ Jesus. (Philippians 3:13)

We do not lose heart. Though outwardly we are wasting away, yet inwardly we are being renewed day by day. For our light and momentary troubles are achieving for us an eternal glory that far outweighs them all. So we fix our eyes not on what is seen, but on what is unseen. For what is seen is temporary, but what is unseen is eternal. (2 Corinthians 4:16–18)

Though we still long for His coming, we also yearn for others to come to know Him as well. Thus, while we wait for His coming, we have kingdom work to do. Jesus' instructions to His disciples—and to us—are crystal clear:

Go and make disciples of all nations, baptizing them in the name of the Father and of the Son and of the Holy Spirit, and teaching them to obey everything I have commanded you. And surely I am with you always, to the very end of the age. (Matthew 28:19–20)

The primary goal of every Christian should therefore be, in accordance with God's expressed will and design, to seek to draw others to Christ.

RUNNING THE RACE

We have watched together as God, through faithful men and women, accomplished His own transcendent and eternal purposes of redemption. The "scorch marks" in each believer's life forever marked him or her, as though with a branding iron, as men and women learning to depend upon and wholly trust in God. These are not stories of "good people" but of a good and gracious God—and of their great faith in Him. Today they are a "great cloud of witnesses," urging us onward, encouraging us to remain faithful. We, too, can persevere in Him because we know He did not fail them and He will not fail us.

So put aside all that hinders. Examine carefully and prayerfully your own life, your heart of hearts. Identify that which distracts you from your calling as a child of God—*and get rid of it.* Are there places or people who draw you back, who tempt you to worship someone or something other than God? *Refuse to give them space in your life.* Are you impatient, bitter, mean-spirited, judgmental, lazy, dishonest? *Repent of these sins and put them behind you.* Scripture teaches us that even if our own eyes or limbs cause us to stray, we would be better off without them than to risk losing our way and so betray the Lord of Life.

The author of Hebrews closes his sweeping account of faith—both God's own faithfulness and the faith of those who chose to follow hard after Him—with the very object and foundation of our faith: the Lord Jesus Christ. It is as though the writer had said, "Now, in light of what you have just heard, run the course God has marked out for you by keeping your eyes fixed on Jesus" (Hebrews 12:1–3). In other words, now that you know what faith looks like, what faith provides, what faith costs—go out in the grace and power of God and *live it,* live a life of faith.

By Faith ...

In the days of grief and doubt after our son Mark was taken from us, it seemed as though an ugly, pitch-black darkness had somehow descended upon us. Where was God? Why had this happened to us? In our anguish, we clung to God's sure promise that He would go before us and level the mountains, break down the gates of bronze, cut through the bars of iron, and give us "the treasures of darkness, riches stored in secret places" so that we would know that He is the Lord, the God of Israel, the One who summons us by name (Isaiah 45:2–3).

When we review the years since Mark's death, we realize that every means of comfort and healing God has applied to our family can be traced back to the covenant promises made and kept in the unfolding history of the church as recorded in Hebrews 11. At the hospital minutes after our son's death, even though we were shaken, confused, and hurting, we sensed, in a fleeting moment of spiritual clarity, that God would use this—*even this*—for good, for the building up of His kingdom. Because of the eternal promises of the covenant, we knew God would not waste the darkness, that it had some greater purpose and meaning for Him. Somehow His light of hope would shine through this ordeal and others would experience Christ as a result of it.

God promised His everlasting presence in His covenant with Abraham, Isaac, Jacob, Moses, Samson, and Rahab; with Margie, Stu, Michelle, Sharon, and Chuck. Though our emotions sometimes accuse God of forsaking and abandoning us, we know that, because of that covenant, we continue to be safely in His grip.

And because of the covenant we know that God also desires for us to walk humbly before Him and share His compassion with a broken world. The way home is very often dark and sad and uncertain. But God is there, and He is greater than the darkness. In Him, truly, the darkness is not so dark, the shadows not quite so threatening as, along the way, we discover "treasures of darkness, riches stored in secret places." God's treasures of faith, the examples and comfort of His people, light our way. As we travel onward, we also draw more deeply upon our Father's love and, empowered by that love, we help others travelling the road with us. Together, we ask God to "fix our eyes on Jesus" and to show us how to build His kingdom. Each task brings us a little closer to our true home, heaven.

Dear brother or sister, just as the patriarchs passed on the promises of God to each succeeding generation, we also affirm to you, through our own sorrows and joys and difficult days, that God is faithful—He is faithful! Do not grow weary. Do not lose heart. *By faith* keep on in your journey. Consider Him who endured so much for us and be encouraged. The lights of His great city can even now be seen, just ahead, just beyond the mountains, just a little farther on. Do not give up now. A few more steps, my friend, just a few more steps—and you'll be home.

> Strong Son of God, Immortal Love,
> Whom we, that have not seen Thy face,
> By faith, and faith alone, embrace,
> Believing where we cannot prove.
>
> We have but faith: we cannot know,
> For knowledge is of things we see;
> And yet we trust it comes from Thee,
> A beam in darkness: let it grow.

Alfred, Lord Tennyson, *In Memoriam*

DIGGING DEEPER

Day One

- ◆ Review Hebrews 11. What strikes you most about God's character throughout this passage?
- ◆ How does a better understanding of God's character equip you to walk the path God has marked out for you?

Day Two

- ◆ Read Hebrews 12:1–3. What does the writer mean by "everything that hinders"?
- ◆ What hindrances do you need to put off? Be specific.

Day Three

- ◆ What does the writer mean by "the sin that so easily entangles"? How and why is unbelief the root cause of sin?

Day Four

- ◆ If we are to put off unbelief, what must we put on in its place? How can we do this?
- ◆ How does keeping our eyes fixed on Jesus enable us to walk with patience the pathway marked out for us?

Day Five

- ◆ What specific promise have you seen God keep in your life?
- ◆ Trace the beginnings of that promise back to the covenant God made with Abraham.

Day Six

- ◆ Why is it important to view your own personal journey as a means God will use to bless other people? How is this a fulfillment of the covenant?
- ◆ How will this understanding make you more intentional in your daily life?

◆ Notes ◆

◆ Notes ◆

◆ Notes ◆

◆ Notes ◆

♦ Notes ♦

◆ Notes ◆

◆ Notes ◆

◆ Notes ◆